SAILING
and
SMALL CRAFT
Down the Ages

SAILING
and
SMALL CRAFT
Down the Ages

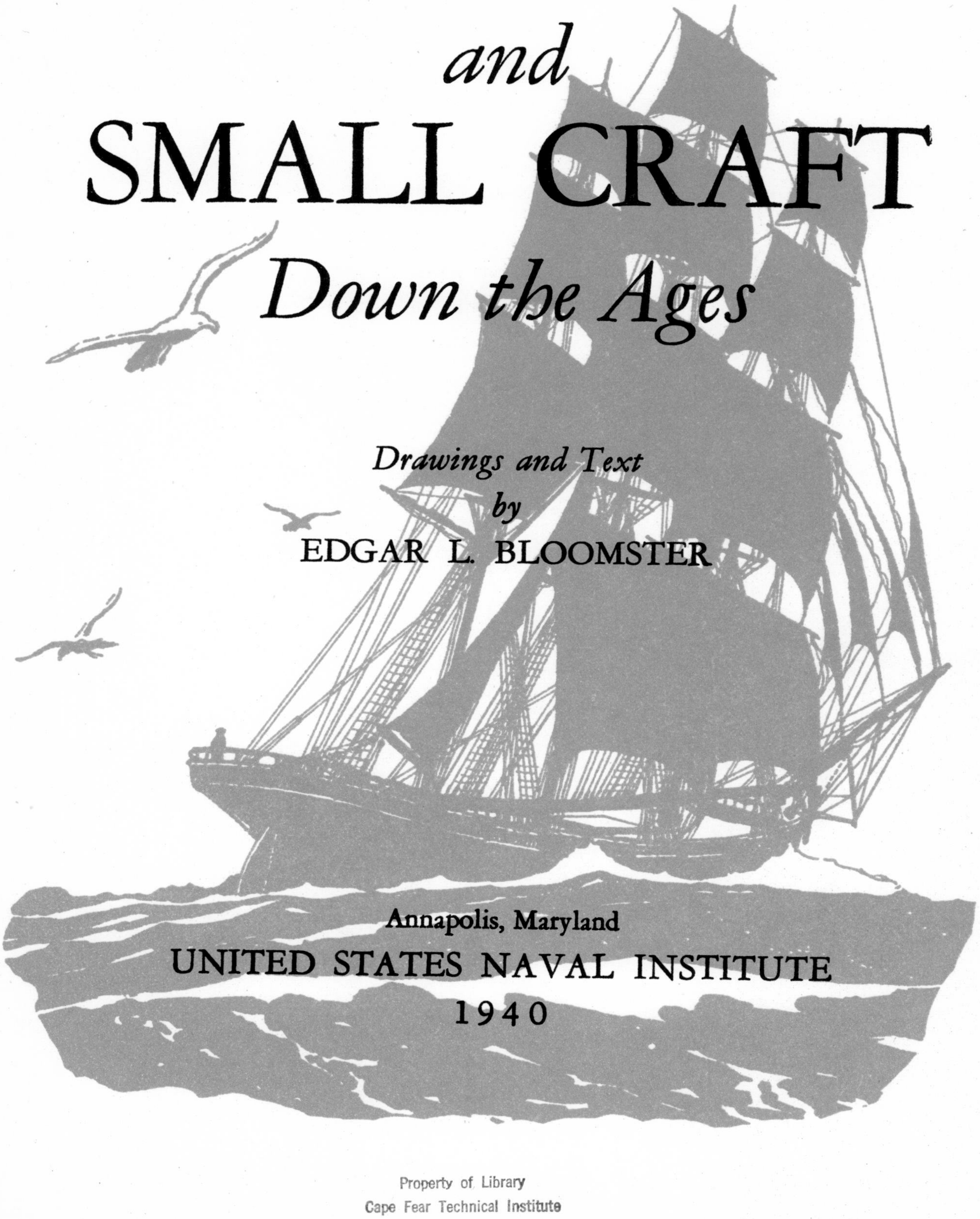

Drawings and Text
by
EDGAR L. BLOOMSTER

Annapolis, Maryland
UNITED STATES NAVAL INSTITUTE
1940

GEORGE BANTA COMPANY, INC., MENASHA, WISCONSIN

PRINTED IN THE UNITED STATES OF AMERICA

TO LORETTA

Foreword

WITH the passing of sail from the seas, except in the fisheries and the coast-wise trades of certain foreign countries where time is of less importance than economy of operation, it is essential that the rigs and appearance of the vessels that for centuries were the sole means of traffic on the oceans of the earth should be preserved. With the passing of only a score of years the rigs of the various craft that carried the commerce of the world are largely unknown to the present generation. Even yachtsmen, familiar only with fore-and-aft sails, hardly know the names of the great variety of square rigs so common around the turn of the century. The difference between a ship and a bark, between a brig, a brigantine and a topsail schooner, can be accurately described by but a few men today whose memory does not go back twenty years. To preserve this knowledge, to know the underlying reasons for the various types and rigs of the ships of the days of sail, is, it seems to me, important. We were, in this country, originally a seafaring people. We are still, as a nation, sea minded. To preserve our heritage we should perpetuate the knowledge of the types of craft which man has sailed and in which he opened the world to our ancestors.

In this volume Edgar Bloomster has made a distinct contribution to this cause. In these pages he shows by accurate drawings the ships that sailed the seas from the time of ancient Greece to those of the present. Reliable records of the earlier ships are scarce, and naturally the bulk of the types and rigs he shows are of a later period. Yet the results of his research into the earliest types are convincing to the sailor of today. That is the best test by which any work can be judged.

The author is well fitted to the task to which he has set himself. A sailor by avocation, a yachtsman by experience and an artist of distinction, he combines the knowledge and the skill which together are necessary to produce a book of this kind. In it, he has done a real service to the sailor of today.

HERBERT L. STONE
Editor, "Yachting"

Preface

I<small>N COMPILING</small> and writing the following pages it is my purpose to include in a single volume a definition or short description of the various types of rowing and sailing craft, as well as their sails, used throughout the ages in different parts of the world. Also to give the reader an idea as to their use and approximate period. In connection with my work as a marine artist, countless hours have been spent in research before portraying a particular ship on canvas, and the idea was born to put in book form much of the data thus garnered to save others from mulling through scores of volumes in an effort to get information which this book contains.

The silhouette drawings should give the reader an impression of the rig and the shape of the hull. To many persons, especially those of a nautical turn of mind, they are by this method more easily retained than if a detailed line sketch were given. To provide a book for ready reference, the subjects are listed alphabetically in the manner of the encyclopedia. In some cases the description is necessarily meagre and perhaps inadequate, due to lack of authentic information.

No attempt has been made to list every local variation of a type or class, as it would be a colossal task to give in every instance the correct native name of a vessel or boat, as that which would be the accurate term in one port or district might be called something entirely different in another, due to dialect or some small feature of construction or rig having no particular bearing on the class as a whole. This is especially true in the Pacific Islands, which spread over a huge expanse—130 degrees of longitude and nearly 80 degrees of latitude. In each of the hundreds of smaller islands and in the shore-bound districts of the larger ones, the natives have developed their own individualities in their water craft. Hence, while bearing an affinity for its neighbor, each one varies and is given a different name. In view of the great number of Oceanic types and the relative unimportance of many, only outstanding craft and those of well-known islands are described and illustrated.

It must be remembered that during the last quarter of a century or so the commercial vessel depending on wind and sail alone for propulsion—especially in occidental countries—has given way largely to power-driven craft. However, among the less mechanical minded sea-faring people of the Orient and other parts of the world, where competition is not so severe and speed is not such an important factor, the sailing craft is still the cargo carrier and the boat of the fisherman as it has been for centuries.

The author of this book has studied many boats and vessels in the course of his wanderings in America and Europe, in an effort to secure first-hand information, but, in view of the extinction of so many types, has been forced to use the records, models, and pictures handed down from generation to generation. Also, due to the impossibility of visiting every seacoast and locality to study and analyze the remaining craft, he must necessarily rely on the contemporary writings, drawings, and photographs of others who have handled their subjects so ably.

To the authors and artists listed in the appendix the writer conveys his especial thanks and records his indebtedness; also to the people in distant lands who have so kindly furnished me with data, and to the United States Naval Institute, for its helpful suggestions and kind coöperation.

Beverly Hills, California　　　　　　　　　　　　　　Edgar L. Bloomster
November, 1940

Contents

American Clipper Ship of 1854

British Clipper Ship of 1869

Three Barks
and a Barkentine

Pictured are the bark and barkentine rigs, examples of combinations of the square rig and fore-and-aft rig as applied to vessels having three or more masts. These were effected mainly for ease in handling and economical reasons, the fore-and-aft rig requiring less crew than the square.

Four-Masted Bark—Typical Australian Grain Ship

Four-Masted Barkentine

Bark

Modern Five-Masted Steel Bark

The Brig Family

The main difference between the brig, brigantine, and hermaphrodite brig is the number or absence of sails on the mainmast. If an auxiliary mast be added just aft of the mainmast of a brig, we would have a "snow"; if a fore-and-aft gaff sail be added to the foremast of a hermaphrodite brig and the fore course discarded, we would have a topsail schooner.

Brig

Brigantine

Hermaphrodite Brig

Early American Types

This group shows a few of the commercial and naval vessels in use during American colonial times and the War of the Revolution.

Sloop Rig 1765

Schooner 1750

Ketch 1760

Snow 1775

Radeau 1776

Continental Galley 1776

American and British Ships of War 1770 to 1830

Here are pictured some early naval vessels—from the tiny Jeffersonian gunboat to the stately, but cumbersome, ship-of-the-line (the mosquito and the elephant).

Frigate 1770

British Brig-Sloop 1830

Cutter Galley 1776

United States Frigate 1803

Ship-of-the-Line 1795

United States Gunboat 1803

Two American Frigates

A frigate of the highly successful *Constitution* class, which did such valiant work against the Barbary pirates and in the War of 1812, and, below, one of the frigates used in the War of the Revolution. Most of the latter were captured or destroyed.

American Frigate of the "Constitution" Class 1800

Continental Frigate of 1778

American Craft

Pictured here are some types from our east, west, and south coasts, from the 17th century to the present time. These were employed mainly in the fishing industry.

Boston Fishing Cutter Galway Hooker

Quoddy

New Orleans Lugger

Key West Smackee

San Francisco Felucca

Fishing Craft of Early 17th Century

Chesapeake Bay Pungy

Chesapeake Bay Schooner

More American Types and the Bermuda Sloop

Here are additional distinctive American types of the past and present, and two stages in the development of the fleety Bermuda sloop.

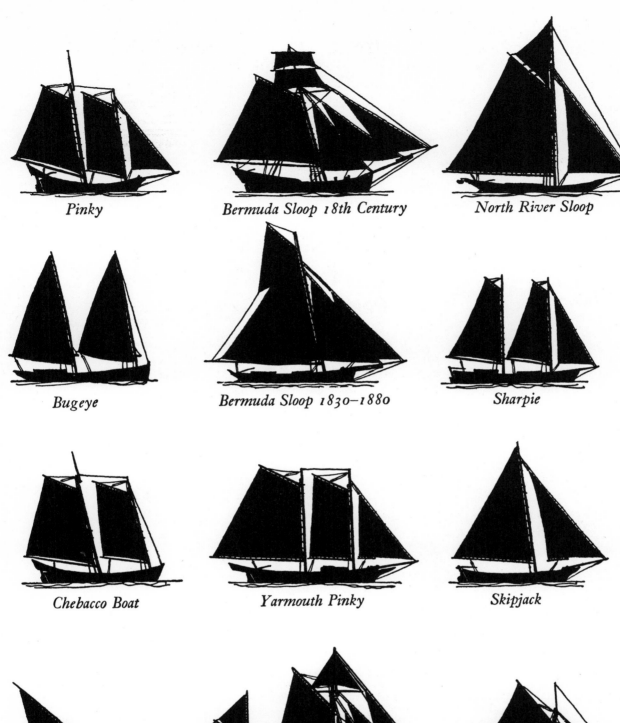

Pinky

Bermuda Sloop 18th Century

North River Sloop

Bugeye

Bermuda Sloop 1830–1880

Sharpie

Chebacco Boat

Yarmouth Pinky

Skipjack

Merrimac Gundalow

Lake Michigan Ketch

Friendship Sloop

A Page of American Schooners

One of the most popular of all rigs, the schooner is now over two centuries old. Pictured here are some examples and adaptations of this highly efficient rig as applied to various types of vessels.

Double Topsail Schooner Used as a Slaver

Single Topsail Schooner Baltimore Clipper

Four-Masted Schooner (Maine-built)

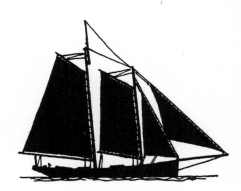

Pilot Boat

Great Lakes Schooner 1850

Gloucester Fishing Schooner

Block Island Schooner 1820

Revenue Cutter

Atlantic Passenger Ships

The British "Blackwaller" and the American packet ship were the transatlantic liners of their day. During the 1850's the fast clipper ships largely supplanted the older type shown in the lower picture.

Blackwall Frigate 1858

American Packet Ship 1830

A Whaler and an East-Indiaman

Shown on the adjacent page is a typical whaling ship, staunch and odoriferous, and an equally staunch, but less odoriferous, cargo carrier of the "Honorable John Company." Both were mighty workers of the sea.

American Whaling Ship of 1840

British East-Indiaman 1730

The Seventy-four Gun Ship
and the Corvette

These two war vessels were popular in the navies of the western European powers. The illustrations show a French "74" and a ship-sloop or corvette of the latter 18th century.

Seventy-four Gun Ship Early 18th Century

Ship-Sloop or Corvette

A Dutch and an English Ship of the Middle 17th Century

Here are two capital ships of the early Dutch and English navies. The ships of the former were of shallower draft, clinker-built above the water line and were somewhat less embellished than those designed by the Pett family at this period.

A Dutch Ship of 1650

An English Ship of 1650

Craft of Southern England

In this group are the picturesque barges of the Thames, the Brixham boats, the "nickey" from the Isle of Man, and the "wherry"—all outstanding, individual English types.

Old Thames Barge 1825

Topsail Barge

Hatch-Boat

Upper Thames Barge

Brixham Trawler

Manx Nickey

Brixham Mumble-bee

Norfolk Wherry

Miscellaneous Craft
of Britain

The lug rig was favored by the Scottish and English fishermen, but each harbor was partial to its own particular style of boat. Today there are a few survivors here and there, but the motor boat has made tremendous inroads in the once large fleets of sailing fishing boats.

Scotch Skaffie 1880

Scotch Zulu 1925

Humber Keel 1930

Brighton Hoggie 1800

Lowestoft Smack 1925

Yorkshire Lugger 1815

Deal Lugger 1870

Yarmouth Yawl 1850

Manx Dandy 1925

Mount's Bay Driver 1920

Mousehole Lugger 1840

Yarmouth Shrimp Boat 1900

More British Craft

Here are additional types from England—fishing boats and carriers—with which their owners glean a livelihood from the sea.

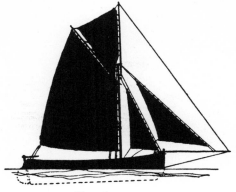

Bawley

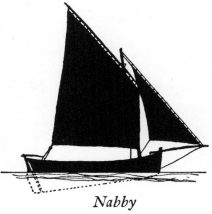

Nabby

Mersey Lighter

Essex Oyster-Boat

Peter Boat

Coble

Yorkshire Billy-Boy

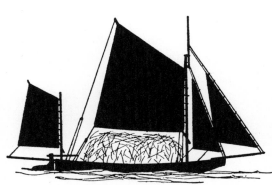

Thames Hay Barge

Tilt-Boat

Some Boats from France and the Mediterranean

The French boats shown worked out of the fishing ports of Brittany (perhaps some still do), while the "tartane," the "barque" and the "barquette" belong to the northern shores of the western Mediterranean.

Normandy Chasse-Marée

Boulogne Drift-Boat

St. Malo Bisquine

Breton Tunny Fisherman

Douarnenez Lugger

Morbihan Lugger

Channel Islander

Etaples Lugger

Havre Trawler

Havre Pilot Boat

Italian Boats

The boats of Italy are of diversified designs and the rig may be that of the lateen, lug, or fore-and-aft. The Latin loves lots of sails and if they are gaily colored, so much the better.

Giglio Trawler

Paranzello

Naples Trawler

Moleta

Topo

Balancelle or Navicello

Bovo

Bragozzi

Trabacola

Italian Coaster

Velocera

Early Dutch Ships

For many years Holland was a powerful maritime nation and her ships roved the Seven Seas. The Dutch vessels have always been beamy, rotund, and shallow. Light draft was necessary in order to clear the shoal spots surrounding the harbors of the low countries.

Buss 17th Century

Galliot 18th Century

Schuyt 17th Century

Hulk 16th Century

Merchant Ship Early 17th Century

Flute 17th Century

Armed Ship End of 17th Century

Craft from the "Low Countries"

The "boeier," "botter," and "hoogaar" are present day pleasure boats of Holland. Comparing the two drawings of the "boeier" it can be seen that they have undergone little change in the past two centuries. The remainder of this group are fishing and commercial vessels of Belgium and Holland through two centuries.

Boeier

Botter

Hoogaar

Dutch Koff *18th Century*

Dutch Boeier *18–19th Centuries*

Dutch Dogger *18th Century*

Haak, Dutch Lighter

Dutch Bombschuite

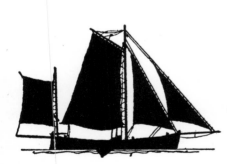

Scheviningen Dum or Pink

Belgian Lugger

Belgian Fishing Boat

Scandinavian Craft

From the time of the Vikings, the Scandinavian sailors have favored the double-ended clinker-built boat. Some of their craft still employ the square sail of their ancestors.

Hornbaek Boat

Baltic Dandy

Skovshoved Herring Boat

Swedish Fishing Boat

Norwegian Jaegt

Nordlands Cod Boat

Arendal Yawl

Söndfjord Yawl

Söndmöersk Boat

Old Hvalor Pilot Boat

Ise Fjord Fishing Boat

Bornholm Herring Boat

Miscellaneous Types of Europe

This group is comprised of odd types which the writer encountered from time to time and assembled in this rather hit and miss fashion.

Norman Cog

Yacht 17th Century

Kurran Kahn

Danish Sound Boat

Breton Lug-rigged Sardine Boat

Butterman Schooner

British Coasting Schooner

Norwegian Bankfiskerskoite

British Collier Brig

Three Ancient Types

Here are three old-timers, covering a period of fourteen centuries—a long era of slow development when we consider the strides made since the Venetian galleys sailed the blue waters of the Mediterranean.

Venetian Galley 15th Century

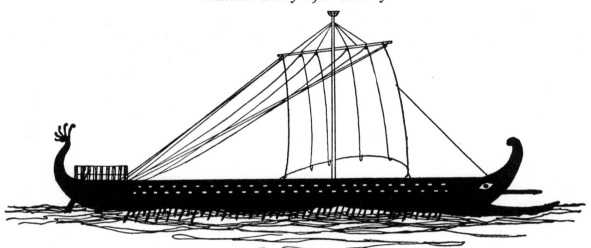

Greek Bireme circa 0 B. C.

Viking Ship or Dragon circa 1100

Ancient Craft

We may scoff at these apparently crude designs, but the vessels pictured performed their functions quite satisfactorily. The Viking "langskip" cruised over thousands of miles of open ocean, the corbita hauled its merchandise, and the galley, trireme and penteconter were formidable instruments of war.

Greek Galley 500 B. C.

Roman Trireme

Galleass 16th Century

Greek Penteconter 1000 B. C.

Galley 17th Century

Viking Long Ship 1000 A. D.

Greek Merchant Ship B. C., 0 A. D.

Roman Corbita 200 A. D.

European Ships 13th to 17th Centuries

The illustrations show the transition of the sailing ship through four centuries. The 13th century English craft is a huskier model of the Viking ship, with fore-and-aft platforms. The carracks and argosies of the 15th century ranged in size up to 1000 tons.

English Warship 13th Century

Merchant Ship Early 15th Century

Merchant Ship Late 15th Century

Carrack or Argosy 14–15th Centuries

English Pinnace 16th Century

Caravel 15–16th Centuries

Cromster 16th Century

Galleon 16th Century

Ketch 17th Century

Miscellaneous European Craft 16th to 19th Centuries

Pictured are some early merchant craft and two warships of Sweden and Russia. A great percentage of the cargoes were carried in small vessels. It will be noticed that the Swedes still clung to their oars and sweeps, even on their naval craft.

Bugalet 18th Century

Howker 16–18th Centuries

Hoy 17–18th Centuries

Bilander 17–18th Centuries

French Shallop 18th Century

Houario 18th Century

Norwegian Cat 17–18th Centuries

Dutch Sloep 17–19th Centuries

Cutter 1820

Russian Shebek Late 18th Century

Swedish Udema Late 18th Century

Boats of the Mediterranean, Adriatic and the Near East

These vessels of yesterday and today have been used by the maritime peoples of Southern Europe from the west to the east, with the exception of the "zarug," which is Arab. The Turkish boats may be seen in the Bosphorus and along the coast, while the "zarug" is an offspring of the dhow and is found in the Red Sea.

Portuguese Muletta 17th Century

Grecian Kaiki

Tartane 1925

Dalmatian Bragagna 19th Century

Tuscan Bombarda

Barquette

Barque Provençale

Italian Trabacoto

Turkish Tchektirmé

Turkish Càïque

Zarug

Mediterranean Types

The Mediterranean vessels of 200 and 300 years ago displayed a variance of hull and rig. The countries of Southern Europe adopted the square rig to a great extent as far back as the 16th century. Some of the sails are shown furled on the illustrations. The term "bark" is generic in the Mediterranean.

Polacre 18th Century

Patache 18th Century

Pink 17–18th Centuries

Saïque 17–18th Centuries

Polacre-Settee

Bark

Some Lateen-Rigged Vessels
of the Mediterranean

With the exception of the "vinco," the types shown are direct descendents of the early galleys, with the bowsprit extending beyond the prolongation of the stem and the projections at the stern. The bow of the "vinco" is reminiscent of the craft of the 17th century.

Italian Square Topsail Lateener

Genoese Vinco 1845

Spanish and Arab Galley with Oars 1600–1800

Tartane

Spanish Felucca 1800

Xebec

Egyptian Craft

The two illustrations at the top of the succeeding page approximate the types of boats of the two periods, and the remainder are modern. The Suez shore-boat is Arab in character. It is an impressive sight to behold a fleet of white-winged gaiassas slowly gliding over the Nile.

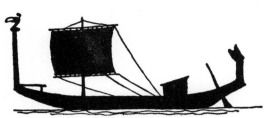

Egyptian Boat 2000 B. C.

Egyptian Galley 1600 B. C.

Gaiassa

Dahabia

Suez Shore-Boat (Arab)

Naggar

Craft of India and the Indian Ocean

Working eastward from Suez into the Red Sea and Indian Ocean we find the dhow family predominant, but among the islands of the Indian Ocean and on the large rivers of India are other types, each individual to its own locality.

Muchva

Tony, Bombay Canoe

Batelo

Bombay Mashva

Malabar Kotia

Three-Masted Malabar Pattamar

Bengal Malar Panshi

Bengal Pulwar

Persian Garukha 1850

Maldive Island Trader

Laccadive Is. Canoe

Ganges Dinghi

Craft of the Red Sea, India and Siam

Here are three more dhow types, and as we leave India we spy a lugger from the Mergui Archipelago. In the Gulf of Siam are seen a "rua pet," a "rua ta" and the half-caste "lorcha," with its western hull and Chinese sails.

Gehazi

Sambuk

Siamese Rua Pet

Bangkok Lorcha

Cambodian Rua Ta

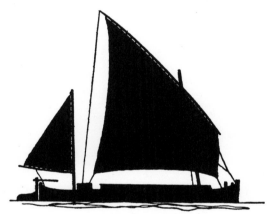

Rangoon Lighter

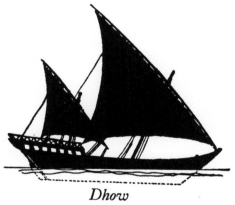

Dhow

Burma Rice Boat

Mergui Pearler

Malayan Craft

Along the coast of Malaya are found interesting native types. The harbor at Singapore abounds with many varieties of hull and rig—a mixture of Malayan, Chinese, and western. What a fascinating sight it would have been to watch (from a well-concealed hiding place) a Malay pirate craft racing toward a becalmed and helpless merchantman.

Malay Penjajap

Malay East Coaster

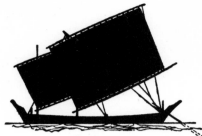

Payang

Singapore Tongkang

Johore Banting (or Atcheen)

Twakow

Bang Choon

Malay Outrigger Canoe

Sampan Panjang

Flying Prau or Malay Pirate Craft

Singora Lake Boat

Junks and Sampans

From the Indies to the North China border the junk plies the eastern seas, as it did before time was recorded. In the harbors of the Orient the little sampans dart here and there, begging for passengers or cargo. The drawings will give an idea of the diversity of design. It would be difficult to find two junks that look alike.

Yangtze River Sampan

Nagasaki, Japan, Sampan

Bangkok, Siam, Sampan

Amoy Junk

Hongkong Cargo Junk

Japanese Junk

West River Chinese Junk

Five-Masted Woosung Junk

North China Junk

Two Junks and a Sampan

Some of the ocean-going junks run to huge proportions, as can be seen by the drawing of the Hylam junk. The living quarters are usually tucked away under the after deck. The junk must be an efficient craft since there has been no change in design for thousands of years.

Hylam Junk in the Gulf of Siam Trade, 90' w.l. x 28' b. x 7'd. (From "Yachting")

Singapore Junk, 72' w.l. x 22' b. x 7'-8" d.

Chinese Sampan, Gulf of Siam, 30' w.l.

Craft of the
Netherlands Indies

Pictured here are some "praus" of the Indies. The outrigger is in evidence on some of the smaller fishing boats, while a strong western influence is manifested in the rigs of the trading vessels. The hulls, however, retain the native aspect.

Javanese Prau

Madura Prau

Bajak

Sumatra Lanchang

Barong or Prau Tukau

Caracore

Prau Bugis

Canoes of Polynesia

When touring the South Pacific Islands in search of native craft, let us start in Polynesia and work westward. It is truly regrettable that "civilization" has caused the extinction of so many types developed by the ingenious natives of the faëry isles. It must be remembered that their materials and tools for boat building were confined to the slender resources provided by each tiny island.

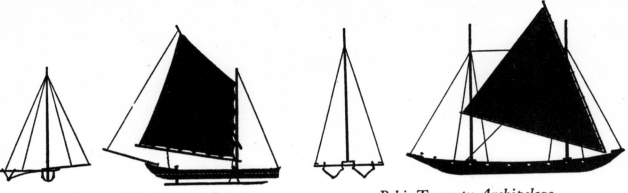

Pahi, Leeward Society Islands   Pahi, Tuamotu Archipelago

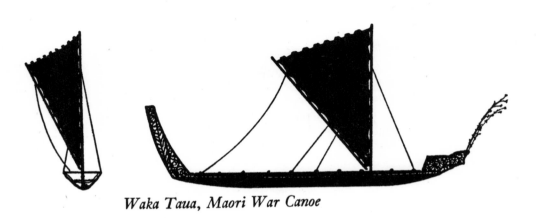

Waka Taua, Maori War Canoe

Thamakau, Fiji

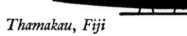

Wa'a, Hawaii

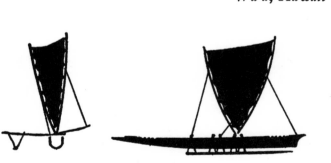

Va'a Motu, Tahiti   Soatau, Samoa

Canoes of Melanesia

The natives of the Melanesian Islands have not displayed the aptness of design of the Polynesians or Micronesians in the construction of their craft. Perhaps the warlike attitude of the people of the black islands prevented any influx of the higher types from southern Asia during their settlement voyages ages ago.

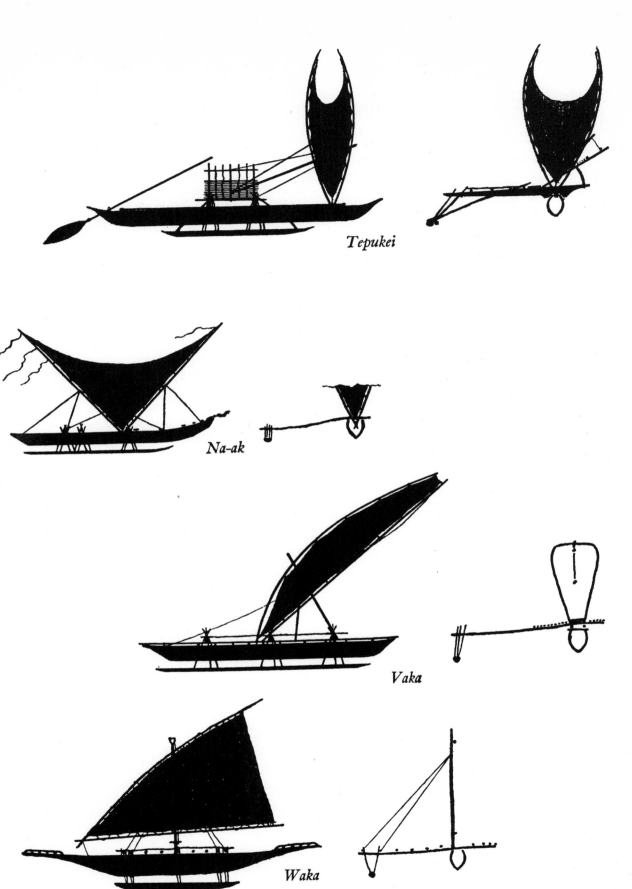

Tepukei

Na-ak

Vaka

Waka

More Canoes
of the Melanesian Islands

Though crude and fantastic, these canoes served their simple purposes. The natives lavished their art on their water craft. Some of the sails bear a resemblance to the lugsail used on the "naggar" of the Nile. The sailing dugout canoe, with outrigger, is prevalent in the islands south of the equator from the Marquesas to the Laccadives off India.

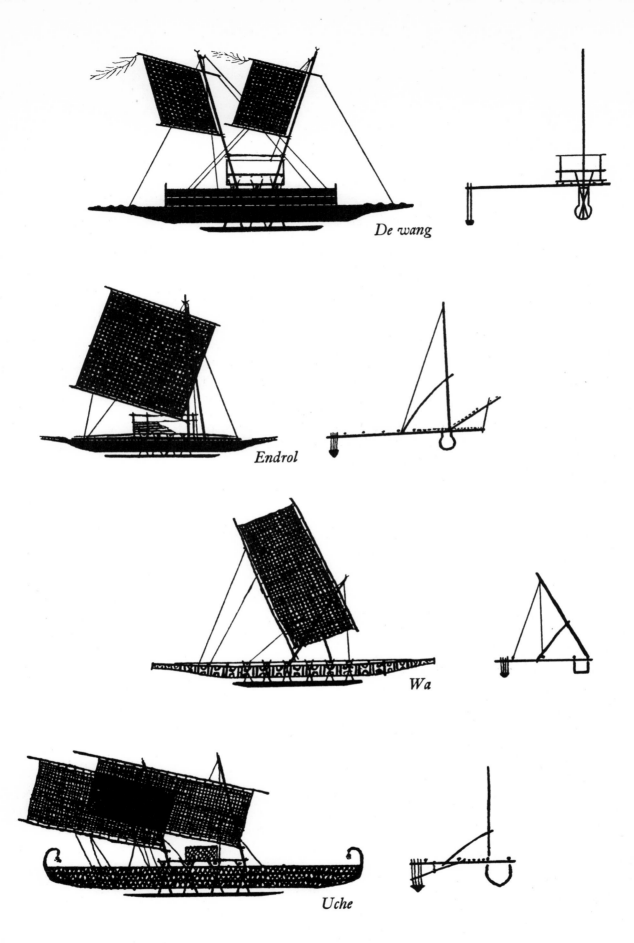

De wang

Endrol

Wa

Uche

Canoes from the
Micronesian Islands

This stretch of islands in the western Pacific is the home of the fast outrigger sailing canoe. The Micronesians (of Malay and Polynesian descent) displayed great talent in the design of their craft. The natives have always been excellent sailors and rovers of the sea, while the Marshall Islanders, perhaps the boldest of them all, worked out their own sea charts and maps.

Popo, Caroline Is.

Wa lap, Marshall Is.

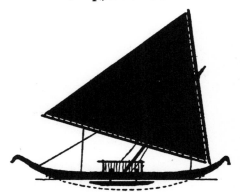

Kaep, Palau Is.

Flying Proa, Marianas

Tsukpin, Yap I.

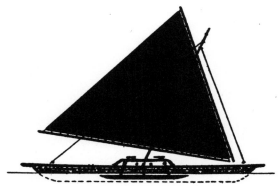

Baurua, Gilbert Is.

Canoes of New Guinea

New Guinea is perhaps most distinguished for the Papuan "lakatoi" of Port Moresby, which is illustrated on page 89, but double canoes are found from the Papuan Gulf to Orangerie Bay, and outrigger canoes of all description are in evidence here and there around the coast.

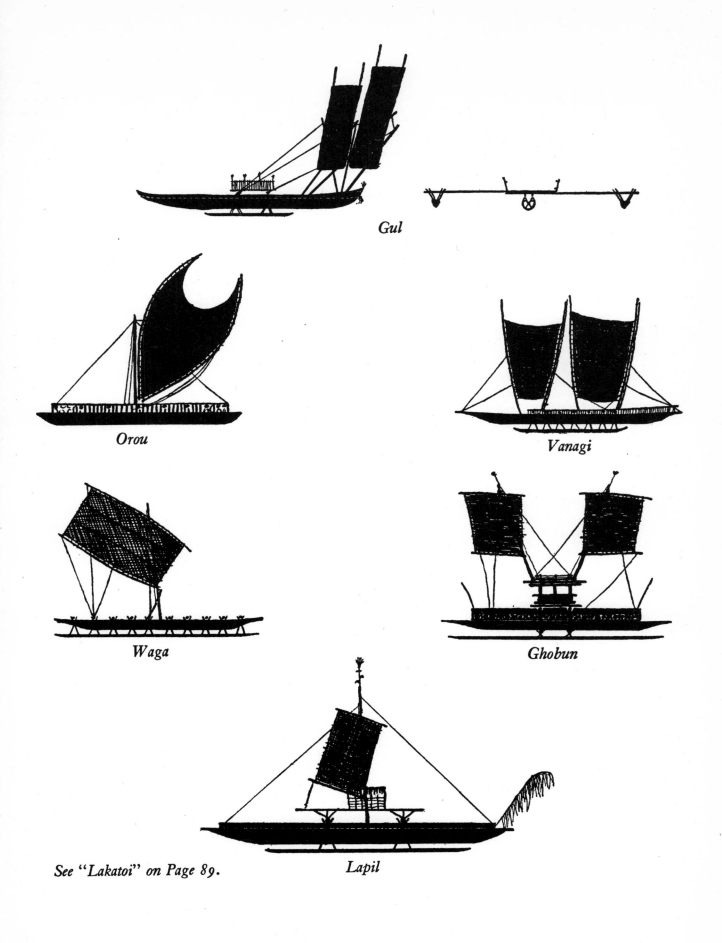

Gul

Orou

Vanagi

Waga

Ghobun

See "Lakatoi" on Page 89.

Lapil

North American Canoes and Small Craft

This group illustrates some examples of small water craft that are (or were) employed for water transportation in the area now comprising the United States, Canada, and Alaska. The dory, while a distinctly American craft, has been adopted by the European "banks" fishermen.

Canadian Birch-Bark Canoe

Haida Indian Dugout Canoes, N. W. America

Kayak with Occupant

Alaskan Umiak with Sail

Kootenay Indian Spruce-Bark Canoe

Louisiana Pirogue (Dugout)

Umiak

Algonquin Bark Canoe

Tlinglit Dugout

Chippewa Dugout

Tule Grass Balsa

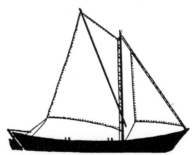

New England Dory with Spritsail and Jib

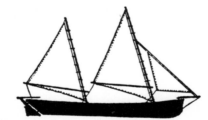

Chesapeake Bay Dugout Canoe with
Leg-of-Mutton Rig

Miscellaneous Craft

On the opposite page is a geographical melange of water craft from odd parts of the world. The "canoa" and "balsa" are indigenous to South America, the "mtepi" is from Kenya in Africa, the four canoes of the Solomon Islands are of the "mon" type, and the "koleh" is a racing canoe of Malaya. The "lakatoi" is found at Port Moresby in Papua, New Guinea.

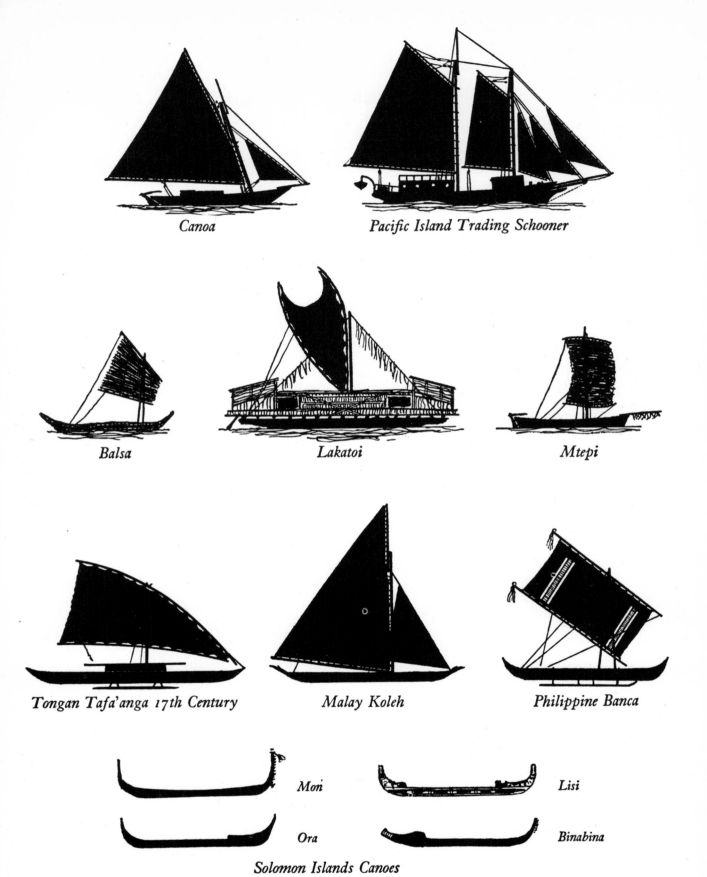

Canoa

Pacific Island Trading Schooner

Balsa

Lakatoi

Mtepi

Tongan Tafa'anga 17th Century

Malay Koleh

Philippine Banca

Mon

Lisi

Ora

Binabina

Solomon Islands Canoes

AMBATCHE   A canoe, or balsa, of the White Nile River, made of bundles of
                 ambatche reeds which are found along the banks. The bow
                 tapers to a point, while the stern is cut off square. See "balsa."

ANGULA   A Singhalese double-dugout, platform canoe used at Kunsdale,
                 Ceylon, for ferrying passengers. The hulls are similar to the
"vāragum oru" except that the bottoms are flat instead of round, making the craft
better adapted to landing on a shallow shore. The canoes lay parallel, with a platform built across amidships, and range from 25 to 30 feet in length and 14 to 16
inches in width, with strongly raking overhangs.

ARENDAL   A sharp-ended, open, clinker-built skiff used in the fishing
   YAWL   industry around Arendal, Norway. The stem and stern are
   Illustration on page 45.   alike with curved raking posts. An outboard rudder is hung
                 from the sternpost. The length is roughly four times the beam.
The rig consists of a single lugsail, wide at the foot, and the boat is also equipped with
two sets of oars and oar locks. It is called the "Norway yawl" by British fishermen.

ARGOSY   A "carrack" (the largest ship of the middle ages) which sailed
   Illustration on page 53.   out of the port of Ragusa, now Dubrovnik, Jugo-Slavia, in the
                 15th, 16th, and 17th centuries. During this period, the "ar-
gosies" of prosperous Ragusa were seen in every port of Europe and the Mediterranean. The name was derived from "Ragusa," which through the centuries was
known to Englishmen as "Argusa" or "Aragusa." No doubt, the rig and structure of
the carrack of western Europe and the argosy differed.

ATCHEEN   See "Banting," illustration on page 69.

AUSTRALIAN   Steel sailing vessels rigged as ships or barks, which annually
GRAIN SHIPS   carry a cargo of grain from the outports of Spencer's Gulf,
   Illustration on page 7.   Australia, to England. Most of the vessels are old, although
                 two have been built since the Great War, and at this writing
a scant two or three may make the voyage this year. For the past twenty years the
Australian grain trade has gone to the windjammers to a great extent because they
will accept a lower rate than the steamship. Also, the grain is loaded in small, out-of-
the-way places and it is expensive for the steamer to lie and wait two or three weeks
while the cargo is being stowed.

   Some of the voyages have resulted in keenly contested races for the honor of
making the best elapsed time. The various vessels usually leave within a short time
of one another and, with few exceptions, take the Cape Horn course.

   Following are some of the ships that were engaged in the Australian grain trade:
Herzogin Cecilie, Lawhill, Ponape, Pamir, Parma, Pommern, Viking, Melbourne, Hougo-

mont (all Finnish), *Abraham Rydberg* (ex-Alaska packer *Star of Greenland*), *C. B. Pedersen* (both Swedish)—all four-masted barks; *Killoran, Penang, Winterhude,* barks; the full-rigged ship *Grace Harwar*. All the Finnish four-masters and the barks belong to Captain Gustaf Erikson, of Maarianhamina, Finland. *Pamir* and *Parma* formerly were nitrate carriers from Chile to Germany.

Many of the grain ships are out of commission or have been lost at sea. The *Parma* seemed to be in good shape when the writer visited her in Hamburg four years ago. This bark made the 16,000-mile voyage in 103 days in 1932, and *Herzogin Cecilie* took but 96 days in 1928. The latter is a former cadet ship of the Norddeutscher Lloyd.

These ships are long, powerful, and slab-sided, with low freeboard when loaded, and have a clipper bow and overhanging stern. The fore-, main-, and mizzenmasts (except on the three-masted barks) carry a course, upper and lower topsails, upper and lower topgallants, and a royal, with four headsails to a spike bowsprit. Spankers vary: ordinary gaff type; divided, with double gaff; trysail and ringtail. Illustration of "bark" on page 7.

AUXILIARY   A sailing vessel having a motor or engine as auxiliary power.

BADANE   A Persian and Arabian dhow. See "dhow."

BAGALA *or*   A large dhow used by the Arabs on the Red Sea. This is a
BUGALA   true dhow. It averages about 85 feet in length, beam one-
                   quarter, with a displacement of 200 tons. See illustration of
                   "dhow" on page 67.

BAGARRA   An Arab dhow similar to the "bagala," having true dhow
                   characteristics—long overhang forward, raking transom stern,
raised poop deck, main- and mizzenmasts. While Arabic in origin, it is found as far east as Rangoon, India. See illustration of "dhow" on page 67.

BAJAK   A native term for a "Dyak prahu" of Borneo. There were
Illustration on page 75.   various models, but usually there was a sharp, curving bow
                   with a long, pointed platform extending forward, which also
supported a bowsprit. The large square stern was the after end of a superstructure which rested on the rear portion of the hull. There were projecting open galleries for oarsmen on each side. The stem was curved and ended in a long, carved head. The sternpost raked severely. The rig consisted of two or three lugsails and two jibs. Length of hull proper averaged 45 to 50 feet, beam somewhat more than one-fourth. The "bajak" was used also by the Dyaks of the Celebes and Sumatra.

BALLAM   A Singhalese dugout canoe of Ceylon, having a round bottom
                (transversely), no sheer, sides that tumble home. It is open,
double-ended, ends vertical above water line, curved below, and has a short solid
section at each end; 20 to 30 feet long, width 2 to 3 feet.

BALANCELLE   See "navicello."
     Illustration on page 39.

BALANDRA   A crude craft used on the west coast of South America, sloop
                or schooner rigged.

BALDIE   A double-ended fishing boat of 25 feet on the keel, and up-
                wards, used on the Scottish east coast from Aberdeenshire to
Fifeshire. The "baldies" are built on the lines of a "fifie," with little or no rake to
the stem, are decked over, and have sleeping and cooking accommodations for a full
crew. They are lug-rigged, the larger ones carrying a mizzen, as well as a jib, which
is extended to a long bowsprit. The mizzen trims to a boomkin. The mainmast is
stepped well forward. The name is a contraction of Garibaldi, by which this type
was known originally in Aberdeenshire. Among the eastern villages of Banffshire,
the "baldies" are known as "skiffs."

BALLINGER   A vessel of about 100 tons used on the Bay of Biscay in the
                14th century. Sails and oars were used and it probably was not
                unlike the Norman vessels of the time.

BALSA   A canoe-shaped boat constructed of bundles of grass or reeds,
     Illustration on page 89.   used in various parts of the world where other materials for
                boat building are not available. In the early days of California,
balsas were an important means of transportation. These grass boats are made in
different manners. The Indians of Western Mexico constructed theirs with two long
and one short bundles of reeds, tapering toward the ends. The short bundle was
placed between the longer ones and lashed together to form an open, pointed canoe.
The sailing balsas used by the natives on Lake Titicaca between Bolivia and Peru,
are, on the other hand, made of two lower bundles of reeds and two other tapering
bundles of much smaller diameter laid on the outer upward sides of the lower two,
the whole lashed firmly together to form a canoe with raking pointed ends. A trapezoidal sail of reeds, with a yard top and bottom, is hung from an inverted-V mast.
   Another type of "balsa" is a sailing raft composed of a few light logs lashed
together and equipped with a crude mast and sail. These are used in parts of South
America, Africa, the Philippines, etc. The balsas of Peru are made of "balsa" logs,
which are as light as cork.

BALTIC DANDY
Illustration on page 45.
A ketch or dandy-rigged, shallow-draft vessel of the Baltic Sea. The mizzenmast is lofty, which sometimes gives the rig the appearance of a schooner. Leeboards are carried on craft of the southern coast. Three or four head sails run to a long jibboom and when running free square sails are often set on the mainmast. The hull is beamy and well-built, with sort of a clipper bow and an old-fashioned round stern with davits and dinghy above. These Baltic vessels are clinker-built with wide strakes in true Scandinavian manner. The flare forward is considerable, as is the sheer, especially in the smaller open boats. The deck houses are gayly painted.

BALTIMORE CLIPPER
Illustration on page 21.
Fast, sharp-hulled vessels originated on Chesapeake Bay. These were used when speed was of prime consideration, as in the slave trade, privateering, the Mediterranean fruit trade, etc. The chief characteristics of the "Baltimore clipper" were: masts with extreme rake aft; raking stem and sternpost; a high bow, with good sheer to a low stern; low freeboard; great dead rise at the midship section; 2 to 5 feet drag to the keel. The beam on the larger vessels was about one-quarter of the length, but this increased to somewhat less than one-third on the smaller ones. The greatest beam was well forward of the center of the length. The schooner rig was the most popular, although some were rigged as brigs, brigantines, and hermaphrodites. While the shipbuilders of Chesapeake Bay produced sharp-hulled vessels of the "Virginia model" as early as the second quarter of the 18th century, this type was not generally known as the "Baltimore clipper" until after the War of 1812. With the popularization of the larger clipper ship in the late 1840's and early 50's, the "Baltimore clipper" as a distinct type passed out of favor.

BANCA
Illustration on page 89.
A double-outrigger canoe of Mindanao Island in the Southern Philippines. Four bamboo outrigger booms to a side are connected directly to long floats, which are upturned at the forward end. A rectangular sail, with a yard laced to each of the longer sides, is set obliquely to a tripod mast. The sail is painted with wide vari-colored stripes and is ornamented with tassels.

BANDAR
See "lanchang to'aru."

BANG CHOON
Illustration on page 69.
A "net boat" used in the fisheries of Singapore. The hull is open, sharp-ended, with a rounded "V" section. Stem and sternpost are straight and raking and extend above the gunwale. There is considerable sheer, the keel is parallel to the gunwale, and when light the forefoot and heel are above the water. The helmsman sits on a small seat set athwart the gunwales at the stern. The net is stowed in a compartment abaft the center of

the boat. It is usually two-masted, the main stepped amidships and the foremast in the bow raked forward, a short, wide spritsail set on each. The rudder is hung outboard. The average size is 35 to 40 feet long, 4 feet 6 inches beam, and about 2 feet in depth.

BANGKONG   A long, canoe-shaped, open boat used by the Dyaks of Borneo for fighting. The larger ones could accommodate eighty men and were often built with a substantial flat roof from which the warriors fought while the others paddled below.

BANKER   A large fishing vessel which frequents the offshore fishing banks of the North Atlantic. See "Gloucester fisherman," illustrated on page 134.

BANKFISKER-
SKOÏTE *or*
BANKSKOÏTE
Illustration on page 47.
     A large decked vessel, rigged variously, used in the cod fishery off the west coast of Norway. The hull has a curved, strongly raking stem, full bow and stern, raking sternpost, moderate sheer, rudder hung outside. The average size is 60 feet over-all by 20 feet 6 inches beam. About thirty years ago a keel of iron was introduced, which helped their speed. At the present, however, the Norwegian "bankers" are motor-driven to a great extent, as is the case in New England.

BANKSKUTA   A Swedish fishing vessel of the Island of Tjorn on the Bohuslan Coast. One voyage is made yearly (April to September) to the Storregan Bank. It is a carvel-built keel vessel with flush deck; beamy and deep; flaring bow with great rake to the stem; stern shaped like bow; narrow rudder; hollow water lines. Ketch-rigged with bowsprit. Fore-and-aft mainsail, spritsail mizzen, two jibs, and square-headed gaff topsails; 60 to 65 feet long on deck.

BANTING *or*
ATCHEEN
Illustration on page 69.
     A fast, open, sailing dugout of Johore, on the southern tip of the Malay Peninsula. It is one of the most remarkable forms of dugout in the world and has fine sailing qualities; 30 to 35 feet long, one-sixth the beam. It has a long, hollow, clipper bow; sharp hollow floor, shaped to form a keel. The rig consists of two balance lug or settee sails and a jib carried to a short bowsprit.

BARCHE   An Italian term for vessels from 10 to 60 tons' displacement. The rigs are diversified. Italian craft are usually highly painted and decorated and the sails are often of a gay color.

BARGE   The term "barge" has been applied to numerous types of vessels through the centuries. In the Middle Ages it was a fighting ship of medium size, with a single mast and square sail. Oars, or sweeps,

[95]

were used. In early Roman times a "barge" was a large, elaborate, and highly decorated rowing vessel—for instance, "Cleopatra's barge." The state "barges" of the present day are of the same type. In the Victoria and Albert Museum in South Kensington, England, rests an 18-oared state barge, built in 1732 for the Prince of Wales, and a still more ancient one is preserved in Greenwich, England. The latter was built by King William III in 1689 and is still in fair condition.

Another type is a long, light boat formerly used in the British Navy for conveying high officers from ship to shore. This type of "barge" pulls ten or more oars.

A flat-bottomed scow used on inland waterways is still another form of barge, while the simple lighters which are used for unloading ships are often referred to as barges. The latter class usually have no motive power of their own and are towed by tugs.

Then there are the sailing barges—those unique English vessels which ply the waters of the Thames and the English Channel, popularly known as the "Thames barge." See "Thames barge," illustrated on page 31.

BARK *or* **BARQUE** *Illustration on page 7.*	A sailing vessel of three or more masts, square-rigged on all masts, except the after one, which is fore-and-aft rigged.

BARK *Illustration on page 59.*	Small Mediterranean craft, with combinations of square, lateen, and fore-and-aft sails; a long beak forward, which provides a stout support for the lower end of the forward lateen sail. The

term is generic and there are many varieties.

Small English ships of the 18th century having no mizzen topsail were also called "barks."

BARK	In the American colonial period the term "bark" was not applied to a rig, but to a type of hull, square-sterned and flush-

decked. The name was often used instead of "ship" or "vessel." According to H. I. Chapelle, the majority of colonial "barks" probably were brigantines, with some rigged as ketches and ships.

BARKALONGA	A western Mediterranean vessel, having two or three lug-rigged masts.

BARKENTINE *or* **BARQUEN-** **TINE** *Illustration on page 7.*	A sailing vessel of three or more masts, having a ship's foremast, that is, square-rigged, the after masts being fore-and-aft rigged. The "barkentine" was very popular on the Pacific Ocean. It was not known previously to 1830.

BARKS of CRA-	Canoes used by the natives of Borneo and the Dutch East In-
CALOA and	dies, with flush decks, a high sheer, and a sharp bow. They had
the STRAITS	one mast and the sail used was similar to that of the "caracore"
OF SUNDA	(illustration on page 75), being long and narrow, and were

kept from upsetting by outriggers on both sides. They are now extinct.

BARONG

Illustration on page 75.

A native fishing craft used by the Milanaus of west Borneo. The hull is square-ended at the gunwales, with V-shaped raking end boards at bow and stern, being similar to the stern of a dory; good rounding sheer, with low freeboard amidships. The thin, flat keel follows the sheer line and is hollowed out of a log. The soft wood planking is fastened to five or six hardwood frames with strips of rattan. A thin plank deck is laid over the crossbeams of the frames. The mid-section forms a wide, rounded "V." On either side, some distance above and extending out from the gunwale, are long, narrow racks of rope lacing running the length of the boat on the starboard side, but with an opening on the port side, through which fishing is done by means of a purse seine. This net is laced to two long poles which form a "V," hinged at the bottom.

A single mast, without shrouds, is stepped forward of amidships, on which is carried a square sail, controlled by sheets and braces. The mast is braced with fore-and-aft backstays. The vessel can be rowed by four oars on either side and is steered by a long oar or twin rudders. The net, sail and spars are stored on two T-shaped rests stepped on the center line of the boat. Projecting aft from the stern is a platform. The average length is about 30 feet, with a beam somewhat less than one-third.

BARQUE

A lateen-rigged, commercial sailing vessel used on the Lake of Geneva, Switzerland. It is two-masted and the hull is decked, with walkways projecting beyond the gunwales on which the scullers stand. The freeboard is low, there is no sheer except at the bow, which rises sharply, meeting the high, concave stem in a point. The slab sides meet the flat bottom in a chine. There is a cabin forward, with a port hole on each side of the stem. Its side view suggests the "gaiassa" of Egypt, illustrated on page 63.

BARQUE
PROVENÇALE

Illustration on page 57.

The "bark" was also a Mediterranean craft of the 18th century. It had three masts and no bowsprit, but sometimes had a long, slender extension protruding from the bow. The mainmast was a pole mast and carried three square sails, like the "polacre" (illustrated on page 59). The foremast had a severe rake forward and carried a lateen sail. The mizzenmast was small and carried a topmast with a lateen course and one or two square topsails.

[97]

BARQUETTE

Illustration on page 57.

A small, half-decked craft, common to the Spanish and French Riviera. They are 18 to 20 feet in length, with high stem post and a sharp, rounded stern. They are carvel-built. The single lugsail has a long yard and a short luff. The Madiera fishing boats and small Portuguese coasters are really "barquettes" about 30 feet long.

BATEAUX

This class of boat was flat-bottomed, sharp at both ends, carried one or two guns, and had weather cloths all around to protect the crew from bullets. They were sometimes equipped with a single lateen sail, and 60-foot lengths were not uncommon. Bateaux were used on Lake Champlain and small lakes and rivers during the American Revolution.

BATELO or BATEELE

Illustration on page 65.

A small dhow of about 35 tons, averaging 50 feet long and 10 feet beam. See "dhow."

BAURUA

Illustration on page 83.

An outrigger sailing canoe of the Gilbert Islands in the western Pacific. The sharp, double-ended hull had the flattened lee side characteristic of the islands of Micronesia. Because of the dearth of timber other than the cocoanut palm, it was carvel-built of varying lengths of planking sewed together and to the ribs. The keel was a sharp "V" in section, preferably of a single length. The types of outrigger differed with locality, but the commonest form consisted of three booms attached to "Y" connectives set in the pointed float. Sometimes a platform projected from the off side.

The rig was of the typical Micronesian type—a triangular sail with boom and yard set on a forwardly raking mast stepped amidships on the weather gunwale. The mast was braced by a shore and two stays to the central outrigger boom and also by fore-and-aft stays.

The "baurua" is now extinct, but it was formerly used for inter-island voyages and warfare. It was as fast as the "popo" and the "flying proa" and could sail very close to the wind. The canoes ranged in length from about 25 feet to three times this figure.

The only canoes which survive in the Gilberts are the tiny dugouts, "wa," and the fishing canoes, "waririk." The latter are 15 to 24 feet in length and their construction is similar to the "baurua."

BAWLEY

Illustration on page 35.

A small English vessel, common to the Thames Estuary, rigged similarly to a cutter, but without a main boom. It is wide-beamed, shallow-draft, with high freeboard forward, designed for fishing and trawling in all kinds of weather. Vertical stem, slightly raking stern-post, some drag to keel, outboard rudder slung to a transom stern, and a long, heavy bowsprit. The lower mast is short, but it carries a long topmast and gaff. The main-sail is sheeted to a horse inboard and brails are used for furling. The "bawleys" range in size from 22 feet by 8 feet by 3 feet draft to 32 feet by 11 feet by about 4 feet; clinker- or carvel-built. The crews generally consist of three men. The "bawleys" of Harwich and the Blackwater are deeper, drawing 3 to 4 feet forward and up to 6 feet aft.

BEAN COD   A small fishing or pilot boat, used by the Portuguese a century or two ago; in rig it was similar to the "tartane" (illustrated on page 57).

BELGIAN
LUGGER   The type illustrated is a three-masted fishing boat found (there may be a few left) off the Belgian coast. It is not unlike
Illustration on page 43.   the French three-masters, such as the Havre trawler. The rig consists of a tall mainmast with a dipping lugsail and topsail for fair weather, a shorter foremast stepped in the bow, a tiny mizzenmast with a triangular sail at the stern, and a jib to a bowsprit. The hull has a transom stern with outboard rudder and a straight stem with a curved forefoot. The three-masted rig makes for a well-balanced boat and a big spread of sail in light weather.

BERMUDA
SLOOP   A type of sloop built and developed in Bermuda, which was popular from about 1690 to about the time of the American
Illustrations on page 19.   Revolution. The type survived, however, in Bermuda well into the 19th century. It was also adopted by the colonists of Chesapeake Bay during the early 18th century. The "Bermuda sloop" was a proto-type of the sharp model schooners and somewhat similar to the Jamaica sloop which preceded it. The mast had a sharp rake aft and later models used a lofty leg-of-mutton mainsail. Earlier models had raised quarter-decks and high bulwarks, but the later ones were flush-decked, with just a low rail. The hulls were beamy and deep, with plenty of drag to the keel, transom sterned, and the stem and sternpost had con-siderable rake. Because of their speed, the "Bermuda sloops" were in great demand by pirates and privateers, and they were used quite extensively as small cruisers by the British Navy in the West Indies, and even in Europe, especially in the early 1800's. In size they ran as long as 75 or 80 feet over-all, and were often rigged with square sails for running before the wind. From about 1830 to the 1880's the smaller Bermudi-ans, with high leg-of-mutton mainsail and overlapping jib, were quite popular as racing boats in the Islands and in England. For beating to windward in smooth water they were considered the fastest boats in the world. Some used an out-and-out jib-headed, loose-footed mainsail with a headboard, and on others a short gaff was employed. In fair weather a peculiar quadrilateral topsail, extended by a diagonal sprit, was set.

Today the "Bermuda sloop" is extinct, as is its smaller and younger cousin, the "Bermuda dinghy," and boat building on the island died a natural death years ago, owing to the dearth of lumber.

BERMUDIAN   The name given to craft of the Bermuda Islands, using the lofty leg-of-mutton sail set on a raking mast.

BERTHON BOAT   A collapsible life boat frequently used on destroyers and small craft.

BIDARKA   The Russian term for a long, narrow canoe, made of skin, used by the Aleuts in Alaska. It is skin-decked, with one to three holes cut for occupants. There is little difference between the "kayak" (illustrated on page 87) and the single-holed "bidarka."

BIDARRA   A Russian name applied by the Aleuts to a large, open, flat-bottomed, double-ended, skin boat, which ranges in length from 20 to 50 feet. It is in general use for transportation and hunting from the Aleutian Islands to north Alaska. Large "bidarras" are employed for carrying freight. To the northern Eskimos, the type is known as "oomiak" or woman's boat. The "bidarra," like the "oomiak" or "umiak," is made by stretching walrus skins over a wooden framework. See "umiak," illustrated on page 87.

BILANDER   A term used as far back as 1550. The 18th century vessel's dis-
Illustration on page 55.   tinguishing feature was a trapezoidal mainsail similar to a cut-off lateen, the forward end going to the middle of the ship. The term "bilander" was used rather ambiguously, but it generally was a two-masted, square-rigged vessel with the above-mentioned mainsail.

BILGE BOARD SCOW   See "scow."

BILLY-BOY   A flat-bottomed, round-ended coasting vessel of Dutch origin,
Illustration on page 35.   used on the east coast of England. The rig is that of a sloop, ketch or yawl, with sometimes a square sail on the foremast. Clinker-built, with high sheer fore and aft. Leeboards are carried.

BINABINA   A canoe of the "mon" type of the Solomon Islands.
Illustration on page 89.

BIREME   A long narrow ship or galley of ancient times having two super-
Illustration on page 49.   imposed banks of oars.
The Phoenicians are credited with the origination of the bireme and perhaps the three-banked vessel, or trireme. The double and triple banks

[100]

gave increased oar-power without lengthening the hull. The earliest representations of the bireme are found on the walls of the palaces of the Assyrians, who were the conquerors of the Phoenicians and made use of their craft. While the latter people employed the bireme centuries before, these relief drawings date back only to the 7th century before Christ.

The war vessels pictured have a beaked prow for ramming, an upturned curved stern, decks fore and aft, an outside gangway, and a mast and square sail. The upper tiers of rowers are exposed to view or "aphract."

The ancient Greeks adopted the bireme and trireme as their vessels for warfare in the 6th or 7th centuries B.C. Their ships followed the lines of the Phoenicians, with the addition on some of an elevated forecastle. The triremes, and perhaps the larger biremes, are thought to have been two-masted. In action the mast and sails were either stowed below or left ashore. Steering was accomplished by means of quarter rudders or oars.

Though the system of protective bulwarks (cataphract) dated from an early period, it is claimed that the Greeks did not adopt it until after the Homeric era. The Athenians employed a girdle of ropes which ran lengthwise around the hull and was tightened by a lever or levers at the stern. This was done to strengthen the vessel and to take up part of the shock when ramming another ship. The average size of an Athenian trireme was about 130 feet in length and one of this dimension could accommodate 225 men, with 54 oars in each bank to a side.

The First Punic War in the 3d century saw the initial employment of the bireme and trireme by the Romans. Their larger war vessels had turreted fighting castles fore and aft from which spears and darts were thrown and they also developed the "corvus" or boarding grappler. Beginning in the 4th century B.C. fighting ships were constructed increasingly larger, but after the victory of the Liburnians with their fast light biremes, in the battle of Actium in 31 B.C., the huge unwieldy triremes became passé. See "galley" and "trireme."

BISQUINE
Illustration on page 37.
A two-masted, lug-rigged fishing boat, used in the vicinity of St. Malo, France. The hull has good sheer, high freeboard forward, straight vertical stem, raking sternpost, long overhanging counter, transom stern, short, straight keel, and much deadrise. The average size is 40 to 45 feet long, one-third to one-quarter the beam, about 6 feet draft, and 15 to 20 tons' displacement. Two lug topsails are sometimes carried on each mast and a single headsail on a very long bowsprit. The Cancale "bisquines" have a foremast right in the bow and a taller mainmast amidships, with a long bowsprit. A few "bisquines" carry a small lug mizzen, sheeted to a long boomkin.

BLACK BALLER A packet ship sailing under the flag of Marshall & Company, of New York, which was known as the "Black Ball Line."

Their ships carried a black ball on the foretopsail and the house flag was red with a black ball in the center of the field.

There was also an English company, of which James Baines was the head, known as the "Australian Black Ball Line," which used the same house flag and whose ships were also known as "Black Ballers," especially in England.

BLACKWALL FRIGATE
Illustration on page 23.

A passenger and cargo ship of England. This fine type of sailing vessel came into being after the East India Company lost its monopoly in the 1830's. The "Blackwallers" represented the supreme development of the packet ship of the period, not only in build, but in the treatment accorded the passengers and crew. These "frigate built" ships resembled those of the Royal Navy and were exceptionally well built of teak. They were great sail carriers and could hold their own against the clipper ships. The first "Blackwaller" launched was the *Seringapatum* in 1837 and the last was *Melbourne* in 1875.

BLOCK ISLAND BOAT
Illustration on page 21.

A sharp-ended, open keel boat, used at Block Island, Rhode Island. It had good sheer, with raking stem and sternpost. The rig was that of a cat schooner, with gaff and boom mainsail and loose-footed gaff foresail. The sails had a high hoist and narrow heads.

BOAT

Any small vessel or water craft propelled by oars, sail, or motor, as a rowboat, sailboat, or motor boat—seldom applied to large vessels.

BOBAO

A crude, outrigger, dugout, paddling canoe of the Tongan Archipelago, which lies between Fiji and Cook Islands. The outrigger has two straight booms with U-type connectives to the float. Round bottom with tumble-home sides. Not over 15 feet long and 16 inches beam.

BOEIER
Illustration on page 43.

A sloop-rigged yacht of the Netherlands. It is a roly-poly craft with a round bottom and is husky and well built, as are all Dutch boats. In plan the ends of the hull are semi-circular, with a diameter somewhat less than the beam. The section shows a round, almost circular bottom, with the sides tumbling home above the main sheer line. The sternpost is straight and practically vertical, while the stem is rounded. There is pronounced sheer forward and aft. The rig consists of two headsails and a loose-footed mainsail with the short curved gaff common to Dutch craft. It is equipped with leeboards and outboard rudder with tiller. The average size of the "boeier" is around 40 feet over-all with a beam about one-third.

BOMBARDA
Illustration on page 57.

An Italian pole-masted, polacre-rigged brigantine.

BOMB KETCH
Illustration on page 11.

A naval ketch, carrying mortars used for bombarding fortifications. It was used mostly in the French Navy in the 18th century, but was not adopted by the Americans.

BOMBSCHUITE
Illustration on page 43.

An odd, decked, tub-shaped fishing craft of the Netherlands; 39 to 35 feet long, with a beam about two-thirds the length; almost square-ended, with large outboard rudder and leeboards. The peculiar yawl rig is seen nowhere else in the world. The mast can be lowered.

BORNHOLM HERRING BOAT
Illustration on page 45.

Typical to the Danish island of Bornholm in the Baltic Sea. It is dandy-rigged, spritsail main and mizzen, with a straight leech. A yard topsail is sometimes used. This has a sliding gunter topmast, the heel of which comes within reach of the deck. The hull is about 22 feet long and 8 feet beam and has straight stem and sternpost.

BOTTER
Illustration on page 43.

A shallow-draft, sloop-rigged yacht of the Netherlands. It is, perhaps, the best sea boat of all Dutch craft. Just to be contrary, the Hollanders designed the "botter" with a rounded bow and a pointed stern. The bottom is flat and the sides are slightly curved and flare out a bit. The stem is gracefully curved and joins the heavy sweep of the forward sheer in a point. An outboard rudder is slung from a raking sternpost. The average size is about 40 feet length over-all with a beam about one-third and a draft of 2 feet with the leeboards raised.

BOULOGNE DRIFT-BOAT
Illustration on page 37.

A ketch-rigged vessel, engaged in the drift net fishery, which works out of the port of Boulogne, France. These drifters are large and husky, ranging in length to over 90 feet. The stem is plumb and a wide stern rises to a high bow. The main- and mizzensails are high peaked and loose-footed. A fore staysail and jib complete the working rig, the jib being extended to a long bowsprit. A white wave line is painted on each side of the bow just above the water line.

BOVO
Illustration on page 39.

A two-masted, lateen-rigged fishing vessel of the Gulf of Genoa, Italy. The rig is comprised of a mainmast, stepped just forward of amidships, with a lateen mainsail, a short mizzenmast on the stern, the lateen mizzen sheeted to a boomkin, and two or three headsails to a long bowsprit. The hull is beamy, with a low raking transom stern; the sheer moderate except at the bow where it rises to meet the stem.

BRAGAGNA
Illustration on page 57.
A three-masted, lateen-rigged sailing vessel similar to the "felucca" (illustrated on page 61) of the Mediterranean. The hull had good sheer, raking convex stem, raking sternpost and overhanging stern, and sometimes a raised poop. The small mizzen was sheeted to a boomkin and the forward raking foremast was stayed to the end of the long bowsprit. The "bragagna" was a native of Dalmatia and it was seen on the Adriatic and the Mediterranean until the middle of the last century.

BRAGOZZI
Illustration on page 39.
A two-masted, double-ended fishing craft of Venice. A very small lug foresail is carried on a mast stepped in the bow and a large balance lugsail is on the mainmast. The boats of Venice have little draft forward with drag to the keel, hence the center of sail effort is placed farther aft than usual. Bow lines are often employed to stretch the sail taut. The stem and sternpost are straight halfway down and then curve into the keel. The stem has a carved head which extends above the rail. The rudder is hung outside. The tack purchases on Italian vessels are set away from the mast to obtain a flatter sail. A feature of the Venetian boats is the painting of the sails in gay colors and designs.

BRAKEKA
An open boat used in the herring fishery from Blekinge, Sweden. It is clinker-built with eight strakes to a side and has a curved and strongly raking stem, flaring sides, and a thin narrow stern. The average size is about 20 feet long, with the beam about one-third. Usually spritsail rigged, with either one mast stepped amidships or a yawl rig with two jibs and sprit topsails.

BRIG
Illustration on page 9.
A two-masted, square-rigged vessel with a spanker and crossjack. A brig's main braces lead foward to the foremast. The brig rig was handy and fast.

BRIGANTINE
Illustration on page 9.
A two-masted vessel, square-rigged, but without a main course, the mainsail being a fore-and-aft sail. Crosstrees are used on the mainmast instead of the usual "top."

BRIG-SLOOP
Illustration on page 13.
In the British Navy, a brig or brigantine.

BRIXHAM TRAWLER
Illustration on page 31.
Large ketch- or dandy-rigged fishing vessels, working out of and originating in Brixham, Devonshire, England. The latter day Brixham boats run up to 70 feet in length and over 60 tons. Built for rough, deep-sea trawling, they are fine sea boats and

are at their best in a stiff breeze and a heavy seaway. A characteristic of the "Brixham trawler" is the forward rake to the masts. The hull is well-proportioned, the mid-section showing good dead rise; straight, slightly raking stem; fine entrance; high freeboard forward; easy sheer; deep forefoot, with considerable drag to the keel; raking sternpost, with overhanging counter and transom stern. The outer jib extends to a long bowsprit, generally without a bobstay. In moderate weather a maintopsail is carried.

Up to 50 or 60 years ago the "Brixham trawlers" were cutter-rigged, but since then the long boom has been discarded, the foot of the mainsail shortened, and the mizzen added. The big North Sea sailing trawlers are almost identical to the Brixham boats.

BROADHORN   A rough scow used in the early days on the Mississippi River. They were guided with long sweeps and floated down stream with the current, carrying passengers and freight from the Ohio River ports to New Orleans, and then sold for lumber at the latter port.

BUCCA   A sailing and rowing ship of the Crusades' period, of Venetian origin.

BUCENTAUR   The state barge of Venice in the time of the Doges. Propelled by sweeps on the main deck. A long upper deck (overhanging aft) extended about two-thirds the length forward from the stern. The whole boat was embellished with carvings and ornaments.

BUGALA   A lateen-rigged Arab trading vessel of the Red Sea, of the true "dhow" type, fast and seaworthy. The hull is very beamy, with a long overhang forward and raking transom stern. There is generally a high poop and a forward deck, the rest of the vessel being open, with battens nailed to the frames to keep the cargo off the bottom. A few planks are laid over crossbeams to afford a fore-and-aft gangway. The hull is double-planked, with a layer of composition between, making a dry and durable craft. The mainmast amidships and the mizzen on the poop rake forward. The Arab "dhows" have been ably handled by the Arabian sailors and, next to the Chinese, they have been the most skillful seamen of the East.

The bugala, bagala, baggalo and baggara vary little as a class, the differences in detail being as to the locality.

BUGALET   Small square-rigged craft used along the coast of Brittany in
Illustration on page 55.   the 17th century. Its rig consisted of a tall aftermast, with a large square sail and topsail; the foremast was much shorter, with a square sail and one or two jibs carried to a bowsprit.

BUGEYE

Illustrations on pages 19 and 221.

A type of vessel typical to and found only in the Chesapeake Bay region, where it is employed largely in the oyster fishery and as a pleasure craft. It is descended from the dugout canoes formerly used for tonging oysters. The "bugeye" derived its name from the old practice of painting an eye or circle on each side of the bow. The hull is shallow, carvel-built and sharp-ended with raking stem and sternpost. There is a fine entrance and run, medium sheer, rather flat floor, centerboard, outboard rudder and bowsprit. The usual rig consists of two leg-of-mutton sails and jib; as a rule the foremast is longer than the mainmast, but the schooner rig is used also. It is decked, with a square cabin house and a hatch to the hold. The clipper bow usually terminates in a long head, often embellished with scrollwork and a figurehead.

There are two classes of the true bugeye—"chunk boats" and "frame boats." The former is so-called because its keelson and bottom are fashioned from hewn logs. Instead of ribs, knees are employed, to which the planking and deck beams are secured. The frame boat is of ordinary construction. The masts of the bugeyes are raked aft excessively, but they sail well, particularly when close-hauled in a fresh breeze.

In the lower Chesapeake there is found a type of bugeye with a gaff foresail and leg-of-mutton mainsail and jib, which is known as a "brogan."

BUIS

Dutch for "buss"; also known as "herring buss" in the 17th century.

BULL BOAT

A North American Indian bowl-shaped "coracle" made of Buffalo hide, stretched over a frame of saplings. This crude craft was used on the Missouri River and its tributaries by the women of the Sioux, Arikara, Mandan, and Hidatsa tribes for carrying their goods. It was very light and could be easily carried by one person.

BUMBOAT

A small craft used to carry peddlers who supply the crews on ships with edibles and merchandise.

BURMA RICE BOAT

See "rice boat."

BUSS

Illustration on page 41.

A small, rotund, bulgy fishing boat, having three masts and a narrow poop. Three courses and sometimes a topsail on the main were used. The largest of this type of ship was about 200 tons, average length being about 50 feet and beam 16 feet. Popular in England and Holland in the 17th century. The "buss" was employed mainly in the herring fishery. It rode to the nets with only the mizzensail set, the bow to the wind.

BUTTERMAN SCHOONER	A topsail schooner used for carrying dairy products from the island of Guernsey to London in the 19th century until the advent of steam. Because of the sharp competition between the

Illustration on page 47.

"buttermen" an enormous spread of sail was carried. The mainmast carried a loose-footed mainsail and large topsail, while on the foremast were a foresail, square topsail, topgallant and royal, five headsails, besides two fisherman staysails. The hull was of a fast model with a sharp entrance, the greatest beam of the lower water lines being well forward, while that of the upper water lines was aft of amidships. The stem and sternpost were slightly raked with an overhanging counter. Typically 85 feet on the water, 100 feet over-all, 20 feet beam, 10½ feet draft.

BUZZO   A capacious cargo carrier of the Venetians, propelled generally by sails, although oars were sometimes used. Also known as the "bucca."

CABALLITO   A Peruvian reed fishing boat—a "balsa" (illustrated on page 89)—composed of cigar-shaped bundles of coarse grass lashed together to form an open boat or canoe. The "caballito" is very light and well adapted to ride the heavy swells of the Pacific. Propelled by a paddle.

CACHE   15th century English for "ketch."

CAÏQUE   A small open Turkish boat with a hull on the order of a skiff and of various sizes and rigs, rowed or sailed. The smaller boats are actually rowboats. The ordinary type of hull is low in the waist, curved stem and sternpost, with good sheer. The oars have blades shaped like mackerels' tails.

Illustration on page 57.

CALIFORNIA CLIPPER   A clipper ship engaged in carrying passengers and cargo from the east coast of the United States around Cape Horn to San Francisco, during the decade following the discovery of gold in California in 1848. This caused a tremendous boom in ship-

Illustration on page 5.

building in the eastern ports. On the return trip the ships usually crossed the Pacific to China and loaded tea and spices to make a profitable homeward voyage. Many famous clippers engaged in the California trade and speed was the watchword. The best time on the run from New York to San Francisco was made by *Flying Cloud*— 89 days, 8 hours—January 19 to April 20, 1853. Considering that the average time for the voyage was around 130 days, the record is remarkable. *Flying Cloud* repeated in 1854 and *Andrew Jackson* equaled it in 1859–60 (actually bettering the former record by a few hours). Passages of 100 days were common by the faster ships. See "tea clipper."

CAMARAE   An ancient rowing boat, broad of beam and tubby, sometimes
                 wholly or partially roofed over, in use in Asia Minor.

CANOA   A sloop-rigged fishing boat used by the natives of the ports of
Illustration on page 89.   the Amazon delta, in northeastern Brazil. When not engaged
                 in fishing, the "canoas" are employed in transporting merchan-
dise and miscellaneous products to Belém on the Para River and other towns around
the mouth of the river. Canoas range in size from a few tons to 30 or more. The
larger ones are also used to transport cattle from the farms on the Island of Marajó
to Belém and even as far as Cayenne, French Guiana. Before leaving for a fishing
trip, the canoas are loaded with ice to prevent the fish from spoiling. The fishermen
call these "geleiras." Those using the town of Vigia as a base are termed "vigilen-
gas."

    The hulls of the canoas have moderate sheer, a 45-degree rake to the stem and
sternpost, and are decked and have a cabin. The mast rakes aft sharply and the hoist
of the high-peaked mainsail is short, being less than one-half the length of the gaff.
The rudder is slung outboard.

CANOE   A light craft, usually sharp-ended, made of a wooden frame
                 over which is stretched a water-tight covering of thin wood,
bark, woven fabrics, hides, etc., or, in the case of the dugout, hollowed out of a log.
The latter was the earliest form of canoe or boat and is in use in many parts of the
world today, including the United States. The canoe is of great importance in the
history of water craft, because it was the main means of water transportation in
America from prehistoric times until the civilization of the white man was well
established.

    The skin and bark canoes developed by the North American Indians were (and
are) admirably suited to the purposes for which they were built and employed. As
the material for the birch-bark canoe was easily obtained, this type was widely used
by the tribes of the territory which is now the northern part of the United States and
Southern Canada, and its design was remarkable for its symmetry, lightness,
strength, buoyancy, and speed. The skin canoe, or kayak, of the natives of the Arctic
regions is another praiseworthy creation.

    The canoes of the Pacific islands vary in design and construction details, but the
outrigged type is used almost exclusively (the seagoing double canoes having disappeared) and the majority of these are dugouts or built-up dugouts. In Micronesia and
parts of the Orient, such as Ceylon and Malaya, an extremely fast outrigged sailing
model has been developed.

    It is worthy of note that in spite of the high degree of perfection to which the
dugout and other forms of canoes were brought by the Indians of the North and
South American continents, none of them had learned the use of sails for the propul-

[108]

sion of their craft until taught by the white man. Even then, the Indian did not take to sail readily and it has always been foreign to his nature.

The modern, carvel-built, plank canoe covered with canvas is the white man's improvement over the Indian's craft of bark. It was originated in Maine in the early 1890's. When sailed, a lateen sail is commonly used, with leeboards, but paddling is the main method of propulsion. The decked canoes, on the other hand, are usually sailed, and the rig generally consists of two masts with jib-headed sails. This type has been in use for the past 70 years, the early ones resembling the Eskimo kayak. The average size of the decked canoe for racing is 16 feet long by 30 inches wide, with a sail area of 90 square feet. They are equipped with centerboard, rudder with tiller ropes, and cross-sliding seat.

Today canoeing is a nation-wide sport and canoe clubs dot the landscape on rivers, streams, and lakes. The modern decked racing canoe requires considerable skill in handling and the sailer is kept more than busy taking care of sheets and tiller, in addition to shifting his weight on the sliding seat to counter-balance the sensitive hull. Illustrations of various canoes on page 87.

See "dugout," "cunner," "kayak," "Malay outrigger canoe," "proa," "Louisiana pirogue," "flying proa," "popo," "kaep," "wa lap," "pu hoe," wa'a," and other canoes of the Pacific Islands.

A canoe is also a light rowboat used by pilots for boarding steamers.

CANOE YAWL   A small English yawl-rigged cruising boat with a keeled-decked hull having a rounded stem and a canoe-shaped stern. These efficient and seaworthy cruisers range in size from 20 feet over-all by 6 feet beam to 30 feet over-all by 10 feet beam.

CARAMOUSEL   Similar to the "saique" (illustrated on page 59) except for a much higher stern.

CARACORE   This was a light vessel of the 18th century used on the Island
Illustration on page 75.   of Borneo and Dutch East Indies and also by the Dutch as coast guards in those latitudes. It was high at each end and propelled chiefly with paddles. To use paddles some of the men sat in the vessels and others on outriggers on both sides of the craft. By placing three or four rows of men on the outriggers and some within the hull, considerable speed could be obtained. The mast was a tripod of bamboo poles supported by shrouds. There was but one sail, an elongated quadrilateral sail bent to a bamboo yard at the head and to a boom at the foot. The boom was hauled aft by a sheet and the yard had a bow line to keep it to windward. Also there was a brace or vang which led aft from the peak or leeward end of the yard. The sail could be rolled up or furled by a crank on the forward end of the boom.

CARAVEL
Illustration on page 53.
One of the most romantic types of ships through the ages. The "caravel" was at its height in the 15th and 16th centuries and was employed to a great extent by the explorers of that period. It was a more able and graceful ship than its contemporaries and a better sailer. It had rather high bulwarks, square stern, a bowsprit with spritsail, and fore-and-aft castles, the latter being high. Three or four masts were carried and the rig varied according to locality and period. The earlier types were lateen-rigged and may have carried a square sail on the foremast for running. The prevailing type seems to have been a four-masted vessel, with a square-rigged foremast and three lateen-rigged masts decreasing in size. A round "top" was carried on the foremast and sometimes on the main. Another type was lateen-rigged on the first mast and aftermast, while the second and third masts were square-rigged. A square topsail was sometimes carried above the forecourse.

CARRACK
Illustration on page 53.
A term generally applied to larger ships of the 14th, 15th, and 16th centuries. They were designed to carry large cargoes. The type was distinctive, in that it had higher topsides and greater draft than other ships of that period. They perhaps reached 1,000 tons' burden and had fore-and-aft castles; also four large wales. The sides of the hull were strengthened with skids. Three, and sometimes four, masts were carried, the main-mast being larger than the others. The form of hull and rigging differed as to locality and period, combinations of square and lateen sails being used.

CARTEL
A vessel used to negotiate with an enemy under a flag of truce and to carry prisoners of war.

CASCO
A canoe about the size of a dory used by the Brazilians of the Amazon delta. It is made of a dugout bottom with flaring sides of planks and raking, V-shaped end pieces. See "montaria."

CAT
Illustration on page 55.
Used widely in marine terminology since the 13th century. An early form of "cat" was a rowing vessel, having a beak like a galley and about fifty sweeps on either side, each sweep being rowed by two men. In the early 18th century it was a three-masted merchant vessel on the order of a Dutch "flute" (illustrated on page 41). This hull was blunt and tub-bish; therefore, very slow, and it was square-rigged. The Norwegian "cat" was a rather large vessel with three masts and a bowsprit and the hull had a heavy sheer. It was rigged like an English ship, having, however, only pole masts (no topmasts), and it carried no topgallant sails. The mizzen was rigged with a gaff sail.

CATASCOP-ISCUS
A fast Roman sailing ship of about 200 A.D. employed for reconnoitering and scouting.

CAT BOAT *Illustration on page 219.*	A small present-day sailboat, very beamy in proportion to its length, having a single mast with a fore-and-aft sail set almost to the bow.
CATAMARAN	A raft of logs lashed together, either sailed or rowed. See "kat-tumaran," "yuloh."
CAT SCHOONER	A two-masted vessel which was cat-rigged, carrying no jib, the foremast being set right in the bow.
CAYUCA	A dugout canoe used by the Indians of Panama.
CELOCES	A swift, single-banked Greek galley.
CHAMPAN	A small flat-bottomed vessel used by the Chinese and Japanese. It had one mast, rigged the same as the mainmast of a "junk,"

with a single sail made of cane. It seldom exceeded 80 tons' burden and was constructed without iron or nails. Owing to the rickety build, the "champan" was unfit for rough weather. It was used in the 18th century and was about the same as the "sampan" of the present day.

CHAMPLONG	A double-ended, decked, keel sailing craft of Java and Pulau Klapa. Curved stem and sternpost, rising above the gunwale,

curving inboard, and terminating in an oval-shaped, elaborately carved end. It has washboards at the quarters, upon which rests a mat roof. Forward of this are tholes for oars. A single cotton lugsail is carried. Average size about 25 feet, with one-third the beam.

CHANGADAM	East Indian for "double canoe."
CHANNEL ISLANDER *Illustration on page 37.*	A local type of fishing and pilot boat typical to the Channel Islands in the English Channel, three-masted and about 36 feet long. Formerly lug-rigged, but lately a boomless fore-and-aft sail with a high peak has been adopted. A jib is carried on a long bowsprit.
CHASSE-MARÉE *Illustration on page 37.*	A French vessel of the lugger type, carrying three masts (each with a lugsail), a bowsprit, and jibs. The fore- and mizzen-masts are stepped in the extreme bow and stern, respectively,

the mizzensail being sheeted to a long boomkin extended beyond the stern. Sometimes one or two lug topsails are carried. The "chasse-marée" is still in use in practically the same form it has been for generations.

CHATTE   A lighter used in loading and unloading larger vessels in French ports.

CHEBACCO
BOAT
Illustration on page 19.

A small sailing vessel originated and built in the parish of Chebacco of Ipswich, Massachusetts (incorporated in the town of Essex since 1819), and used extensively in the fisheries of New England during the half century following the Revolutionary War. It was characterized by a narrow overhanging "pink" stern and "cat-schooner" rig—no bowsprit nor headsails. These boats were rarely over 40 feet long, rigged with two raking pole masts, the foremast stepped in the bow and the mainmast amidships; outboard rudder with tiller; full round bow with curved stem; raking sternpost; narrow beam. Each boat had two or more "standing rooms" or cockpits, in which the men stood and fished with hand lines. The floor of the standing rooms was just above the keelson. Many of the larger boats were flush-decked, however. The "Chebacco boat" and its square-sterned first cousin, the "dogbody," handled most of the fish caught off the New England shores until they gave way to the "pinky" (illustration on page 19) about 1820. Both types were fine sailers and seaworthy.

CHESAPEAKE
BAY
SCHOONER
Illustration on page 17.

A type of schooner extensively used in the oyster fishery of Chesapeake Bay and tributaries. Moderately sharp bow and sharp stern; flat floor and low bilge; lofty schooner rig; masts rake aft sharply; maintopsail carried. Average size 45 to 55 feet, with one-fourth the beam.

CLIPPER
PACKET

See "packet ship."

CLIPPER
SCHOONER

A Baltimore-built, centerboard fishing schooner used in the Cape Cod mackerel fishery in summer and for transporting oysters from Chesapeake Bay to New England ports in the winter. With few exceptions, this type was a shallow-keeled, beamy craft, about 60 feet long, one-third the beam, with flat, sharp floors and long easy lines forward and aft; raking curved stem; light square stern; schooner-rigged. From 1845 to 1855 an effort was made by New Englanders to improve the speed of their vessels and the clipper schooner type was tried out. While they were fast, they were wet and uncomfortable in a blow and they were soon replaced by stauncher New England built vessels.

CLIPPER SHIP
Illustration on page 5.

A large, sharp-modeled, ship-rigged sailing vessel of great sail carrying capacity. The "clipper ship" was developed by American shipbuilders in response to a growing demand for larger and faster ships. The clipper ship (as a distinct type) era began with the launching of the *Rainbow* in 1845 and ended about 1860, although by 1854 the boom was over and decadence in the American merchant marine set in. No new out-and-out clippers were launched in America after 1857. The design of the clipper ship was an outgrowth of the Baltimore clipper and the later fast packet ship.

The essentials of a "clipper ship" were: firstly, that its rig was loftier, more heavily sparred, and carried a larger area of canvas than other ships of the same size; and secondly, that the hull was more sharply built. The stem was sharp, usually concave, but never convex; very little, if any, rake to the sternpost; varying sheer; short broad counter; sharp-ended, with often a hollow entrance; and clean, but rather short run. The length was five to six times the beam. The greatest breadth was about amidships. The early clippers had rather severe dead-rise but the later models had long flat floors. Although the clipper was a very fast model, it was hard driving on the part of the skipper that made the highly advertised quick passages possible. Because the design reached an uneconomic development, the extreme clipper did not influence future shipbuilding to any great extent in America. The financial depression, foreign competition, the opening of the West, the steamship, diminished California and Australian trade, the Panama railroad (opened in 1855) all contributed to end the glamorous epoch of the American clipper ship.

Following is a list of some record passages made by clipper ships:

New York to San Francisco—Andrew Jackson, 89 days 4 hours, March 23, 1860 (finished). *Flying Cloud*, 89 days 8 hours, April, 1854, and 89 days 21 hours, August, 1851.

San Francisco to New York—Comet, 76 days, March, 1854.

San Francisco to Boston—Northern Light, 76 days 6 hours, March, 1853.

San Francisco to Shanghai—Swordfish, 32 days, July, 1853.

Hongkong to New York—Sea Witch, 74 days 14 hours, March, 1849.

Liverpool to Melbourne—James Baines, 63 days, February, 1855.

New York to Equator—Great Republic, 15 days 19 hours, December, 1856.

New York to Bombay—Sweepstakes, 74 days, July, 1857.

Liverpool to New York (westward)—*Andrew Jackson*, 15 days, November, 1860.

San Francisco to Honolulu—Flying Cloud, 8 days 8 hours, September, 1852.

See "China clipper," "California clipper," "tea clipper," "packet ship."

COASTER	A vessel used in the coastwise trade.
Illustrations on pages 39, 47 and 69.	
COBLE	A small, distinctive, open boat of both Durham and York-
Illustration on page 35.	shire, England, 20 to 30 feet in length and 5 to 10 feet beam. It was designed to be launched from the shore against heavy

seas—hence, the high flaring bow and fine hollow entrance, running away to clean, flat stern section. The stem is curved and the sternpost straight, both raked. It is clinker-built and on either side of the bottom, running aft from amidships, are two "shorvels," or shallow keels to assist in keeping the boat upright when beached. A deep forefoot makes the "coble" a fine boat on the wind. The sterns are either square or round, the latter preferred because of superior running power. An outboard rudder is carried, drawing 3 to 4 feet. The rig is a single dipping lugsail on a raking mast. For every reef taken in the sail, the mast is given a greater rake aft, to assist in lifting her over head seas. The "cobles" have been extinct for several years.

COBRE A Dutch fishing craft of the early 16th century, similar to the "dogger."

COCK A small sailboat from 2 to 6 tons' burden, used in the herring fishery out of Brighton, England, in the middle 19th century.

COCK BOAT A small dinghy or rowboat used as a tender.

CODICARIAE A flat-bottomed boat used in ferrying and general cargo carrying on the Tiber River by the ancient Romans.

COG
Illustration on page 47. A double-ended, bluff-bowed, full-lined vessel in use in the 11th to 14th centuries in Northwestern Europe. This clinker-built craft made its appearance in the Mediterranean in the 14th century. The Norman "cogs" of the 13th century had raised platforms fore and aft and rows of shields along the outside of the bulwarks. Merchantmen probably did not carry this "pavese." The larger "cogs" were three-masted, with observation and fighting "tops" at the heads, and each mast carried a single square sail.

COLLIER BRIG
Illustration on page 47. A brig used in the coal trade on the Thames River and English coast in the 18th and 19th centuries. A huge single headsail and large topsails were carried.

CORACLE A primitive bowl-shaped, basket-like craft made of woven grasses or reeds, either oval or round. See "bull boat," "courache," "corita."

CORBITA
Illustration on page 51. A heavily-built, slow-sailing merchant ship of ancient Rome. The name was derived from the Roman "corbis" or basket, one of which was carried at the masthead to indicate that they carried merchandise and passengers. The "corbita" was a "round" ship, with a high, curved stern, and considerable sheer to a raking stem. A pole mast, stepped amid-

ships, was stayed by fore- and backstays and shrouds set up with lanyards and dead-eyes. It carried a square sail hung from a horizontal yard and was furled to the yard with vertical brails, which passed through rings on the sail. A topsail of two triangular halves was carried above the lower sail. An "artemon," a sail similar to the later spritsail, was hung beneath a bowsprit. The vessel was steered by a large oar on the quarter.

CORITA — A large, basket-like "coracle" formerly used by the Indians of south central California and the lower Colorado River for fording streams with passengers and merchandise. The outside was water-proofed, usually with bitumen.

CORNER BOAT — A skipjack type called "corner boat" at Provincetown, Massachusetts, because the topsides meet the bottom at an angle, or chine, forming a corner. It is a compromise between the flat-bottom and round-bottom boat.

CORNWALL DRIVER — A lug-rigged fishing ketch of Cornwall, England, with double headsails.

CORSAIR — A privateer of the Mediterranean. Its activities were mostly of a piratical nature.

CORVETTE
Illustration on page 27. — A ship common in the French Navy. Generally, it was a "sloop of war," with low freeboard, no high quarter-deck, and the guns were carried on the upper deck. The masts and sails were rigged similarly to a frigate and it mounted 14 to 32 guns. The U.S.S. *Saratoga*, Captain Macdonough's flagship in the Battle of Lake Champlain, War of 1812, was a "corvette," but the term was not used extensively in the American Navy.

COURACHE — An early Irish "coracle." Oval-shaped, covered with hide, tarred canvas, or made of wicker. It carried but one person and was fitted with a pair of oars.

CRABBER — A small, open sailboat used in setting out and collecting crabs from "crab pots," which were weighted and buoyed, set out and emptied each morning. "Crabbers" were 20 to 23 feet long, with lug or sloop rig, depending on locality. See "langoustier."

CRAYER — A small coasting vessel of England and Western Europe, which preceded the "hoy." It was a rotund craft, with rounded bow and stern, and a square sail was carried from a single mast. The "crayer" might be called a small "cog." The tonnage ranged from 15 to perhaps 60.

[115]

CROMSTER
Illustration on page 53.
A popular two-masted vessel used in England and Holland during Elizabethan days. It was rigged as follows: a jib, or forestaysail, extended on a stay running to a long bowsprit; a hoy mainsail (one extended on a sprit), a square course and topsail on the mainmast and a lateen mizzen. The bow was bluff, with a curved stem and beakhead. There was a raised foredeck and the sheer rose to a high poop. Naval "cromsters" were armed on the upper and lower decks. They were not unlike a large "hoy." The Dutch name was "cromsteven."

CUNNER
A dugout sailing canoe used in the oyster fishery of Chesapeake Bay, 25 to 30 feet long, cat-schooner-rigged, with leg-of-mutton sails, and sometimes a jib.

CURRAGH
A boat-shaped coracle used by the fishermen of the west coast of Ireland. It is made of light sticks and boards covered with canvas and smeared with pitch. Though rather crude in construction, it is easily carried by one man and remarkably buoyant, having the ability to ride the huge waves of the Atlantic.

CUTTER
Illustration on page 55.
A single-masted sailing vessel with a deep underbody, rather narrow beam and heavy keel. Generally, the stem is vertical and the transom stern is very raking. The bow is drawn out sharply. The rig consists of four sails, gaff and boom mainsail, foresail, jib and gaff topsail to a topmast, and the bowsprit is long. The main boom extends a little way beyond the stern. This is the old style type of hull and rig.

The cutter rig in Northern Europe probably descended from the lateen sail of the Mediterranean. Owing to its speed and handiness, the "cutter" has been much in favor for yacht racing and this improved the type greatly.

In the earlier days, it was used by smugglers and as revenue cutters by western European nations. The "cutter" is essentially an English type and was probably in use as early as Elizabeth's time.

In the Navy, a cutter is a ship's boat for rowing or sailing—strongly built and capable of carrying heavy weights of men and stores.

CUTTER GALLEY
Illustration on page 13.
A small galley about 43 feet long, with a short quarter-deck, four gun ports, and three sweep ports to a side. Cutter-rigged with square topsails. Continental cutter galleys were used by General Benedict Arnold on Lake Champlain in 1776.

CUTWATER
A Yorkshire, England, term for a small, sharp-bowed "coble," 18 feet long and 7 feet beam.

DAHABIA
Illustration on page 63.
A lateen-rigged, long-hulled house boat used on the Nile.

DANDY
Illustration on page 33.
A cutter or sloop-rigged vessel, used in British waters, with a mizzenmast abaft. A true "dandy" is lug-rigged, but a fore-and-aft mainsail and a leg-of-mutton mizzen are now generally used. The term "dandy" is sometimes applied by British fishermen to any ketch or yawl.

DEAL LUGGER
Illustration on page 33.
Open clinker-built boat used in the port of Deal in Southern England since the 13th century. It formerly carried three lugsails, with no jib. Later models discarded the mainmast amidships. A small forecastle is built forward and a small removable deck house amidships. This type was used by the Kentish boatmen for life saving and carrying pilots, as well as "hovelling." By 1880 the "Deal lugger" was on the wane. See "hoveller."

DE WANG
Illustration on page 81.
A two-masted sailing dugout canoe with outrigger used in the Sassi Islands in the Bismarck Archipelago. The hull has rounded sides and bottom, with ends that terminate in sharp beaks, flat on top, usually carved, as are the sides of the canoe. Two strakes are sewn on above the gunwales. A heavy outrigger float is supported by three transverse booms placed fairly close together on the upper strakes. A double platform, with rail around, usually sits on the booms amidships. Two oppositely raking masts are stepped on the floor. The small woven pandanus sails, rectangular in shape, are set from the upper half of the masts. Each sail has an upper and lower yard.

The one-masted canoes (known as "gaw gawn-nasalin") are similar to the two-masted canoes, the mast being lashed to the front of the platform.

DGHAISA
Pronounced dīcer. A gondola-like, lateen-rigged boat peculiar to Valetta, Malta.

DHOW
Illustration on page 67.
Since time immemorial the "dhow" has sailed the waters of the Red Sea and the Indian Ocean—from Rangoon to Zanzibar. The general characteristics of a "dhow" (which may vary in detail according to locale, but little as a class) are a sharp bow, with a long overhang forward, great beam, raking transom stern, considerable sheer rising to a high poop, and the lateen rig. There is generally a forecastle deck, but between this and the poop deck the waist is practically open, planks being laid over the crossbeams for a fore-and-aft gangway. The poop is often highly ornamented and studded with windows. "Dhows" are usually double-planked, with composition between, making for great durability. The keel is straight or arched.

The rig is a lateen, with main and mizzen, although many of the Arab or Red Sea "dhows" have but a single mast. Most of the Indian seagoing "dhows" carry a mizzen, as well as a small jib to a short bowsprit. The mainmast is a heavy, tall spar with a great forward rake. The lateen yard is about the length of the hull and is made up of two or three pieces lashed together. The halyard, single or double, is a heavy rope, which passes through a sheave in the masthead from the forward side to a purchase leading to the front of the poop. The mizzenmast is a smaller spar, stepped either through the poop deck or just ahead of it, and has less rake than the mainmast. The standing rigging is scant, consisting mainly of shrouds on either side, and perhaps a forestay. The mizzensail is much smaller than the mainsail. When desiring to change tack, the Arab wears around, the sail flying forward, the yard then swung, and the sheet hauled in. The sails are seldom reefed. Instead various sizes are carried and used according to the strength of the wind. The sails are often bent with the yards standing. Owing to the great weight of the main yard and sail, a large crew is necessary for hoisting. If the Arab is not the most efficient sailor in the world, he is without a doubt the most vociferous and excitable. See "bugala," "kotia," "patta-mar," etc.

DINGHI
Illustration on page 65.

A boat used for transportation on the Ganges and Hugli Rivers in India. The open hull is not unlike the early Egyptian craft in form—crescentic sheer meeting the straight and strongly raking stem and sternpost in a point. A simple square sail hung from a horizontal yard is supported by a mast stepped just forward of a rounded cabin. Sometimes a square topsail is set. Steered with a sweep.

DINGHY
Illustration on page 223.

A small row boat used as a tender. Dinghies are popular as small racing craft. Then they are equipped with a sail and an outboard rudder.

DJONG

A "junk."

DOGBODY

Similar to a "chebacco" boat, but square-sterned, cat schooner-rigged, about 36 feet long and 11 feet beam, with full rounding bow and a little "cuddy" forward with berth, and sometimes a fireplace for cooking. Used extensively in cod and mackerel fishing. See illustration of "chebacco boat" on page 19.

DOGGER
Illustration on page 43.

A sturdy two-masted vessel used by the Dutch and other nearby peoples for fishing in the German seas and on the Dogger Banks. On the mainmast were set two square sails; on the mizzenmast was a gaff sail, and above that a topsail was carried. The "dogger" also had a bowsprit, with a spritsail and two or three jibs.

DONGA   A peculiar type of dugout canoe made from the trunk of the
               tar palm tree and used by the native fishermen of Jessor, Ben-
gal, India. Due to the shape of the tree, the prow of the canoe has a diameter of about
2 feet 4 inches and the stern only 11 inches, the length being 12 or 13 feet.

DORY   A small, flat-bottomed boat used extensively in the fisheries
Illustration on page 87.   of the United States, especially in the New England States. It
               is open, keelless, clinker-built of rather wide planks; double-
ended, both ends raking severely; sharp bow; narrow, V-shaped stern; slightly
rounded flaring sides; sharp rounding sheer. Lengths up to about 22 feet, with one-
fourth the beam. Rowed or sailed. It is readily stowed into "nests" by removing the
thwarts. Very seaworthy, at least three having been known to cross the Atlantic.
The dory was originated in Newburyport, Massachusetts, about 1800, but it did
not become popular in the fisheries until the middle of the last century. It is used by
American, Canadian, and French "bankers."

DOUARNENEZ   A two-masted, cat-rigged lugger used in the mackerel and
   LUGGER   sardine fisheries out of the port of Douarnenez, on the west
Illustration on page 37.   coast of Brittany, France. The bow is high, with a straight
               stem, slightly raked; the sheer line is almost straight, running
to a low stern, which is either transom or sharp; carvel-built. The sternpost has a
terrific rake, the rudder being slung outside; steered with a tiller; 22 to 40 feet long;
beam over one-third the length. Deepest draft is aft and ranges from 2 feet for the
smaller sizes to about 7 feet for the 36 and 40 footers. The forefoot is very shallow,
hence there is much drag to the keel. There is a hard turn to the bilges. Inside ballast
only. Decked or open. These luggers are very fast to windward and are fine weather
boats. The masts rake aft, the mainmast being stepped amidships and the fore in the
bow. The dipping lugsails are lofty and highly peaked. The tack of the foresail is
secured to the head of the stem, and the main lugsail is sheeted to the heavy rudder
post. The luff rope is laced to a heavy line, which extends from the lower end of the
yard to the point of the tack. Generally the only stay is the halyard and its purchase.
The sails are of about equal size and are tanned.

   The port of Douarnenez has long been known for its luggers and the Breton
coast is the last stronghold of the commercial sailing vessel in Europe, but there,
too, power-driven craft have made vast inroads in the picturesque fleets of sailing
luggers.

   Across Douarnenez Bay at Morgat the type varies somewhat, the bow being
almost of the clipper type and the mainsail is nearly always larger than the fore. The
luggers of the west coast of Brittany have the same characteristics as a class, but
vary in detail in the different ports.

   See also "Morbihan lugger" and "sardinier."

[119]

DOUBLE
CANOE
Illustration on page 77.
A craft made up of two canoes of equal or nearly equal lengths placed parallel with one another and connected a short distance apart by two or more transversely placed booms. The hulls were usually dugouts or partial dougouts with planks sewn on to form the sides, as in the case of the "pahi" of the Tuamotu Archipelago. The types of double canoe ranged from the simple "wa'a kaulua" of Hawaii to the large platformed voyaging vessels, such as the "tipairua" of the Society Islands, "alia" of Samoa, and the Fijian "ndrua," the latter being the finest and largest native double canoe built by the people of Oceania. These vessels were usually equipped for sailing. The rig in Hawaii, Marquesas, Cook, and Society Islands and New Zealand was the Oceanic spritsail, while the Oceanic lateen, in various forms, was used in Fiji, Tonga, Samoa, Tuamotus, Ellice Islands and Papua. Double canoes were prevalent in all the Polynesian Islands, but were rare in Melanesia and Micronesia, except in New Guinea. They are practically extinct in Polynesia.

DRAGON
Illustration on page 49.
A large Viking ship used in warfare. These war vessels were elaborately carved and decorated. The sides gleamed with their stripes of color and gold, topped off by the warriors' shields hung along the gunwales. The figureheads were of gold and the sails of rich-colored embroidered cloth.

DRIVER
A fishing boat engaged in the drift-net fisheries in English waters. A drift-net is a long net, 9 to 12 feet deep, with about 30 meshes per running yard, used for catching herring, mackerel, etc. The top edge of the net is floated by corks and the bottom weighted by sinkers, suspending it vertically. A number of nets are used by each boat and they are fastened together, end to end, making a continuous net a mile or more in length. It is shot or set where the fish are supposed to be running (generally at night), the boat riding to a line at the leeward end, the boat and nets drifting along until the nets are full. Then they are hauled and the catch taken aboard, the meshes being alive with the fish caught by their gills. The last quarter of a century has seen the gradual abandonment of the lug-rigged fishing boat and the drift, or gill, net, in favor of the steamers and motor boats equipped with purse-seines or trawls. See "Cornwall driver," "Mount's Bay driver," etc.

DROMON
A large galley of the Crusades' period of Roman origin, with two rows of twenty-five oars each on either side. Probably three-masted, lateen-rigged. There was a deck above the rowers for fighting purposes.

DROGHER *or*
DROGER
A bluff-modeled vessel used in transporting heavy cargoes, as a "stone drogher"; also a type of West Indian trader.

DUGOUT A canoe or boat made by hollowing out a log and shaping it into the form of a vessel, usually sharp-ended. The dugout was the earliest form of hollow water craft and by the Stone Age it had reached a well-developed state of efficiency. It followed the prehistoric raft. To make a dugout canoe, a tree trunk is scooped out with an adz or mattock, burned out with fire, then chipped with a small axe and finally scraped with a piece of broken glass or scraper, making a smoth hard surface. It is a long tedious process.

The hollowed-out canoe is used throughout the world. It was brought to a high degree of perfection by the Indians of various parts of North America and is still to be found in the bayous of Louisiana, the waters of Chesapeake Bay, the west coast of Canada and Alaska, and on Pátzcuaro and other lakes of Mexico. The paddling and sailing canoes—outrigged and voyaging—of Oceania and Indonesia were and are predominantly dugouts and in some places, as Micronesia, Malaya and Ceylon, an extremely fast model has been developed.

The natives in parts of South America and Africa also employ the dugout to a great extent. Fine large canoes were made in the past by the Indians on the coast of Oregon and northern California. These were usually made from giant cedar trees and ranged up to 100 feet in length.

The size of a dugout is, of course, limited by the length and breadth of the trees available, being constructed from a single tree trunk. When trunks of sufficient size are not obtainable, partial or built-up dugouts are made by using one or more logs fashioned into a base, with sides of planks built on above. Most of the Oceanic sailing dugout canoes have washstrakes above the topsides to increase the freeboard.

See "ballam," "cunner," "donga," "jalor penjalap," "Louisiana pirogue," "Malar panchi," "Malay outrigger canoe," "mtepi," "piragua," "proa," "tony," "kaep," "flying proa," "wa'a," and canoes of the Pacific islands.

DUM
Illustration on page 43.
A Dutch fishing boat of Scheveningen, husky and clinker-built, beamy and shallow-draft. It is sloop-rigged with the short curved gaff and long boom on the mainsail, one or two headsails and long bowsprit. An outboard rudder is slung from a transom stern. Leeboards are used as in most Dutch craft.

DUNDEE
The name given to the large ketches formerly used by the Bretons in the fisheries off Iceland.

EAST-INDIAMAN
Illustration on page 25.
The large, armed, cargo-carrying ships that were owned and operated by the British East India Company were known as Indiamen. At a distance they might be taken for ships of war, but closer inspection would disprove this, as the deck arrange-

ment was different and the rig was that of a merchantman. The hulls had full underbodies, flat floors, sharp turns to the bilges and quick rises, all of which make for a slow vessel, but ample room for a large cargo. The Indiamen were heavily armed and manned to be able to resist any attacks by pirates or ships of hostile nations whose officers might covet the immensely valuable cargoes from the far off Indies. Studding sails were an important part of the equipment, as great distances could be sailed before a prevailing breeze.

EGYPTIAN CRAFT
circa 2000 B.C. and circa 1600 B.C.
Illustration on page 63.

The illustration of the Nile boat of 4000 years ago represents the oldest known record of a sailing craft. The prehistoric tomb carving which shows a boat of this type pictures a more exaggerated spoon-shaped hull, which could scarcely be expected to remain upright unless very heavily ballasted. The bow terminated to a high post, while the stern curved back, finishing in a carving of a bird or beast, or perhaps a lotus flower. A square sail and oars were the means of propulsion.

The Egyptian galley of fourteen centuries later, more or less, was apparently a larger vessel, as the carvings show as many as twenty-six oars to a side, besides four steersmen and a cargo of cattle. As the fore-and-aft portions of the hull were unsupported by the water, a rope truss supported by crutches extended from stem to stern to prevent hogging. A wide square sail, usually with a yard top and bottom, was used when the wind was favorable, and reefing probably was accomplished by lowering the upper yard. One or two men to a side did the steering, each with a paddle to which a tiller was attached.

Sea fights evidently were not an uncommon occurrence and the early Egyptians seem to have been able adversaries, as the Pharaohs recorded victories over the combined forces of the Persians, Mysians, and Taucrians. The war galleys were equipped with a metal beak projecting from the bow for ramming.[1]

EKA

A clinker-built, flat-bottomed rowing boat used for fishing on the small lakes of Sweden. The bottom curves up at the ends to a narrow, square bow and stern, and there is good sheer. The average length is from 15 to 16 feet, with a beam of 5 feet 6 inches.

EKTA

A primitive form of dugout canoe used at Patna, Bengal, India, made from the stem of the semul tree.

ENDROL
Illustration on page 81.

The native term for canoe in the Admiralty Islands, which form a portion of the Bismarck Archipelago. The outrigger sailing canoe illustrated is a dugout, the ends being formed by inserting long blocks of wood into the open ends of the hollowed log. These blocks are carved and painted to represent a crocodile's head. A long, narrow washstrake, higher in the center, extends along each side of the hull. Three to five booms support a canoe-shaped outrigger float, each attachment consisting of several crossed pairs of sticks. A platform of poles is usually laid over the booms.

A mast about one-half the length of the hull is stepped in the bottom of the hull against the front of the platform. The mast is steadied by four stays and an inclined pole to the masthead. A rectangular lugsail of matting, with upper and lower yards, sets obliquely. The large "endrols" are often two-masted and are manned by as many as fifteen men. The paddles are used more on the order of rowing than paddling.

ESNECCA   A craft of the Crusades' period, propelled by sweeps and sail. It was, in all probability, a huskier and larger model of the Viking ship, and it may have had a short raised deck fore and aft. "Esneccas" were among the ships used by Richard, the Lion-hearted, in his great mass voyage to the Holy Land.

ESSEX OYSTER-   A cutter-rigged craft used in the oyster fisheries of Burnham,
BOAT   Mersea, Brightlingsea, and other ports on the Thames estuary.
Illustration on page 35.   These smart boats somewhat resemble the "bawleys," except that their rig is yachtier in appearance and the boom mainsails have a loftier cut. They have the old-fashioned counter stern and a short sliding bowsprit, are decked, the stem is vertical, the sternpost raking, and there is little drag.

ETAPLES   A two-masted, lug-rigged fishing boat working out of Etaples,
LUGGER   France. The higher foremast is set well in the bow, carrying a
Illustration on page 37.   standing lugsail and a jib to a bowsprit. The mizzen, set in the stern, is sheeted to a boomkin. The hull has a straight stem, transom stern and raking sternpost. It will be noticed that the English and Scottish sails are peaked higher and sharper than the square-cut French lugsails, and, hence, are better for windward work.

ETEA   A small, light, extremely narrow (10 to 12 inch) dugout canoe used at San Cristobal Island and one or two other islands in the Solomon group. A long, slender outrigger float, usually made from the middle rib of a frond of the sago palm, is supported by a main central boom by means of two U-shaped connectives and another slender boom projecting from the bow. The ends of the hull are pointed and raked. The occupant sits on a board placed on the gunwales amidships.

FASSONE   A reed rowing boat, or balsa, of Sardinia. It is made in the typical balsa manner—bundles of reeds fashioned and lashed together to make a boat with a curved bow terminating to a point and a square stern. It is rowed and wooden outriggers extend outward from the sides to carry the oarlocks and oars.

FELOUQUE A "felucca" of Southern France and Spain.

FELUCCA A Mediterranean vessel of many varieties—one or two masts,
Illustration on page 61. lateen sails, with or without oars. A large "felucca" of former days might have an apostis—galley-like—as a part of the superstructure built above the hull, with the after part of the deck drawn out to a tapering, overhanging platform beyond the transom stern. The stem would rake and terminate into a long bowsprit, which would take the forestay. It would be two-masted carrying high lateens and the hull might be embellished with carving and gold work. When the wind was unfavorable for sailing, the stately craft would be propelled by many sweeps.

FIFIE A 19th century Scotch fishing boat, double-ended, stern and stem straight, the former raked. Up to the middle 1860's the "fifies" were open boats of light draft, clinker-built, and rather tub-shaped. As the fishermen were forced to go farther out to sea for the shoals of herring and cod, the size of the boats was necessarily increased and they were decked over. A gradual transition in the model took place—deeper draft and bilges; finer lines; longer keels, and carvel-built—making a better sailer to windward in a head sea. The older models were about 30 feet long, but they finally reached a length of 70 feet. The "fifie" was lug-rigged, with jib and mizzen. Different sizes of mizzensails were carried and used according to the weather, but a small mizzen was always used when close hauled. The bowsprits and boomkins were long, and if the weather was rough were taken in. The mainmast was set fairly well forward. The rudder was slung outboard. It might be added that the lug rig and pointed stern still remain the favorites among the Scottish east-coast fishermen.

FILE-BOTTOM A nickname given to the early Gloucester fishing schooners
Illustration on page 134. because of the great dead rise. Afterwards called "sharpshooters." These "file-bottoms" or "sharpshooters" had low freeboard, raking stem and sternpost, with less rake to the latter; deep drag to the keel, sharp on the water line, with great flare to the bow The stern had little overhang. The "file-bottoms" had the old-fashioned transom, with the lower portion set at a more acute angle than the upper, and the transom was square-cornered until 1853 when the elliptical style was introduced. A quarter-deck extended to a point just forward of the mainmast. The heads were long with cheek knees, single rail, carved trail boards and simple billet head. The masts had a strong rake aft and the large

jib had a bonnet, the schooner rig being similar to the pilot-boat rig, except that one or two topsails were carried. The popular lengths were from 60 to 75 feet, with a beam about 30 per cent of the length. Depth of hold 5 to 6 feet 6 inches. See "Gloucester fishing schooner".

FIRE SHIP Generally an old coaster, or merchant craft, filled with combustibles, sent out to grapple enemy ships and then set afire. The British built a few special ship sloops which were used as fire ships.

FISHING BARK A small vessel used for fishing by the Spaniards and others. On a single mast was set one square sail, with a jib and bowsprit.

FISHING CUTTER
Illustration on page 17.

A cutter type of vessel modeled after the "Galway hooker," introduced in the United States from Ireland about 1857, after which time it was used extensively by the Irish fishermen of Massachusetts Bay. The model was much improved by the U. S. builders and was fast and seaworthy. The average length was about 36 feet with one-fourth the beam, draft forward a little under 3 feet with 3 feet drag to the keel. The bow was sharp with a straight, vertical stem above the water line; deep, square, raking, heart-shaped stern; decked over the forward half, balance open; medium sheer; outboard rudder; cutter-rigged, usually without a topsail. There was a cockpit aft and the middle portion of the hull was bulkheaded off for fish. Due to their speed, some were purchased and used as yachts.

FISHING SCHOONER
Illustrations on page 21.

For types of schooners used in the New England offshore and Grand Banks fisheries after 1850 see "Gloucester fisherman" (illustrated on page 134). For the type in use in the 17th century see "Fishing vessel of the 17th century" (illustrated on page 17). The general type of schooner employed in the last third of the 18th century and well into the 19th had a large square stern, a high quarter-deck extending to the mainmast, full round bow with gammon knee at top of a curved stem, vertical or slightly raked sternpost, low round bilge, straight sides, short run, long floor. The masts had a sharp rake and a large jib was set to a bowsprit. One or two topmasts were carried. Lengths varied up to 65 feet or so and was about three and one-half times the beam. Because of the high quarter-deck, the vessels having the shorter ones were called "heel tappers." In the 1830's and '40's the fishing schooners were built with low quarter-decks. Fishing was done from the deck with hand lines.

FISHING SLOOP Called "sloop-boats" by Gloucestermen. This type of sloop was popular in the shore fisheries out of Gloucester and Beverly, Massachusetts. They ranged up to 60 feet in length and were similar to the

[125]

Maine-built "Friendship sloops" but larger. They were built with a clipper bow, high concave floor, graceful sheer, deep narrow overhanging stern to a raking stern-post, sharp entrance and considerable drag to the keel.

FISHING VESSEL of the 17th Century
Illustration on page 17.
A type of vessel employed in the fisheries off the American east coast in the early days of the Colonies. The *Sparrow Hawk*, wrecked on Cape Cod in 1626, the remains of which were uncovered in 1863, is a typical example. It was a carvel-built, keel vessel, with a rather full convex bow and strongly raking curved stem; short run; square stern with no overhang to counter; considerable sheer; high quarter-deck; rail open amidships. The rig consisted of a single mast, with one square sail and a jib extended to a bowsprit. It was 40 feet long, 14 feet beam, 7 feet moulded depth, mast 45 feet above deck, yard 32 feet long.

FLEWER
A sailing craft of 8 to 20 tons' burden, used in the herring fishery out of Brighton, England, in the middle 19th century.

FLUTE
Illustration on page 41.
A Dutch merchant ship and trader of the 17th century. Ship-rigged, with generous sheer, a stubby round bow. Above the rounding stern and almost vertical sternpost was a high narrow transom which formed the after part of a lofty poop deck. A curved beakhead projected forward from the bow. A lateen mizzen course was carried on the after mast and on the highly steeved bowsprit was a spritsail, as well as a sprit-topsail. When armed, guns were carried on the upper deck only, the lower decks holding the cargo. This is armed *"en flute."* The "flute" was a favorite type in Holland.

FLYBOAT
A storeship of the 16th century.

FLYING PRAU
Illustration on page 69.
See "prahu," Malay pirate vessel.

FLYING PROA
Illustration on page 83.
An extremely fast outrigger sailing canoe formerly in use in the Marianas Islands (or Ladrone Islands). The hull was either a dugout or a partial dugout with sides of planks built above the edges. The leeward side was flat and the weather or outrigger side was curved in the normal manner. Two or three outrigger booms were attached to a boat-shaped float, each by two obliquely and transversly placed stanchion connectives. These "proas" ranged in length from 27 to over 40 feet, with a beam from 18 to 24 inches and a depth from 3 to 5 feet. A lateen sail or a settee with a very short luff, of fine matting, with a boom and yard, comprised the rig. A raking pole mast was stepped amidships on the outrigger side within the hull. The heel of the yard was confined

in a shoe placed in each end of the hull. When coming about, the craft was maneuvered so that the bow became the stern. The sail was reversed by raising the yard and walking the lower end along the gunwale to the other end of the canoe, where it was fixed in a shoe as before. At the same time the boom was hauled around by another sheet. Steering was done with a paddle. Assertions have been made that the "flying proas" could travel 20 knots. They have been extinct for over a century.

FOIST — A type of barge.

FRENCH SHALLOP
Illustration on page 55.

A large, decked merchant sloop used in Holland and Flanders in the 18th century, having one mast and carrying a gaff mainsail, with no boom. On the forward side of the mast, above the gaff, was a short spar projecting forward, to which was bent a long, narrow sail. The tack of this sail was made fast to the stem, and the sheet to the side near the shrouds. On the bowsprit were set two or three jibs. A small mast was often fixed in the stern that carried a mizzensail, generally a spritsail.

FRIENDSHIP SLOOP
Illustration on page 19.

A type of sloop built in Friendship, Maine, and near-by towns. They were copies of the larger Gloucester sloops, but were lighter built and were of a cheaper construction. They were built with a clipper bow and had a long bowsprit and a gaff mainsail with two jibs. This type was rarely more than 40 feet in length. Many of them were used as pleasure craft.

FRIGATE
Illustrations on pages 13, 15 and 23.

A type of sailing warship in size and armament between the sloop-of-war and the ship-of-the-line, the cruiser of the day. Frigates or "frigots" were known as early as the Spanish Armada, but the term was probably used rather loosely. Originally, a frigate was a light vessel propelled by sails and oars. The decks of a frigate were flush; "frigate-fashion" means decks running from bow to stern with no rises or falls.

Although the huge fleet of Louis XV of France is said to have included twenty-nine frigates in the 17th century, circa 1760 marked the adoption of the frigate as a standard class of war vessel in the navies of the western European powers. The frigates of the 1760's were ship-rigged, with a barrel-shaped bow having a head ornamented with an elaborate figurehead, rails and brackets; a forecastle deck and a poop deck, with perhaps a cabin aft. The usual armament consisted of 30 to 40 cannon.

Among the first frigates built for the Continental Navy during the American Revolutionary War were the *Hancock* and *Raleigh*, 32 guns. These two vessels are good examples of typical American-built frigates of this period and a description of them may prove interesting. *Hancock*, incidentally, turned out to be the fastest ship in the American and British fleets. *Raleigh* measured 131 feet 5 inches on the lower deck, 34 feet 5 inches beam, 11 feet depth of hold and a tonnage of 697. *Hancock* was 5 feet 2 inches longer.

The hulls of these two vessels had good sheer rising to a stern higher than the bow; moderate rake to the sternpost; a stem curved below the water line, but almost straight and with slight rake above; a head projected forward from the stem; easy runs, making for fast hulls. The entrance was quite full, not nearly as sharp as the later *Constitution* and *Constellation* classes. The bow was embellished with decorated trail boards, rails, brackets and a figurehead. The keel was straight with some drag.

Hancock had more dead rise than *Raleigh*, that of the former being about one foot rise in four. There was plenty of tumble home, more on *Raleigh*. A narrow poop or quarter-deck extended almost to the mainmast, there was a raised forecastle deck forward and a lower or berth deck ran the whole length of the hull. The steering wheel was located just ahead of the mizzenmast, and the stove and ovens in the after part of the forecastle. The quarter galleries at the stern butted against a broad high decorated transom, which was studded with five rectangular windows on *Raleigh*, seven on *Hancock*, with two gun ports above. Each side of the gun or main deck showed thirteen ports for long 12-pounders, in addition to three ports in each bulwark on the quarter-deck for long "nines."

The bowsprit and jibboom were sharply steeved and a spritsail hung just forward of the double bobstay. The bowsprit was also held down by gammon lashings through slots in the head. While the rig was that of a ship, Chapelle states that *Hancock* carried a small lateen sail and mast in place of the flag staff. The mizzenmast of this vessel was rigged with a topsail and a loose-footed fore-and-aft spanker bent to a lateen yard. An Admiralty sail plan of *Raleigh* shows a gaff spanker, topsail, topgallant and royal on the mizzen. In all probability *Hancock* carried a loftier rig at times. Hammocks were stowed on the bulwark rails between two longitudinal rows of netting. This afforded further protection from shot and was common practice on sailing men-of-war.

Hancock was taken in action by the British in 1777 and *Raleigh* in 1778. The Continental Navy was very unsuccessful, only two ships being left at the end of the war. Were it not for the glamorous exploits of a few men like John Paul Jones, Conyngham, Barry, Biddle and Barney, its history would make sorry reading. The Marine Committee of the Continental Congress and the local Navy Boards intrusted commands of ships to some quaint characters, indeed, and jealousy, incompetence, intrigue, lack of discipline and politics ran rife in the young Navy.

The United States had no Navy between 1783 and 1796.

The French were credited with some fast ships in the latter part of the 18th century, for example the 36-gun frigate *Insurgente*, reputed to be the fastest ship in the world at the time. She was taken in action in 1799 by the U.S.S. *Constellation*, but foundered at sea the following year.

The most notable example of a late 18th and early 19th century frigate is the U.S.S. *Constitution*, a 44-gun ship built in 1797, now completely rebuilt and overhauled and lying in the Boston Navy Yard. She was designed by Joshua Humphries, built in the yard of Edmund, Joseph and Edward Hartt of Boston, and was a departure from the then accepted mould and type of the larger ship of war, having finer lines and less freeboard. *Constitution*, along with her sister-ships, represented the highest type of frigate design, combining maximum speed without a sacrifice of fighting qualities. Under favorable conditions these ships could do 14 knots in a fresh breeze.

Constitution is 173 feet 3 inches long on the lower deck (approximately at the water line); 44 feet 4 inches extreme breadth; 13 feet 11 inches depth of hold; 1,533 ton's burden; carried 30 long 24-pounders on the gun deck; 20 to 22 32-pounder carronades on the spar deck, as well as two long chase guns on the forecastle. The 44- and 38-gun frigates of the United States Navy had three decks running the full length of the hull and a partial orlop deck at each end for stowage, stores, surgeon's operating room, etc.

Aside from the *Constitution*, the following frigates were on the U. S. navy list in 1800: *President* and *United States*, 44's; *Constellation*, *Chesapeake*, *Congress*, *Philadelphia*, and *New York*, 38's; *Essex*, 32; *John Adams*, 28.

If the Continental Navy was a disappointment, the new Navy covered itself with glory against the North African Berbers and in the War of 1812. The teachings of Truxtun and Preble infused a spirit into the hearts of the officers that was indomitable. Decatur, Stewart, Hull, Bainbridge, Perry, Rodgers, Jacob Jones, Porter, Blakeley, Lawrence, Macdonough, Warrington—these, and more too, with deeds carved their names in imperishable rock down the aisles of fame's hall of immortality.

Between 1820 and 1850 one 36-gun and twelve 44-gun frigates were added to the United States fleet. In 1855, '56 and '57 five steam screw frigates of the powerful *Minnesota* (40) type were built. Twelve of these eighteen vessels took part in the Civil War. A large screw frigate *Franklin*, 5170 tons, was completed in 1865 and 3200-ton wooden frigate *Trenton*—the last one in the Navy—was added to the roster in 1870. With the exception of *Constitution*, *Constellation*, *Hartford*, *Franklin*, *Essex*, *Santee*, *Monongahela*, *Yantic*, *Mohican*, *Nipsic*, and *Alliance*, all of the wooden sailing warships were broken up or sold out of the Navy by 1900.

Frigates always formed the most important part of the American Navy during the era of the sailing warship.

FRIGATOON   A square-sterned vessel of Venetian days, having a mainmast, jigger, and bowsprit.

FRUITERER The name given the two- and three-masted schooners employed in the fruit trade from Italy, Malta, and other orange-growing countries of Europe to London, England. These vessels were fast and beautifully modeled. In the 1850's over 300 were thus employed, but they were gradually displaced by steamships in the 1880's and '90's.

FULK Turkish for "ship."

FUSTA An early Italian "bireme."

GAFFER A fishing boat used in drift-net and long-line fisheries at Polperro, Cornwall, England. The hull is carvel-built, with a square transom, and ranges from 26 to 30 feet in length. The rig consisted of a boomless gaff mainsail and a jib. These boats are now fitted with motors. A "long line" is fitted with 3,000 to 4,000 hooks.

GAIASSA *or*
GYASSA
Illustration on page 63. A cargo boat or sailing lighter of the Nile River. The barge-like hull has little freeboard and no sheer, except at the bow, which curves up strongly, meeting the rounded stem in a point. An outboard rudder is slung from a short, straight sternpost. Two or three high narrow lateen sails comprise the rig. These vessels sail up the river and drift down with the current.[2]

GALIA SOTTIL An early Italian "trireme."

GALLEASS
Illustration on page 51. A larger and stronger "galley," used as a ship-of-war in the late 15th and through the 16th century. An early Venetian "galleass" carried three lateen sails, and there were large platforms, or decks, fore and aft, upon which artillery and soldiers were carried. A solid deck covered the waist of the ship above the rowers. The "galleass" played an important part in all great naval engagements of that period. By the end of the 16th century, however, the term was generally confined to a large ship of high freeboard, propelled by oars, with or without sails. Mediterranean "galleasses" were lateen-rigged. They were used also by the English in the 16th century. A "galleass" of 400 tons and twenty oars to a side required five men at each oar.

GALLEON
Illustration on page 53. A second-class war vessel of the 16th and 17th centuries, generally with three decks. (A "great" or "capital" ship had four decks.) The forecastle ended at her stem, while a long, slim beak projected forward under the bowsprit. "Galleons" carried courses and topsails on the main and foremasts and one, and sometimes two, lateen-rigged mizzenmast.

GALLEY

Illustrations on pages 11, 49, 51 and 61.

A long single or partially decked vessel of war, which depended chiefly on oars or sweeps for propulsion, but had a mast and sail for use when the wind was favorable.

The origination of the galley must be credited to the early Egyptians, more than forty centuries ago. It was adopted and improved upon by the Phoenicians, and from it they evolved the bireme and trireme, which were actually multi-banked galleys. The trireme largely supplanted the single-banked galley in the navies of the early Greeks, Carthaginians, Romans, etc., but later it again came to the fore as a war vessel. It was common to the Mediterranean countries, although used by western Europeans to some extent with variations in design. Because of its superiority in speed over the early sailing ships, the galley remained an instrument of war until its disappearance from the seas in the latter 18th century.

The proportion of the length of the hull to its breadth ranged from a ratio of from five, up to nine, to one, making a fast, but rather poor, sea vessel. It was carvel-built and there was, no doubt, some camber to the keel. On the early fighting galleys a metal beak was built forward from the bow, at or below the water line, for ramming an enemy craft. The Romans employed a hinged drawbridge, or "corvus," with spikes on the under side, which could be dropped on the deck of an adversary, holding the two vessels together for boarding and hand-to-hand fighting.

A fundamental part of the galley was the "apostis," which was a platform constructed along and extending beyond the sides of the vessel. This furnished an extended support for the fulcrum of the oars well outside of the hull proper. This was necessary, especially when the size of the galleys increased and longer oars were used. The benches for the oarsmen were distributed athwartships at a slight angle within the apostis, leaving a gangway, or "coursier," between them down the center. The horizontal distance between the seats was approximately 3 feet, the width of the seat itself being 9 inches. Each man had a foot rest, which was attached to the bench ahead.[3]

The number of oars varied with the size of the vessel, but the larger galleys had twenty-five to a side. The early galleys used a single square sail, bent to an upper yard, but this was later replaced by one or two lateen sails. When this transition took place is not known, but it perhaps happened in the 5th or 6th century. The mast was a heavy short pole, terminating aloft with a square block or head. In this head several sheaves were mortised in, through which passed the halyards and other lines. The masts were supported by shrouds set up by lanyards on each side. The lanyards were reeved through long, flat, double blocks, one fixed to the lower end of the shroud, the other by a toggle to a timber head or eyebolt on the outside of the apostis. The lateen yards of the later galleys were composed of two members, lashed together to form a single spar. Double guys held down the heel of the yard, while other tackles controlled it laterally. The upper end of the yard was controlled by vangs and the sail was furled by means of brails. Steering was accomplished with rudders on each after quarter. Later a stern rudder was employed.

While the galley did not undergo many radical changes, there were some modifications, due to changes in battle tactics and the introduction of cannon. The hull remained long and narrow, and sharp at both ends. While the ram was dispensed with, the galleys of the Middle Ages and later were built with a long, slender beak projecting from the bow on a line with the gunwales, on which was located the tackle for controlling the lower end of the forward lateen yard. There was an after structure and perhaps one forward, and crow's-nest tops were at the mast heads. See "trireme" and "bireme."

Another type of "galley" was a craft of light draft used in the Revolutionary War. They were fitted for rowing and were variously rigged with one or two masts, sometimes with lateen sails or as cutters, sloops, or schooners. They ranged in size from 40 to 75 feet long on deck and carried 1 to 12 guns. After the Revolutionary War the galley was used in the West Indian service and existed until about 1825.

GALLEY PUNT An English clinker-built boat, which can be sailed or rowed, 21 to 30 feet long, rigged with a long-yarded, dipping lugsail on a short mast set amidships.

GALLIOT
Illustration on page 41. An 18th century Dutch craft of 50 to 300 tons, two-masted, square-rigged on the foremast, with several jibs running to a rather long bowsprit. The aftermast carried a fore-and-aft mizzen sail. The "galliot" was equipped with leeboards. Bluff, round bow and stern.

GALLIOTE a BOMBES A French bomb ketch.

GALWAY HOOKER
Illustration on page 17. A cutter-rigged fishing craft used off the Galway coast in Ireland in the 19th century. This type was introduced into New England about 1857. See "fishing cutter" for further information.

GARUKHA
Illustration on page 65. A "dhow" type of the Persian Gulf, still existent. The steering gear is peculiar, having a pair of tackles leading from a short horizontal spar on each quarter to the back of the rudder.

GEHAZI
Illustration on page 67. Local name of an Arab "dhow" of the same type as the "sambuk" (illustrated on page 67), with a high pooped hull. A mizzenmast is sometimes used. Employed on the African coast as far south as Zanzibar.

[132]

GELEIRA A "canoa" of the Amazon delta which carries ice on fishing trips to prevent spoilage of the fish. See "canoa" (illustrated on page 89).

GHARAWA An Arab dugout, with outriggers on both sides. About 17 feet long, 2 feet 6 inches beam. An upper strake is pegged on.

GHOBONG A long, narrow dugout canoe used on the rivers and streams of Borneo by the natives. It has long, tapering, graceful, overhanging ends, which terminate in a small up-facing square, sharp-edged on the forward side. Bow and stern alike. Of various lengths to accommodate two to eight persons. Paddles are used for propulsion.

GHOBUN The native name for canoe in the Astrolabe Bay district in the
Illustration on page 85. Mandated Territory of New Guinea. The outrigger sailing canoe pictured is a dugout with long-pointed, solid ends, having decorated washstrakes and high breakwaters above the hull. Set amidships on the washstrakes is a two-storied platform, on which two oppositely raking masts are stepped, each carrying a small, square mat sail. The masts are stayed with shrouds and stays. The outrigger float is as long as the hull and is connected to two booms by means of double under-crossed attachments. The canoes in this district are employed mainly in the pottery trade.

GIG A small boat formerly carried on shipboard and meant for use when in port. Generally the captain's boat.

GIGLIO TRAWLER Italian fishing craft, single-masted, lateen mainsail and large jib carried on a bowsprit. Clipper bow and outboard rudder.
Illustration on page 39.

GLOUCESTER FISHING SCHOONER or FISHERMAN A schooner developed in and sailed out of Gloucester and other Massachusetts Bay ports. This type of vessel, designed for market fishing, offshore fishing and service on the Grand Banks, started with the building of the *Romp* at Essex, Massachusetts, in 1846–47. The *Romp* was a new idea in fishing schooner design, conceived by Andrew Story, and was modeled somewhat after the "Baltimore clipper," having great dead rise and sharp ends. It was a success and during the following 13 years or so many schooners were built after the lines of the *Romp*. The rig resembled that of the pilot schooner, having a single huge jib and main topsail. This type was known as "file-bottoms" or "sharpshooters" because of the sharpness and great dead rise of the hull. The size range was from 60 to 75 feet in length, 18 to 22 feet beam.[4]

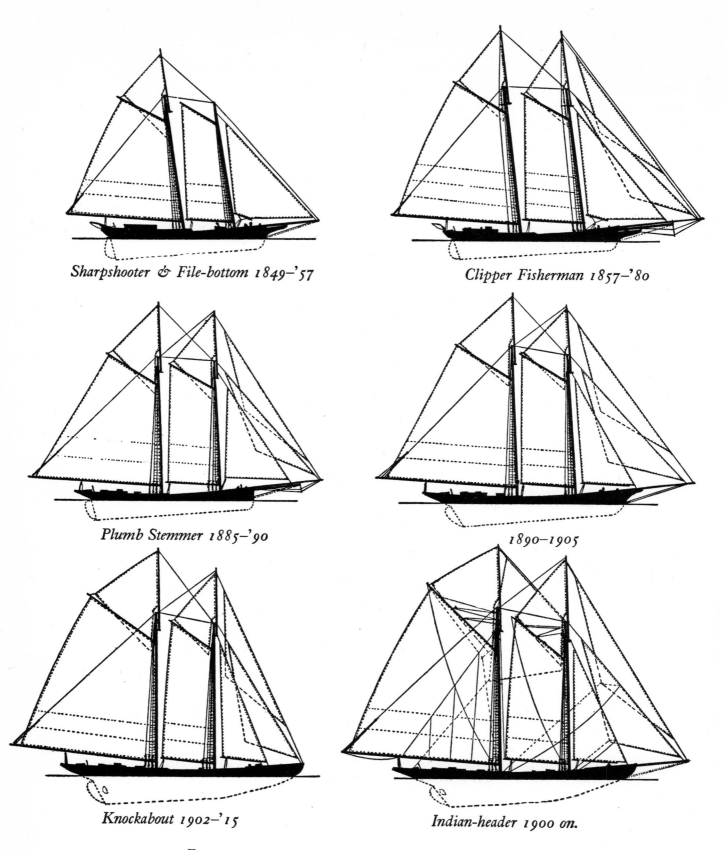

Sharpshooter & File-bottom 1849–'57

Clipper Fisherman 1857–'80

Plumb Stemmer 1885–'90

1890–1905

Knockabout 1902–'15

Indian-header 1900 on.

EVOLUTION OF THE GLOUCESTER FISHING SCHOONER

The demand for speedier ships increased and the "fisherman" became sharper, beamier, and shoaler, and about 1857 a new type, the "clipper fisherman," made its appearance. For the next quarter of a century the "clipper" was the popular model. As time went on they became even more extreme, especially the market schooners. These "clippers" had a shallow hull, beam about 30 per cent of the length, average length 70 to 85 feet, hollow water line at bow and stern, little dead rise, long, straight run, heavy quarters, little drag to keel, low freeboard, short counter, a sort of "clipper" bow, with a long, heavy head, having one or two rails and trail board, a wide and almost square stern, some rake to stem and sternpost. The sail plan was large, with long main boom, long bowsprit and jibboom, huge forestaysail and smaller jib. The market schooners carried fore- and maintopmasts, but the former was usually omitted on the "Bankers." This type, though very fast, was dangerous, as it was liable to capsize if heeled over too far and many lives were lost because of this fault. It endured, however, until the early 1880's, when the trend changed to a safer model.

In 1884 a fishing schooner was built in East Boston, with a hull patterned after the pilot schooners, having a straight vertical stem, deeper hold, long, overhanging, narrow "V" transom stern, a big jib and smaller staysail. The head rails and trail boards were discontinued. This type was fast and successful, but the vertical stem did not last, and in 1890 the clipper bow was again introduced, which lasted well into the 1900's. About 1890 the last fishing schooner with a jibboom was built, the spike bowsprit, with a spreader through the stem, having been introduced in 1886 or 1887. The big jib disappeared and the modern double-headsail rig came into being. The size of the vessels gradually increased. Auxiliary power was experimented with at the turn of the century and shortly became common.

The familiar round stem was introduced in the late 1890's and proved popular. The first schooners built with this type of bow were given Indian names and were known as "Indian-headers." The earlier "Indian-headers" had a keel that formed a sweeping curve from stem to sternpost, but owing to difficulty in handling on the marine railway, the later schooners were built with a short, straight keel. They had a long bowsprit which was dangerous to life in a heavy seaway. To overcome this, T. F. McManus, of Boston, in 1901 designed a "knockabout" schooner, the *Helen B. Thomas*, eliminating the bowsprit and increasing the overhang of the bow. This type was popular up to 1915 or 1916. A fine example of a successful "knockabout" Gloucesterman is the *Arethusa*, built in 1910 at Essex, Massachusetts. She was 114 feet long over-all, 25 feet 7 inches beam, 12 feet 6 inches draft, 107 net tons. She had a high bow with the curved stem, raking sternpost, low freeboard amidships, considerable rounded sheer to a transom stern, which had a yacht-like overhang. The midsection shows great dead rise. The bow was very sharp. The keel was short and straight, with drag, the buttocks long and flat, making for a very fast hull. Double headsails were carried, as were main- and fore-topmasts, and it had the typical long mainboom. *Arethusa* was an auxiliary.

"Gloucester" schooners were also built with a bowsprit of medium length, the forward triangle being shorter on the base (mast to stem) than that of the "knockabouts." The later type is represented by such famous fast vessels as the *Elsie* (designed by McManus in 1910 and the first schooner to represent Gloucester in the "Fishermen's Race"), *Henry Ford, Mayflower, Columbia,* and the *Gertrude Thebaud.* The *Elsie* and other schooners mentioned above carried a bowsprit. Another famous schooner of the Gloucester fisherman type is the *Bluenose,* which sails out of Lunenburg, Nova Scotia, and made her reputation in the International Fishermen's Races against the well-known Gloucester boats. The above schooners represent the highest development of the Gloucester fisherman.

After the War, fishing schooners were built with large power plants and reduced rigs until at present, with a few exceptions, the "Gloucester fishermen" are little more than power boats. At this writing the only full-rigged Gloucester schooner left is the *Gertrude Thebaud.* Its only mate is the *Bluenose,* except for the *We're Here,* owned by a Hollywood movie studio and out of service.

A word about cod fishing should have a place here as the Gloucester schooners were (and still are) used to transport the fishermen to the cod grounds on the Grand Banks south of Newfoundland. St. George's Bank on the southeast corner of the Banks furnishes the finest cod in the world. Codding begins in June and lasts for about six months. Each vessel carries six to eighteen dories (stored in nests on deck when not in use) from which the actual fishing is done. Cod are caught with hand lines and French trawls. In the former case, the fisherman rows his dory some distance away from the large vessel, throws in his line, and pulls in the cod. When a convenient load is obtained, he is picked up and the catch put in the hold. In the case of French trawling, long lines, each bearing 200 or 300 short lines with hooks, are set out to a buoy. Each line is emptied into a dory, which, when full, takes its catch back to the large vessel.

See also "Indian-header," and "file-bottom," both illustrated on page 134.

GOELETTE   The French term for "schooner."

GONDOLA   A flat-bottomed, double-ended vessel, 40 to 60 feet long, cutter-, sloop-, or hoy-rigged, with deep bulwarks and gun ports. Used in the American Revolution on Lake Champlain. The gondola *Philadelphia* has recently been raised from the bottom of Lake Champlain.

GONDOLA   A double-ended Venetian craft, with high ornamental posts in the bow and stern, propelled by one or two oarsmen, each with a single oar or sweep. It is used in the canals of Venice, more or less as taxicabs are used in our streets.

GORLESTON LIFEBOAT	A sailing "beach yawl" used in the life-saving service out of Gorleston, England. Two lugsails are used.

GRASS BOAT
or **BALSA**
Illustration on page 87.

A grass boat made of bundles of reeds lashed together. Three bundles are used, the center one being about one-third the length of the two outer ones. The greatest width is about one-ninth of the length, which varies from 20 to 30 feet. Used by the Mexican Seri Indians on the Gulf of California.

GREAT LAKES SCHOONER
Illustration on page 21.

Two- and three-masted schooners were used to a great extent on the Great Lakes from the early 19th century until they gradually gave way to the steamboat. The design depended on the kind of cargo to be carried, but they were usually of shallow or medium draft, flat-floored, sharp-ended, with a clipper bow and transom stern. Those built with a centerboard were common. The earlier schooners carried square topsails and perhaps a raffee on the foremast. The three-masters had spars of different heights, the mainmast being the tallest and the mizzen the shortest. The clipper type of centerboard schooners built at Manitowoc, Wisconsin, in the 1850's were very successful and fast, 13 and even 14 knots being made in a good breeze. Four- and five-masted schooners were built as trade became heavier.

The writer recalls seeing an old three-master sailing down the Straits of Mackinac about ten years ago. As recently as 1910 several could be seen along the docks of Milwaukee, Chicago, and other Lake ports.

GREEK MERCHANT SHIP
Illustration on page 51.

This Corinthian cargo-carrier, circa 1st century, shows a hull with generous sheer, a "clipper bow" and a raking stern terminating in a high, curved board. The beam was liberal and a single mast carried a wide square sail hung from a yard. It was furled by means of buntlines. Wicker sides were sometimes built above the deck to increase the carrying capacity. An eye was painted on each side of the bow, in the manner of the Chinese craft. Steered by a quarter rudder.

GUFFA

A bowl-shaped craft, or coracle, of Bagdad, made of woven switches and lined with bitumen. Guffas have been in use on the Tigris River since antiquity and are still employed commercially.

GUL
Illustration on page 85.

An outrigger dugout sailing canoe of the islands lying in Torres Straits, between Queensland, Australia, and New Guinea.

Some canoes had double outriggers, some single. The number of outrigger booms varied, as did the short connectives. The hulls were long, ranging up to 50 and 60 feet in length. The transverse section was U-shaped, open at the top. There was no sheer except at the ends which was formed by triangular washboards. The bow and stern terminated in a blunt point. Often a washstrake was sewed on the edges of the hull running the full length of the canoe. The rig was peculiar. Two high, oblong mat sails were carried on an arrangement of masts and struts stepped in the bow. The backstays were carried to the outrigger booms. This rig is now extinct, being supplanted by western fore-and-aft sails.

GUNBOAT
Illustration on page 13.
A small, armed, open sailing vessel used in the Navy of the United States from 1803 through the War of 1812. They ranged from 45 to 75 feet in length and could accommodate 30 to 50 men. The armament varied, though they were usually equipped with a 24- or 32-pounder mounted on a pivot and a small carronade. When needed, a bulwark of sand bags was built along the gunwales. They were rigged as lateeners, sloops, cutters and the largest, schooners. Sweeps were also used.

GUNDALOW
Illustration on page 19.
Also called a "Merrimac gundalow." A river barge used on the Merrimac and other rivers of New England in the 18th century. A short mast carried a lateen sail with a counter-balance on the lower end of the yard.

HAAK
Illustration on page 43.
A large Dutch sailing lighter. Average length about 120 feet by 20 feet beam. Considerable sheer at ends and with very little freeboard amidships; flat-bottomed and square-ended. The mainmast carries a fore-and-aft mainsail, topsail, foresail, and jib to a bowsprit; small mizzen. Outside rudder. Nowadays the hull is usually built of steel.

HALF-CLIPPER
This type of merchant vessel was designed to have greater cargo-carrying capacity than the extreme clipper ships of the 1850's and hence were not quite so fast, although they were second in speed and sailing qualities only to the latter. "Half-clippers" were used in the '70's and '80's and superseded the extreme clippers, which were unprofitable to operate because of their uneconomical design and lower freight rates. The floor of the "half-clipper" was almost flat and long, the sides high and straight, the run rather long and finely formed, the bow moderately sharp and flaring and the rig was generally that of a ship or bark.

HAMPTON
BOAT
A type of small, centerboard fishing boat used on certain sections of the New England coast, having two small masts and carrying spritsails.

HARENGUIER   French "herring boat."

HATCH-BOAT   A fishing and commercial vessel of from 7 to 10 tons, used on
Illustration on page 31.   the lower Thames River in the 18th and 19th centuries.
Hatches covered a portion or all of the deck. Earlier types were
spritsail-rigged, but later a gaff mainsail, with brails and without boom, was adopted.
A mizzen was sometimes used, as were double headsails.

HAVRE   A cutter-rigged, keel sailing vessel, used in piloting out of
PILOT BOAT   Havre, France, before power boats came into use. It was a fast,
Illustration on page 37.   seaworthy vessel, with straight stem, overhanging transom
stern, sharp bow, deep-bodied, considerable drag to keel, about
50 feet long, 15 feet beam, and about 8 feet draft. In fair weather a lug topsail was
carried.

HAVRE   A lug-rigged French "trawler" used in the vicinity of Havre.
TRAWLER   It was double-ended, with straight stem and sternpost and two
Illustration on page 37.   or three masts and a single headsail to a long bowsprit. A gaff
topsail was sometimes carried.

HAY BARGE   A Thames barge built for carrying hay from the east-coast
Illustration on page 35.   towns of England. The hull is of the "barge" type, but of
shallower draft in order that it may enter the little creeks and
inlets of the Thames estuary. The hay barges are often square-ended, with a "swim-
head" bow. There is special gear for holding the load of hay in place. The rig,
similar to the regular Thames barges of the period (usually that of a spritsail yawl
with a diminutive mizzen), has a mainsail with the foot cut off high above the deck
to accommodate the high stack of hay. There may be a few of these unique craft still
plowing up and down the Thames. If so, it is worth one's while to see the skipper
taking orders from a man perched high on the stack conning the vessel.

HEEL-TAPPER   A local name for a fishing schooner of the Massachusetts coast
in the 1820's, having a square stern and a short, high quarter-
deck. They were rarely over 50 feet long.

HENGST   A Dutch pleasure craft on the order of the "hoogaar" (illustrated on page 43), but with less overhang forward and it is
stubbier in appearance.

HERMAPHRO-   A two-masted vessel, square-rigged on the foremast, and fore-
DITE   and-aft rigged on the mainmast.
Illustration on page 9.

HEMMEMA   A Swedish armed craft of the latter 18th century. A combination of the "galley" and "man-of-war." Armed with 26 guns, with sweeps in pairs between the guns. Three-masted, square-rigged.

HIPPAGI   A Roman horse barge.

HOECKER   Dutch for "howker," illustrated on page 55.

HOGGIE
Illustration on page 33.   A fishing craft peculiar to Brighton, England, up to the 1850's. It was of great beam, clinker-built, flat-floored, and round-ended. It carried a gaff or sprit mainsail and often a sprit or lug mizzen, with a large jib set to a bowsprit.

HOOGAAR
Illustration on page 43.   A sloop of Dutch design used mainly for pleasure purposes in Holland and Belgium. The hull is flat-bottomed, keelless, decked, with cabin top and cockpit, and has generous sheer. The stem has tremendous rake, the bow terminating in sort of a snout. There is slight rake to sternpost. The wide upper plank tumbles home sharply and forms a chine with the flaring side below. The outboard rudder is large and deep leeboards ("zitzwaarden" in Dutch) are used when close-hauled. The average size is 35 to 40 feet long, beam about one-third. The mainsail is loose-footed with a short, curved gaff, there are no shrouds nor stays and two headsails are carried.

HOOKER   A contemptuous slang term for a boat of any kind. Also a small fishing craft local to Polperro, Cornwall, England, used for "long-line" fishing. Sloop-rigged, with boomless mainsail. A "long-line" is frequently over two miles in length and carries from 3,000 to 4,000 hooks.

HORNBAEK
BOAT
Illustration on page 45.   A sailing boat used in the plaice fishery of Hornbaek, Denmark. The average size was about 36 feet long, 13 feet 8 inches beam, by 5 feet draft. Clinker-built, with stem and stern alike, considerable sheer, flaring bow and quarters. The sternpost is very raked and the top is rounded up and cut off below the top of the rail, the tiller passing through an open cut in the bulwark beneath the rail. Cutter-rigged, gaff and boom mainsail, and a yard topsail set on a pole mast.

HOUARIO
Illustration on page 55.   A small vessel with two masts and a bowsprit, sometimes used as a coasting vessel, or pleasure boat, in the inlets and rivers of the Mediterranean in the 18th century. On the masts were set sails with sliding topmasts (see "sliding gunter sails"). On the bowsprit was spread a jib. The masts were braced by three or four shrouds, with ratlines;

there was considerable sheer to the hull, and sometimes a large lantern was carried above the stern.

HOUCRE *or* French for "howker," illustrated on page 55.
HOURQUE

HOVELLER A term used in Southern England for the lug-rigged sailing craft on the lookout for shipping and hauling jobs. Also a term applied colloquially to vagrants which formerly plied the English coast in bad weather for plunder from wrecks.

HOWKER A round-sterned merchant craft of the 17th and 18th centuries,
Illustration on page 55. used by the Dutch and other northern nations of Europe. It was a relative of the "buss" and "dogger," having two masts and ranging in size from 50 to 200 tons. The rig varied according to locality and period. In the 18th century it generally resembled a ketch. The mainmast was a single stick, on which were carried two or three square sails. The mizzenmast had a topmast, with a topsail, and rigged abaft was a sail similar to a ship's driver or spanker. There was a long, slender bowsprit, on which was set two or three jibs and a spritsail.

The "howker" of the Danes of the 18th century was similar to a "sloop-of-war," with three masts.

HOY A coasting vessel in which much of the freight was carried
Illustration on page 55. between English ports and those of the Continent in the 16th, 17th, and 18th centuries. The rig was usually that of a fore-and-aft spritsail with a single pole mast. The tonnage of the "hoys" ranged from 25 to perhaps 100, although in the latter part of the 16th century larger ones were known to have existed.

From 1700 to 1740 the tenders used in the British Navy were known as "hoys." They were approximately 80 feet long and 20 feet beam, and carried a brailed, fore-and-aft, boomless mainsail, a square sail, two jibs, and a topsail.

The sailing lighters of the old East India Company, used for unloading their ships, were called "hoys."

HULK A round-sterned, square-tucked, high-pooped vessel of the 18th
Illustration on page 41. century, ranging in size from 100 to 800 tons. Square-rigged on main- and foremasts, lateen-rigged on the mizzen.

HUMBER KEEL A flat-bottomed sailing barge, or keel, typical to the Humber
Illustration on page 33. River in England. The rig consists of a single mast on which is a large square sail and a small square topsail. See "keel."

HVALOR-	A spritsail-rigged, decked craft of Southern Norway formerly
BAAD	used extensively as a pilot boat. Very broad, bluff, and deep,
Illustration on page 45.	it was a fine sea boat. Clinker-built, double-ended, with curved

stem and sternpost; outboard rudder. A square-cut spritsail, with peak lower than the throat, as a mainsail, staysail, and jib to a bowsprit were carried. Only standing rigging was a forestay and one shroud on each side.

INDIAN-	A Gloucester fishing schooner, built with the now familiar
HEADER	round stem, known by this name locally to the Gloucester and
Illustration on page 134.	Salem neighborhoods after the introduction of this type of stem

in the late 1890's, as the first ones built had Indian names.

ISE FJORD	A Danish craft, similar to the "Hornbaek" boat, but with a
FISHING	beamier and shallower hull. Used on the fishing grounds of
BOAT	Kattegat.
Illustration on page 45.	

| ISOBUNE | A rowboat used in the fisheries and on the coast of Japan. About 20 feet long. |

ITALIAN	This type could be called a lateen-rigged yawl with a square
LATEENER	maintopsail. A single broad jib is carried to a spike bowsprit.
Illustration on page 61.	The hull has a low transom stern with the sheer line rising to a

higher bow having a curved stem.

| JACKASS | A term used occasionally for a "schooner" without a main- |
| SCHOONER | topmast. |

JAEGT	A Norwegian craft of former days, used in the coastwise trade.
Illustration on page 45.	Single-masted, with a course and small topsail. The course was
	reefed by means of bonnets along the foot. A forestaysail was

sometimes used. The hull was heavy, beamy, and of generous sheer. A pole mast was stayed by four shrouds on each side.

JALOR	An open, double-ended, keelless dugout canoe of Johore. Used
PENJALA	by natives for fishing with a small net. Long, raking ends; bot-
	tom curved up at each end; sharp floor; moderate sheer. Aver-

age length about 20 feet, with one-fifth the beam.

JAMAICA
SLOOP
A sharp-modeled sloop developed in Jamaica, West Indies, popular previous to 1700. It had much dead rise, a raking stem and sternpost, low freeboard, and was very fast. The mast raked aft considerably. It was generally sharp-ended and was a good weather boat.

JANGADA *or*
JANGODA
A raft-like boat or catamaran which is used in certain parts of South America, mainly Brazil and Peru. The natives around Bahia, Brazil, employ the "jangada" for offshore fishing. They stay on the fishing grounds for several days at a time and once a day other natives make their rounds in a dugout sailing canoe, buying the fish and then taking the catch to market ashore. The "jangada" is usually constructed of six or more logs, pointed at the ends. A sail is employed and there may be a short keel, or "dagger board."

JAVANESE
PRAU
Illlustration on page 75.
A native outrigger sailing craft, or "prau," of the Island of Java, rigged similarly to the "Madura prau," except that the tack of the foresail is supported by a bowsprit. The hull is generally built of teak, double-ended, with little sheer, strong rake to the stem and less to the sternpost, from which a rudder is hung. A long bamboo float is supported by two outriggers. Cabin with matting roof amid ships. See "Madura prau," illustrated on page 75.

JESSOR BOAT
A rowing or paddling boat built of teak, used for fishing and other purposes in the vicinity of Jessor on the Bengal coast, India. It is carvel-built, the planks being fastened together with staples clenched over on the opposite side. The sides are braced by half frames and thwarts. Each end is decked for about 3 feet. The cross section is semi-circular and the hull tapers from the center, terminating in long, pointed, overhanging ends; some sheer. The average length over-all is about 35 feet, beam one-seventh.

JIGGER
A fishing schooner of Massachusetts, developed from the "chebacco boat" (illustrated on page 19), but carrying a bowsprit and jib. First known about 1820 and later called the "pink" or "pinky" (illustrated on page 19). The length ranged from 40 to 50 feet.

Also the fourth mast of a five- or six-masted schooner. The small after mast of a yawl or ketch. Sometimes applied to the last mast of a four-masted "bark."

JOLLY BOAT
A boat corresponding to a dinghy; also a work boat carried by a merchantman, usually at the stern of a schooner.

JUNK
Illustrations on pages 71 and 73.
A sailing vessel used through the ages by the Chinese and other Mongolian people for trading, transportation of goods and humans, fishing, warfare, pirating, etc. Even today it is com-

mon on the eastern seas and rivers. Though ungainly in appearance, the junk is a remarkably seaworthy craft. The designs vary and scarcely two may be found alike, but usually there is a high transom stern with an overhanging poop deck and curving sheer to a low bow.

Junks are carvel- or clinker-built, or a combination of both; round- or flat-bottomed and frequently keelless. The lack of a keel is partially compensated by a deep heavy rudder which is lowered by a tackle or windlass when in sufficiently deep water, and sometimes by a short keel forward which may vary in length from a few feet to half the length of the hull. This keel is really an extension of the forefoot. Some junks are built with a centerboard. Others without a keel may be found using leeboards.

The square blunt "swim-head" bow, with the lower edge meeting the flat bottom just above the water, is often seen in northern Chinese waters, while the southern junks usually have a raking stem, curved or straight. Often a washboard or wing is built on each side of the bow and there may be a horizontal pole between these boards at the forward end to which the anchor hoisting tackle is secured.

The rig consists of one to five masts, some raking and some vertical, each carrying a single battened lugsail of matting or perhaps canvas. The sails are controlled by multiple sheets extending to the boom and to the ends of the battens at the leech. As a rule the sails of the northern junks are high and narrow, with many battens, while those of the south are ordinarily high-peaked with lots of roach to the leech.

Most Chinese craft have an eye painted on each topside near the bow, so the vessel can see where it is going—according to the Chinaman.

Up to about two centuries back, the Chinese were superior to other peoples in the scientific principles of fore-and-aft sailing, but beyond the junk and the sampan, they have progressed little in ship architecture.

KAEP
Illustration on page 83.

An outrigger sailing canoe of the Palau Archipelago, which lies eastward of Mindanao, Philippine Islands. The canoes of the Palau Islands do not have the asymmetric hull of other Micronesian craft. It is extremely narrow, the beam being about one twenty-eighth of the length. Transversely the hull is wedge-shaped, while longitudinally the sharp keel is crescentic. The gunwales are parallel up to a block cutwater at each end and the sheer is rounding. Two heavy outrigger booms, with a grating laid between and a platform above, are connected to a heavy short float with a "Y" attachment and a double yoke above. An Oceanic lateen sail to a raking mast of bamboo, stepped amidships, comprises the rig. The canoe can sail either end forward. The four men comprising the crew sit well aft and the craft is sailed with the bow well out of water. Many people who have seen the "kaep" consider it one of the finest canoes of Oceania and it was one of the fastest. It is not made any more, its cousin, the beamier "ka-traol," surviving.

KAIKI
Illustration on page 57.
A small sailing craft of Greece. High-ended, of great sheer, and having very little freeboard amidships, necessitating the use of weather cloths. A single lateen sail and a jib set to a steeved bowsprit comprise the rig. It is generally steered with an oar or paddle.

KAKAP JERAM
A fishing canoe of the Malayan east coast and Selangor. The stem and sternpost are high and ornamented, with considerable rake. Single lugsail carried. A washstrake formed of a strong lacing of split bamboo strips, stoutly sewed together and filled in with palm leaf comprises the gunwale on either side of the boat, the whole being held in position by lashings to knees brought up from the boat's ribs. This form of washstrake is used by the sea-dwelling Malays of the Selangor coast. It is steered by one or two paddles.

KATTUMARAN
Tamil (Ceylon) term for "catamaran." The Singhalese term is "theppama." A Ceylonese "kattumaran" is a sailing raft 20 to 30 feet long, used for boarding ships when the surf is too heavy to effect a landing. It is generally made of five logs lashed together. A false bow or breakwater is built on the forward end. The rig consists of a single triangular sail, dyed red, with a yard on the foot, stepped amidships. It is steered with an oar.

KAWASAKI
A flat-bottomed, keelless sailing boat, with a long, sharp bow, used in the trawl-line cod fishery of Northern Japan. A long, narrow-bladed rudder is used and there is one mast stepped aft of the center, on which is set a large, rectangular lugsail. Also propelled by sculling. The bottom of the boat is very heavily built in order to withstand being bumped on the beach by the surf. The average size is about 40 feet in length, with one-quarter the beam.

KAYAK
Illustration on page 87.
A skin canoe with a single manhole used extensively by the Eskimos of the Arctic regions of North America. Though the type varies somewhat in design and build in different localities, all forms are intimately related and the same general design has been faithfully adhered to for centuries. The "kayak" is not unlike the single-seated racing shell. It is admirably suited to the needs of the natives of the far North, while the skins of the numerous seals, sea lions and walrus provide ample material for its construction. The canoe is made by covering a light, wooden frame with skins sewed together with sinews and stretched while "green." When dry, the covering becomes taut, and is kept water-tight by being well oiled. The hull is decked over, the only opening being the circular opening, or hatch, in the center. To prevent its filling with water if cap-

[145]

sized or if high waves are encountered, the occupant's outer garment is often snugly secured to the edge of the manhole. In general, the bow is long and very sharp, curving upwards from below; the stern sharp with vertical or raking ends; flaring sides; no keel; deck ridged or flat; bottom round or flat. Double-bladed paddles are the usual means of propulsion. Average lengths 15 to 18 feet, width 19 to 30 inches, depth 7 to 18 inches. The kayak of the west coast of Greenland is considered superior in finish and symmetry to all other skin canoes of North America.

KEEL   A flat-bottomed, sailing cargo barge of Durham and Yorkshire, England, used mostly for inland navigation. The hull is blunt, bow and stern alike with low freeboard and an outboard rudder. One or two square sails are carried on a single pole mast, set a little forward of amidships. The average size of the "keel" is about 60 feet in length, with one-quarter the beam. Leeboards are used when on the open sea. See "Humber keel" (illustrated on page 33), "Tyne keel."

KEELE   An old British term for the long boats used by the Saxons and Danes.

KETCH   Literally, a "ship" without a foremast. In the 17th and 18th
Illustrations on pages 11, centuries commercial ketches were popular as traders and
19, 53, 219 and 221. cargo boats in Europe and America. They were employed to quite an extent in the New England offshore fisheries until the beginning of the 18th century when they fell into disfavor. Ketches were used a good deal in the navies of European nations. The early ketch was, of course, a two-masted vessel, square-rigged on the mainmast, with a lateen on the mizzenmast, and sometimes a topsail, and a spritsail forward.

The rig of the naval ketch was more complicated than that of the commercial type, especially after the adoption of the jib about 1750. The mainmast was stepped about amidships and on it were set a square course, topsail and topgallant with two or three large head sails forward (after 1750). After 1725 a boomless fore-and-aft gaff sail, known as a "wingsail" on a ketch, was also set from the mainmast. The mizzenmast was rigged the same as a "ship's" square-rigged mizzen, with a spanker or "mizzen course." On the smaller fishing and commercial ketches the topgallant was omitted, the mainmast stepped farther forward and on the mizzen perhaps just a fore-and-aft lateen, gaff or spritsail, according to the period. Large ketches carrying mortars, known as "bomb ketches," were used in the navies of Europe, especially France, for bombarding fortifications.

A modern ketch is fore-and-aft rigged, with the mainmast forward and the shorter mizzenmast stepped just ahead of the helmsman. The ketch rig is in great favor at the present time for yachts, especially those used for cruising.

[146]

Ketches were also employed in the lumber trade on Lakes Huron and Michigan, especially the latter. They were huskily built, with heavy gear and were from 80 to over 100 feet long. The stern was broad and the bow was of the "clipper" type. The working canvas consisted of a mainsail, raffee, mizzensail, mizzen staysail, and four headsails. The writer saw the last survivor of these Grand Haven ketches, as they were called by the sailors, slowly sloshing along loaded with logs, early in the 1920's while sailing in the Chicago-Mackinac Race.

KETTLE-BOTTOM A vessel with unusual depth, considerable tumble home, making less beam on deck, full bow, little sheer, heavy square stern and long flat floor. While slow and unwieldy, a vessel of this type was designed to obtain the greatest depth and carrying capacity for a given beam on deck, as the United States tonnage laws of the time (1830's and '40's) estimated the depth for tonnage from the breadth on deck, and the deeper she was in proportion to her beam, in addition to the extra width obtained by the tumble home, the more cargo capacity she would have for a given measurement. John N. Cushing, a shipowner and merchant of Newburyport, Massachusetts, owned a fleet of a dozen "kettle-bottom" brigs. These were about 110 feet long, with a moulded beam of 25 feet.

KIEL Danish or Swedish for "vessel."

KING'S CUTTER A bluff-bowed, cutter-rigged vessel used in the Revenue Service of England during the late 18th and early 19th centuries. Rigged with fore-and-aft mainsail, two square topsails, staysail, and jib. See illustration of "cutter" on page 55.

KJOLL Icelandic for "barge" or "ship."

KNOCKABOUT A sloop or schooner having no bowsprit.
Illustrations on pages 134 and 223.

KNÖRR A large Viking ship, essentially a sailing ship, but oars were also used, for ocean trading and over-seas warfare. Some were capable of carrying 150 men.

KOFF Similar to the "galliot" (illustrated on page 41), but having no leeboards. Either schooner- or ketch-rigged.
Illustration on page 43.

KOFF-TJALK A "koff" with leeboards.

KOLEH
Illustration on page 89.

A Malay racing canoe, "koleh" being the Malayan term for canoe. The hull is narrow in proportion to its length and transversely the section is V-shaped, with round flaring sides. The stem and sternpost are curved and raking and a carved projection extends above the gunwales on each end. The rig around Singapore consists of a tall, leg-of-mutton mainsail and overlapping jib. A high-peaked spritsail and jib were formerly employed. The smaller canoes are about 18 feet long, while the larger ones range up to 45 feet. They are extremely fast, but they cannot come about. See "kolek."

KOLEK

A seagoing canoe of Singapore rigged with an odd-shaped spritsail and a jib. It is double-ended, with an outboard rudder. If a forward "hornbill" projection (a sort of short bowsprit) is used, the natives call the type a "prahu buaya." A half-decked "kolek" is a "katop luan."

KOTIA
Illustration on page 65.

A two-masted Indian "dhow" of the Malabar coast. A large lateen mainsail is carried on a forward-raked mast stepped amidships; also a small lateen mizzen and triangular jib. The hull is sharp forward, with a raking, curved stem and a poop deck aft. The square, heavy transom stern was often embellished with carving. Steered with a wheel. The distinctive mark of all "kotias" is the parrot beak at the stem head.

KURRAN KAHN
Illustration on page 47.

A type of small, open fishing boat, used off the coast of Lithuania, named for the net it operates—"kahn" meaning "boat." A sprit mainsail, an insignificant sprit foresail, and jib are carried. The "kurre," or trawl net, is about 70 feet long, its mouth 30 to 40 feet wide and 2 to 3 feet deep.

LACCADIVE ISLANDS CANOE
Illustration on page 65.

A crude dugout canoe used in the lagoons of the Laccadive Islands, which lie west of India in the Indian Ocean. A large settee sail is used on a mast which rakes forward strongly and is stepped amidships.

LAKATOI
Illustration on page 89.

A picturesque sailing raft of Port Moresby, Papua, British New Guinea, used by the Motu natives for transporting cargoes of earthenware pots and ornaments from the above port and adjacent villages to the settlements at the mouths of the rivers on the Papuan Gulf. There the natives barter for sago and the right to make the dugout canoes ("asi") which form the floating portion of the "lakatoi." These are made from the large ilimo trees found along the rivers.

[148]

The "lakatoi" is composed of three or more long, roughly hewn dugout canoes placed side by side about 6 inches apart. The canoes are secured together by cross-beams which pass through holes in the gunwales. Over the canoes is placed a heavy platform strong enough to take the strain caused by the heavy seas. It extends well beyond the canoes. On each side of the platforms are sturdy crates to hold the pottery and at each end is a bamboo and pandanus-leaf deck house. A weather screen, constructed of thatched palm leaves, runs along the sides to protect the cargo from spray. Two mangrove masts, stepped amidships conveniently apart, each carry an Oceanic "crab-claw" lateen sail. The size of the platforms ranges up to 50 by 60 feet.

Each year, at the end of the southeast trade winds (about the first of October), a fleet of "lakatoi" leaves Port Moresby for the gulf villages, going as far west as Port Romilly. The vessels are decorated with streamers and clan badges, and before sailing for and upon arriving at their destinations rituals are performed. After the ceremonies the trading begins and the new dugouts are made, replacing the old.

LANCHA or LANCHANG — A Malay seagoing craft with two lugsails of equal size. The spars are raked. The hull has an extended "clipper" stem, which acts as a bowsprit for the tack of the foresail. A stern gallery extends over a straight sternpost. The type varies with different localities. The illustration on page 75 shows a "lanchang" of Siak, on the coast of Sumatra.

LANCHANG TO'ARU — A Malay vessel similar to the "lancha," but it is fore-and-aft rigged and carries long topmasts.

LANGOUSTIER — A craft used in the crab fishery off Land's End and the Scilly Islands by Breton fishermen. The larger boats are ketch-rigged, of great beam, decked, with a high bow, counter stern, deep draft, about 50 feet long. There is also a smaller type about 35 feet long, cutter-rigged, with a pole mast, raking transom stern, lug topsail, roller reef on mainsail.

LANGSKIP — *Illustration on page 51.* A Viking "long ship," a fighting ship. See "Viking ship," illustrated on page 49.

LANON — A type of Malay craft formerly used by the native pirates of Johore, at the southern tip of the Malay peninsula, for attacking merchant vessels. It was similar to the Malay "flying prau" (illustrated on page 69). In appearance the hull was junk-like, with a sharp and very hollow bow having a recurved stem, over which was a projecting platform; a square, heavy-carved stern; a gallery extended along either side for an upper bank of oars; high poop deck; strong sheer, especially aft; steering oar with a horizontal tiller. Two square sails were carried on masts which were supported by sheer poles on each side abaft the mast, the

[149]

base being pivoted so that they could be quickly lowered to the deck. The after sail was very small. See "prau," illustrated on page 69.

LAPIL *or*
LEPALEPA
Illustration on page 85.
"Lapil" is the term for "canoe" on Tumelo (Tamara) Island and "lepalepa" on Angel, Ali, and adjacent islands in the Aitape (Berlin Harbor) district off the north coast of Northwest New Guinea. The large dugout sailing canoe from these islands, illustrated on page 85, is used for trading purposes, transporting pots to the mainland in exchange for sago. These canoes range up to 50 feet long and 30 inches wide, and are capable of carrying up to 2 tons. The hull is about 1½ inches thick. The trees from which they are made are obtained from the mainland, as the islands are devoid of large timber. The ends of the canoe round up from the bottom in a yacht-like fashion, terminating to a blunt point. There is tumble home to the sides and a decorated washstrake extends nearly the full length of each gunwale, joining a small breakwater at the ends. A raised central platform is built amidships, with a crate on each side for holding the cargo. Three outrigger booms, lying across the washstrakes and projecting on the off side, are connected to the float with attachments, each consisting of two pairs of under-crossed sticks. A rectangular lugsail, made of coconut cloth, is supported by a mast stepped amidships. The latter is secured to the canoe by an arrangement of crossbeams and is braced by rope and cane stays fore and aft. These canoes cannot tack and are paddled against the wind.

LEMBUS
An ancient boat with a sharp bow and fine lines used by the Illyrians east of the Adriatic Sea at the time of the early Romans.

LEMMERAAK
A Dutch pleasure craft of the Lemster district of Holland, similar to the "boeier" (illustrated on page 43), but having somewhat straighter lines and a finer stern. It is usually built of steel.

LIFEBOAT
An open boat especially designed for seaworthiness and heavy weather, such as used by the Coast Guards and steamers.

LIGHTER
Illustrations on pages 35 and 43.
A small vessel used for loading and unloading larger vessels lying in the open roadstead.

LIME JUICER
A nickname for a British vessel. The British law requires a daily ration of lime juice to prevent scurvy, hence the name.

LISI
Illustration on page 89.
A plank-built "mon" type canoe of the southeastern Solomon Islands. The upturned peaks at the ends are formed by the washboards. They are often highly decorated and carved. No outrigger is employed. See "mon."

[150]

LOBSTER BOAT   A class of small, sloop-rigged boats with centerboard in general use in the lobster fishery of New England. It varies somewhat according to locality. The average size is about 25 feet in length, with a beam of from 8 to 10 feet. One or two jibs are carried to a bowsprit, but it is manageable under mainsail alone. On each side of the centerboard is an open lobster well, with perforated bottom. Fast and able under sail.

LODSBAAD   A Norwegian pilot boat, fore-and-aft rigged, with staysail, jib, and a loose-footed mainsail. A topsail is often carried. Developed from the "Hvalor boat" (illustrated on page 45), but the speed and weather qualities are superior to the older type.

LORCHA   A sailing vessel, typical to Bangkok, Siam. The hull is of western model, with a vertical stem and overhanging transom stern, but the rig is that of the Chinese lug, with one, two, or three masts. Sometimes a bowsprit and jib are carried.
Illustration on page 67.

LOUISIANA PIROGUE   A dugout canoe, made from a cypress log, used for fishing and transportation in the bayous and swamps south of New Orleans, Louisiana. It is an open, keelless, flat-bottomed canoe, with a sharp bow, which is straight and vertical above the water line and curved below. The stern resembles the bow. The sides are round and flaring. Moderate sheer. These "pirogues" range in length from 6 to 20 feet, with the beam about one-seventh the length. A paddle or oars are used.
Illustration on page 87.

Pirogue races are an annual affair on Bayou Barataria, Louisiana, the former stamping ground of the pirates Jean LaFitte and his brother.

LOWESTOFT SMACK   A ketch-rigged trawler typical to Norfolk, England. Formerly lug-rigged, but fore-and-aft sails are now carried on the main and mizzenmasts, with topsails and two headsails, as well as a mizzen staysail. Bonnets are often used to reef the main and mizzen sails. The powerful hull is carvel-built.
Illustration on page 33.

LUGGER   A vessel with one or more masts, rigged with "lugsails." Illustrations on pages 31, 33, 35, 37, 39, 43, 47, 57, 67, and 69.

LURKER   A row boat used in the pilchard fisheries of England, from which the skipper gives his orders and superintends the manipulation of the seine-net. This net is about 1,000 feet long, 50 feet deep at the middle, and 35 feet at the ends. It is carried on a "seine-boat," which is a heavy craft 30 to 35 feet long, manned by a crew of eight, six to row and two to manage the gear.

Two other shorter boats accompany the seine-boat, each with six men aboard. The "lurker" is towed by the largest boat. A watch is kept on shore and when a shoal of pilchards is seen, the boats put out. The net, with a shorter "stop seine" on either end, is shot around the shoal, the whole forming the letter "D." The nets are then towed to shallow water near shore where they are moored in a circle, the fish being confined in the enclosure. The seine is cleared by means of a "tuck-net," and the pilchards bailed out into baskets and taken ashore to the curing yard.

MACHVA   See "muchva."

MADURA PRAU   A native sailing craft used in Madura, an island near the east-
Illustration on page 75.   ern end of Java. It is built of teak and no frames are employed
in its construction, the hull being held together with transverse timbers secured to the sides. The edges of the planks are doweled together. It is double-ended with overhanging bow and stern, the stem and sternpost strongly raking. Moderate sheer. A cabin house is usually built amidships and is roofed over with matting. Equipped with outrigger and two quarter rudders, but only the leeward one is used when sailing. The bow and stern are usually elaborately carved. Rigged with two long, narrow lateen sails, with curved yards along the top and bottom, the forward ends being set from very short masts. The after part of the upper yard is supported by a strut to the hull. Average lengths range between 50 and 60 feet, with the beam about one-quarter of the length. The hull amidships has a wide "U" section.

MAHONA   The Turkish equivalent of the Venetian "galleass" (illustrated
on page 51). The present-day types are fishing and cargo boats of the Bosphorus. The hulls have a generous sheer, good lines, and carry a sprit mainsail or lateen rig, with one or two jibs.

MAIN TOPSAIL   An obsolete type on which square topsails were carried on
SCHOONER   both the fore- and mainmasts. Also known as "two- or double-
Illustration on page 21.   topsail schooners."

MALAR PANSHI   A primitive Bengal boat. The hull is a dugout or is built on a
Illustration on page 65.   dugout frame. There is a high steering platform aft with a
fixed steering oar. One or two square sails on a single mast.

MALAY   A fast, outrigger sailing canoe used by the natives on the Straits
OUTRIGGER   of Malacca. The canoe is double-ended, long and extremely
CANOE   narrow, a 25-footer being but 9 inches wide. It is made of a
Illustration on page 69.   sharp-ended dugout bottom with strakes sewed on above. The

ends are strongly raked, rounding into the keel. A pointed float, about two-thirds the length of the canoe, is supported by two curved outrigger booms on the windward side. A sail, usually a lugsail, is set on a mast stepped amidships. This type has remained unchanged for many centuries. It is claimed that this canoe has been known to make twenty knots under favorable circumstances, which compares very favorably with the "popo" (illustrated on page 83) of the Caroline Islands and the "flying proa" (illustrated on page 83) of the Marianas.

MALDIVE ISLANDS TRADER *Illustration on page 65.*	A large, three-masted, decked trading vessel of 100 tons or more of the Maldive Islands, which lie southwest of India in the Indian Ocean. The hull and rig resemble the 15th century *Santa Maria* of Columbus' time, with poop and overhanging forecastle, a high square mainsail and main topsail, a raking

foremast with a square sail well out over the bow, and a lateen mizzen. From where and whence came this craft?

MAN-OF-WAR	An armed naval vessel. Illustrations on pages 13, 15, 23, 27, 29 and 53.

MAOTA	An outrigger canoe of the island of Napuka, one of the northernmost of the atolls of the Tuamotu Archipelago. These

canoes are formed of a single dugout without end pieces, keel or thwarts. Often a washboard is sewed on above each side. The ends are pointed, curving up from the bottom. An outrigger boom is attached to the gunwales close to each end of the hull. The booms are lashed directly to the float in the Hawaiian manner. These canoes are in use at the present time by the natives for collecting clams found in the lagoon. There has been no change in the primitive design since the island was first visited by white men. Unlike most Tuamotuan craft, the "maota" is free from Tahitian influence. The maximum length is 16 feet, with a beam of 1 foot 8 inches.

MARKET FISHERMAN	A fishing craft which markets its fish as soon as a catch is made. Fast vessels are used in order to reach the marketing port as quickly as possible to prevent spoilage of the fish.

MARSILLIAN	A Mediterranean vessel of the 16th century, similar to the "hulk" (illustrated on page 41).

MASH-HUF	An open boat used by the farmers of Southern Iraq. It is similar to the "tarada," but is wider and undecorated. See "tarada."

MASHWA *or* **MASHUWA**	A term employed on the East African coast to any round-sterned vessel, originally meaning a fishing boat.

[153]

MASULA
MANCHA
A light, wide, flat-bottomed scow used for conveying passengers and cargo through the surf to and from ships on the Madras (India) coast. They range from 28 to 35 feet in length and one-third the beam. No frames are used in the hull, with the exception of the raking end posts, the planks being sewed together with coir yarn and the seams calked with coir. Rowed by twelve men, with two steersmen.

MATAPA
A light open boat used on the northeast coast of Africa. It is of primitive canoe type and has a single square sail. It is employed by the Somalis for fishing and general use.

MELON-SEED
A small, wide, shallow-draft, centerboard boat used for hunting ducks and other sea fowl in the shallow waters of the New Jersey coast. A typical size would be 13 feet long, 4 feet beam, 13 inches draft and having a rather sharp bow, square stern, and rigged with a single spritsail or gaff and boom sail. It is decked except for a cockpit.

MERCHANT-
MAN
A commercial vessel.

MERCHANT
SHIP of EARLY
15th CENTURY
Illustration on page 53.
The ships of this period were awkward looking craft with a blunt bow, round stem, slightly raking sternpost, no forecastle, high sloping and overhanging poop deck and heavy wales and skids on the sides. A high mast, with a "top" at the masthead, was rigged with a large square sail. The larger vessels often had a short square-rigged foremast in addition. A carved steeved bowsprit was stepped alongside the extended stem. Lanterns decorated the after poop deck.

MERCHANT
SHIP of LATE
15th CENTURY
Illustration on page 53.
During this period the ships were round in section and had heavy rounding sheer. There was a poop deck and on the larger vessels a quarter-deck. A fore deck extended over and beyond the forecastle. The sides had the usual heavy wales and skids. The rig on the voyaging ships consisted of a tall pole mainmast, having a "top" aloft and a huge mainsail, sometimes with a tiny topmast arising from and stayed to the "top"; a foremast with a single square sail and a lateen-rigged mizzen. No ratlines were on the shrouds—ascension aloft was done on a Jacob's ladder. Henry Culver maintains that Columbus made his voyages in a ship of this type.

MERGUI
PEARLING
VESSEL
Illustration on page 67.
A small sailing craft used in the pearl fishery of the Mergui Archipelago in the Indian Ocean, just off the lower Burma coast. In general, it is Malayan in character, with the clipper bow and overhanging counter. It is decked, of shallow draft

and the larger pearlers have a cabin house between the helm and the mainmast. The mainmast is stepped amidships and the foremast in the bow, both lug-rigged. A lug-rigged dugout canoe is also used in the pearl industry of this archipelago.

MERSEY LIGHTER
Illustration on page 35.

A sailing barge or lighter used on the Mersey River, England. It is similar to the "keel," except that the fore-and-aft rig is employed.

MOLETA
Illustration on page 39.

A fishing boat of the Tagus, Portugal. A mainmast, stepped amidships, carried a lateen mainsail, a short forward-raking mast in the bow had a small square sail, a jib-shaped sail led from a boomkin to the upper part of the lateen yard and other kites were hoisted here and there wherever possible when the weather was moderate. The hull had little sheer and rounded stem and sternpost. The rudder was slung outside.

MON
Illustration on page 89.

A plank-built canoe, without an outrigger, used in the central portion of the Solomon Islands and in New Ireland in the Bismarck Archipelago. The typical "mon" has high upturned ends, with the sheer line approximating a flattened crescent. The "mon" war canoes are highly decorated with carving and inlay. See "ora" and "lisi."

MONSOON JUNK

A type of Chinese junk, making but one voyage a year from Canton during the favorable direction of the "monsoon" or eastern trade winds. The model in the National Museum has a square, V-shaped bow and stern, with the keel on the forward half only, which is counter-balanced when the huge rudder is down (before tacking the rudder is lifted and the junk comes about quickly); round bottom curving up sharply at the stern; carvel-built; decked, with cabin aft; three-masted "lorcha" (illustrated on page 67) or Chinese balance lug rig.

MONTARIA

An open canoe used by the Brazilians of the Amazon delta. It has a dugout bottom, with boards forming the flaring sides, which connect to V-shaped end pieces that form the raking bow and stern. There is no sheer. When the canoe is about the size of a dory, it is termed "montaria fundo de casco," or simply "casco." The solid bottom was adapted from the Indian "ubá."

MONTYCAT

A small, cat-rigged racing boat about 15 feet long.

MORBIHAN LUGGER
Illustration on page 37.

A two-masted, lug-rigged fishing boat typical to part of the coast of Brittany, France. It is rigged with curious, tall, narrow lugsails, almost rectangular in shape. The boats are fast and seaworthy.

MOUSEHOLE
LUGGER
Illustration on page 33.
A lug-rigged fishing boat working out of the port of Mouse-hole, Cornwall, England. The majority are (or were) 30 to 33 feet long on deck, beam one-third the length, straight stem and transom stern. The older types were three-masted with standing lug main and mizzen, and dipping lug foresail.

MOUNT'S BAY
DRIVER
Illustration on page 33.
A Cornish fishing boat, ketch-rigged without bowsprit, gaff-topsail carried on mizzenmast, which is controlled from a long after boomkin. The hull has high freeboard, a straight stem, and wide rubbing strakes. Length up to 50 feet, beam about one-third.

MTEPI
Illustration on page 89.
An East African dugout canoe, with a single, square matting sail. The hull is sharp-ended and a useless bowsprit is carried, which is decorated with a fringe of grass or reed. Upper and lower yards are used on the sail. This type is used in the Lamu Islands off the coast of Kenya.

MUCHVA *or*
MASHVA
Illustration on page 65.
This peculiar craft, used by fishermen in the vicinity of Bombay, India, is one of the most distinctive types of fishing boat in the world. It is reputed to be the fastest boat of the Orient, excluding certain outrigger canoes. The "muchva" cannot "come about," owing to the deep, angular, fin-like projection where the stem meets the forward end of the hollow arched keel. Because of this feature it is necessary to "wear" or "jibe." It is an open, carvel-built boat, commonly built of teak, having a long, sharp, overhanging bow with a strongly raking stem; sternpost straight and moderately raking; rounded "V" section; hollow run; round stern; rudder slung outside. The usual rig is a large settee sail set on a strongly forward-raking mast stepped nearly amidships. There are thwarts between the sides. The average length is about 40 feet with one-fourth the beam. It is often crudely built.

MULE
A fast, ketch-rigged trawler working out of Brixham, England, of less than 40 tons' displacement, those above this tonnage being called "smacks" locally. The "Brixham trawler" is gradually disappearing. Illustration of "Brixham trawler" on page 31.

MULETTA
Illustration on page 57.
A small Portuguese fishing boat, now quite scarce. The mainmast was stepped about amidships, raking forward and carrying a lateen sail and also a staysail suspended from the top of the yard to the stern of the boat and sheeted to a long boomkin, extending aft from the stern. A small mast was carried in the bow, with a violent forward rake. This

had a square sail, and a spritsail was carried underneath a bowsprit. Staysails were also carried between the masts. The hull had considerable sheer, a pointed bow, a rounding stem adorned with spikes, an outboard rudder and leeboards.[5]

MUMBLE-BEE
Illustration on page 31.
An English cutter-rigged trawler, typical of the southern coast, whose mast is stepped well aft. A beamy boat of from 15 to 30 tons, with a full, high bow, straight keel, and raking sternpost.

MYOPARO
A ship of about 200 A.D. used by Mediterranean pirates.

NA-AK
Illustration on page 79.
The term for "canoe" in Atchin Island, which lies off the northeast coast of Malekula in the New Hebrides group. There were two kinds of canoes used on Atchin Island—the large seagoing canoe (now extinct, being supplanted by whaleboats) and the small coastal canoe, which is still in use. The hull is of a hollowed log of mish-mash wood; its section that of a rounded "V"; double-ended, with outrigger. The seagoing canoes had two washstrakes on either side, the coastal canoes one or none. The outrigger float is supported by three or four booms, the connectives being three or four pairs of crossed (x) sticks lashed to the end of each boom, the lower ends being inserted into the float. Carved figureheads are used and the sides of the hull decorated with figures of fish, etc.

The sail ("na-mban") is a V-shaped spritsail made of pandanus strips pleated and is supported by two spars or sprits which cross at the foot of the sail. They are made fast to the forward outrigger boom inside the canoe. There is no need for a mast. The sail is stayed and operated by three lines from a spar to thwarts and outrigger.

NABBY
Illustration on page 35.
An open sailing skiff used on the Firth of Clyde and Loch Fyne on the west coast of Scotland, from 32 to 34 feet long, carrying a single lugsail and jib on a very raking mast. It dates from 1880. This type of boat was, and is to a lesser extent, used in the herring and "long-line" fisheries. It is double-ended, either carvel- or clinker-built, has a shallow forefoot, with great drag to the keel, drawing 3 to 6 feet aft. Straight, vertical stem and good rake to the sternpost. Some have a small fore deck. The "nabby" resembles the "zulu" (illustrated on page 33), except that it has less rake to the sternpost and more rake to the mast. The mast is stepped well forward and the jib is extended to a long bowsprit. The sail is a standing lug, rather high peaked. In summer a mizzen is added. Average length about 33 feet over-all, 27 feet on the keel. Four men comprise the usual crew for "long-line" or herring fishing, while three men are sufficient for drift-net fishing, which is one man less than is used on the east-coast boats of similar

size. The "nabby" is an outgrowth of the "smack" rig (any fore-and-aft rig, such as cutter or ketch) and the old "short-line" boat model used on the Firth of Clyde.

NADIR	A shallow draft Malay fishing boat of the Malacca coast. The hull is about 24 feet long, carvel-built, with straight stem and sternpost. The rig is a single lug.

NAGGAR *Illustration on page 63.*	A cargo boat of the upper Nile with a sharp-bowed hull and a large outboard rudder. The rig is a simple balance lugsail, set obliquely, with a boom along the foot parallel with the head.

NAO
Illustration on page 185.

A generic term for medium-sized sailing vessels of the Middle Ages—more heavily built than "caravels," but smaller than a "carrack" (both illustrated on page 53). Some authorities maintain that Columbus' flagship, *Santa Maria*, was a "nao" and not a "caravel." If it was the former, the *Santa Maria* might have resembled the drawing on page 185, which shows a ship, or "nao," of the late 15th century. At any rate, both sides of the nao-caravel controversy agree on the rig, which was a square-rigged fore- and main-mast, with a small topmast and topsail on the latter, and a spritsail on the bowsprit. The vessels of that period were steered with a whipstaff, as the steering wheel did not come into use until about 1711. "Nao" is another term for "nef" (illustrated on page 185), although the "nao" may be considered smaller.

NAPLES
  TRAWLER
Illustration on page 39.

A double-ended boat employed in the fisheries of the Bay of Naples. A typical Naples trawler has a single lateen-rigged mast, with two or three auxiliary sails hung about in moderate weather, as is customary with Tuscan and Portuguese craft.[5] The Naples trawlers are fine weather boats.

NAURI	A "dhow" of Baluchistan, exceptionally fast. It has an ornamented stem head and is steered by a wheel.

NAVICELLO *or*
  BALANCELLE
Illustration on page 39.

A two-masted Italian coasting vessel, rigged with a fore-and-aft mainsail, with a short hoist and a long gaff, maintopsail, a forward-raking foremast, stepped well up in the bow, with a staysail set in much the same manner as the rig on the present day "staysail-rigged" schooner yachts, and a triangular jib to a long bowsprit. The long main gaff is kept standing and is hung from one-third to one-half of the lower mast length below the heel of the main topmast. The mainsail travels on rings and is hauled out along the gaff when set. No boom is used and the peak is controlled by vangs. The "navicello" was in use in the 19th century, as well as at the present time. In former times a lateen sail was carried instead of the staysail.

NDRUA   A large, finely constructed double canoe of the Fiji Islands. The dugout hulls, usually of unequal length, had a "U" section (transversely) with some tumble home, and deep washstrakes above. The sterns and the bow of the small hull had a fine run with a small truncate end, while the bow of the larger hull had a vertical cutwater. Both hulls were strengthened internally with ribs and were planked over the full length. A large platform, built amidships over the crossbeams connecting the hulls, had a bailing hatch in each corner and a thatched hut over the middle. The rig was the same as that of the "thamakau" (illustrated on page 77). The canoe was steered with a huge paddle, one-third to one-half the over-all length, one fitted to each end of the larger hull, that at the functional bow being lifted clear of the water. With a fresh breeze on the after quarter, this craft could attain a speed of 10 to 15 knots, but it could not sail before the wind as the bow would bury itself. It could beat to windward fairly well, but, being keelless, made much leeway. On the large "ndrua" of former times as many as 100 persons could be transported, and this type of craft ranged up to 100 feet in length. Two to three years were consumed in the building of such a canoe. When not in the water, the "ndrua" was housed in an immense shed, with low walls and a great arched thatched roof. This type of canoe is no longer in existence.

NEF
Illustration on page 185.

The term applied generally to nearly all sailing vessels from the 14th to 16th centuries, although it probably referred to the larger classes, but somewhat smaller than a "carrack." The "great nef" shown on page 185 was of about 800 tons, with rounding sheer to a high, narrow stern. There was a high forecastle and a long, double-decked after castle, or poop deck, which overhung the stern proper. The hull was strengthened with heavy wales and skids.

The rig consisted of square-rigged fore- and mainmasts, with lateen sails on the mizzen and bonaventure masts. "Nefs" were employed both as commercial and naval vessels. See "nao."

NEW ORLEANS LUGGER
Illustration on page 17.

A single-masted, shallow-draft, lug-rigged boat used in the coast fisheries in the vicinity of New Orleans, Louisiana, on the Gulf of Mexico. Of European origin, and usually manned by southern Europeans. It is carvel-built, half-decked, with centerboard, with a coaming around an elliptical-shaped cockpit, and a covered hatch forward. The bow is sharp with a concave water line and vertical stem; outboard rudder; various lengths.

NICKEY
Illustration on page 31.

A double-ended, two-masted fishing boat of the Isle of Man, England. Present-day types are lug-rigged, without headsails, a gaff topsail being carried on the mizzenmast.

[159]

NOBBIE — A dandy-rigged craft of Hoylake, England, descended from and similar to the "Manx nickey" (illustrated on page 31). Average size about 40 feet by 12 feet by 6 feet draft.

NORDLANDS COD BOAT
Illustration on page 45. — A double-ended, open boat used in the cod fishery on the west coast of Norway, similar in line to the old Viking "long ship." Clinker-built with wide planks (15 or 16 inches); great sheer at ends, with high stem and sternpost; straight keel; low free-board amidships and outside rudder. A single mast, with a tall square sail, is stepped somewhat forward of the center. It is equipped with oars and rowed against the wind. It ranges in size from 20 to 60 feet in length, with narrow beam. Sometimes a small cabin is built in the after end.

NORWEGIAN CAT
Illustration on page 55. — See description under "cat."

NORTH RIVER SLOOP
Illustration on page 19. — A large shoal-draft, centerboard sloop, used on the Hudson River for carrying passengers and freight before the advent of steam. These sloops were 70 to 90 feet long on deck, were fast, and fine weather boats. The square topsail was replaced by a triangular topsail after the War of 1812.

OOMIAK — See "umiak," illustrated on page 87.

OPIUM CLIPPER A fast sailing ship engaged in transporting opium from India to China from about 1830 to 1855. The opium clippers were small vessels, averaging about 100 tons, and were, for the most part, "brigs" and "schooners," with a few "barks," and only one "ship," the *Falcon*, of 351 tons. Inasmuch as the traffic in opium was illicit, speed was the prime requisite of the vessels therein engaged, and due to this necessity some fine ships were produced and the men who sailed them were incomparable seamen. Strange as it may seem, the officers, especially of the British ships, were usually of good family and many of them were former navy men. The pay was large.

Large ships were not required as an opium cargo rarely exceeded 300 chests, and due to the danger from pirates, always lurking in the eastern seas, a larger cargo meant a greater loss. To overcome the hazard of attack when becalmed, the vessels were equipped with sweeps and were armed with small cannon.

Upon reaching Macao or Linton, off the China coast, the opium cargo was put on receiving ships, which were stationary gunboats or converted "Indiamen," with

[160]

armed crews, as well as business clerks. Smaller vessels then would take a portion of the cargo from the receiving ship and distribute it to other clippers waiting along the China coast between Hainan and Woosung. The latter vessels would then transport the opium to various Chinese ports. These ships were picked for their speed and seaworthiness, as they had to run the gauntlet of fleets of pirates, armed "junks" of hostile Mandarins and typhoons.

In the early 1850's, steamers began to compete with the "opium clippers" and soon they had disappeared from the seas. The last American "opium clippers" were the 300-ton schooners *Minna* and *Brenda*, built in 1851 at Portsmouth, New Hampshire.

ORA
Illustration on page 89.
A plank-built "mon" type canoe of San Cristobal Island in the Solomon group. The "ora" has the typical "mon" peak aft, but the peak at the forward end is formed by the upturned washboards. There is no outrigger. See "mon."

ORANG LAUT BOAT
A type of Malay fishing craft used by the Orang Laut natives on the west coast of the Malay Peninsula, and very often used as their homes. The hull has long overhangs and is open, except for a "kadjang," or thatched awning. The mast is stepped somewhat forward of amidships and carries a large matting square sail, with upper and lower yards—a true Malay sail—which can also be used as a dipping lugsail; controlled by a sheet and a vang at the peak.

ORKNEY SKIFF
A small, open skiff used in the fisheries off the Orkney Islands, Scotland, quite beamy in proportion to its length, clinker-built, raking stem, rigged with two rather high-peaked spritsails, and outboard rudder.

OROU
Illustration on page 85.
A double sailing canoe used by the Mailu Islanders of Papua (British New Guinea). It is constructed of two dugout canoes of nearly equal size, placed parallel to each other and connected by 6 to 12 booms for a distance apart of half the length of the hulls. The booms pass through the washstrakes, which are 14 to 18 inches high and run practically the full length of the hulls, terminating at and joined to tall carved breakwaters. The booms project beyond the hull on the side opposite the mast. A plank deck is laid between the hulls over the boom projections. The ends of the hulls are bluntly rounded and raked. A large crab-claw Oceanic lateen sail, of matting made of split rushes, is hung from a sapling mast, the roots cut off forming a buttress base, which is lashed firmly to the adjacent booms and hull. The mast, stepped amidships of the larger canoe, is braced by rattan fore-and-aft stays. These are double and twisted for strength, and they are festooned with streamers fashioned from leaves. The sail is

twice the height of the mast and it is hoisted sideways by two or three halyards made fast to the longer yard about two-thirds up from the foot. The foot of the sail is hauled down by a line and then lashed to the mast. Two lines are attached to the outer yard, one of which acts as a sheet and the other as a forward guy. When coming about the steering paddle is unshipped and slung on the opposite end, the bow becoming the stern, the main sheet becoming the guy. The "orou" can also be rowed. It is quite fast, doing 8 knots in a fresh breeze, and can sail close to the wind, making little leeway. It is used for trading and cargo carrying.

OUTRIGGER CANOE	A canoe with a boom, or float, running parallel with it, some distance away, and secured to outriggers, extending at right angles, to prevent its overturning.

OYSTER SCHOONER	A type of two-masted schooner designed for carrying oysters from the fishing grounds of Chesapeake Bay to Baltimore. Average size about 75 feet long, by 22 feet beam, with sharp

bow and slightly raking stem; long, well-formed run; wide, square stern; moderate sheer; long, low quarter-deck and carvel-built. A "Bay boat" is of the same type.

PACIFIC ISLANDS TRADING SCHOONER *Illustration on page 89.*	The schooners used for inter-island transportation of copra, general merchandise, and passengers in the South Pacific are of varied hull design and the length may be from 60 to 90 feet. The few the writer has seen have had a clipper bow, one or two tall deck houses, plenty of hold space, and are heavily built to withstand the buffeting received during the summer gales.

Motors are essential in order to work out of currents when becalmed. The eastern side of Christmas Island, for instance, is lined with wrecked vessels swept ashore by the strong current, which runs about 96 miles per day. Any ship without a strong motor is doomed to be lost if caught within 10 miles eastward of the Island.

PACKET SHIP *Illustration on page 23.*	The passenger ship of the period from 1816 until the 1860's when the sailing vessel made way for the steamship. The early packets were small, three-masted, square-rigged ships, from

300 to 500 tons' register, but the size increased until many were over 1,000 tons. They were full-bodied ships, could carry a big spread of canvas, and although the hulls were slow, they were driven hard, and the New York-Liverpool run in 16 days was not uncommon. Formerly flush-decked, a poop was added about 1830, and this was followed by other deck houses.

In the late 1840's the old type packet was supplanted by the fast "clipper" ship, and the average running time was cut down by several days. The fastest passages made by the "clipper-packets" were those of the *Lightning*, *James Baines* and *Dreadnought*. *Lightning*, an American clipper, built by Donald McKay in 1854 for James Baines of the Australian Black Ball Line, made the passage from New York to Liverpool in 13 days 19½ hours, in 1855. Her highest 24-hour run was 436 nautical miles, at an average of 18 knots.

In March, 1855, the American "clipper-packet" *Dreadnought* made the 3,018-mile trip from New York to Northwest Lightship, off Liverpool, in 13 days 8 hours. Captain Samuels claimed he made the run from Sandy Hook to Queenstown, Ireland, in 9 days 17 hours, in 1862.

The *James Baines*, American-McKay built clipper-packet, of the Australian Black Ball Line, made the run from Boston Light to Rock Light in 12 days 6 hours, in September, 1854, making 20 knots on several occasions.

The American packet ships (and the "Blackwallers") were the finest afloat. They were fast and dry, ably managed, the passenger accommodations were sumptuously fitted up and they carried the best officers and the largest crews. Because of these distinctions, the American lines gained a virtual monopoly of the transatlantic passenger and mail trade. Some of the prominent packet lines established from New York during the period from 1816 to 1821 were: The Black Ball Line, Red Star Line, Swallow-tail Line, and the Dramatic Line.

PADA A "padow."

PADDA BOAT An open, square-ended, flat-bottomed canal boat of Ceylon used for transporting freight, with sharply raking ends, having graceful sheer. Roofed over with rattan or bamboo frame. Paddled. Usually 25 to 30 feet long and about 6½ feet beam.

PADOW A large trading "dhow" of India, north of Bombay, generally having painted ports along under the poop.

PAHI A term applied by Tahitians to any larger vessel. "Pahi"
Illustration on page 77. is the name of the large seagoing double canoes formerly used by the natives of the Tuamotu Archipelago and Tahiti. These were large vessels, ranging up to 75 feet in length, constructed with a keel, frames, and a skin of planking neatly and painstakingly sewed together. The twin hulls were connected by two heavy planks and a platform laid between the adjacent gunwales. There were two masts, one stepped on each connecting plank midway between the canoes and each was braced by three vine or rope shrouds to a side and a forestay. According to a model in the Marine Museum in the Louvre, the sail was a triangular Oceanic lateen. At each end of the hull was a head fitting peculiar

[163]

to the Tuamotus, formed by an extension of the upper plank meeting the upper end of the raking cutwater. A heavy steering oar was lashed to the stern piece. The "pahi" of Tahiti had a high curved stern. One of the last of these voyaging "pahi" is preserved in the museum at Papeete, Tahiti.

The present-day outrigger, dugout sailing canoes of the Leeward Group, Society Islands, are also known as "pahi." These craft are very fast, handy and well built. They have been known to make 14 knots. The hull is formed of a dugout with one or two washboards sewed on for additional freeboard, and it sheers up strongly at the stern. The bow is sharp with a vertical, slightly concave cutwater, while the stern is pointed. The outrigger, with one curved and one straight boom, is permanently fitted to the port side and the attachments are typical to the island to which the canoe belongs. The straight fore boom has a connective to the float, the after one attached directly. The rig is that of a boomed spritsail, the upper end of the sprit being guyed to a long boomkin. A balance spar is lashed to the fore boom and projects from the starboard side.

PALACCA   An Italian "polacre" with three pole masts, the foremast being lateen-rigged, the main square-rigged with a topsail, and the mizzen lateen-rigged with a square topsail.

PANGA   A flat-bottomed rowboat of Central America.

PARACHAL   An open, circular, saucer-shaped coracle used on the Bowani River, Coimbatore, India. Made by covering a rattan frame with oilcloth.

PARANZELLO   An Italian two-masted trawler, with a large lateen mainsail on
Illustration on page 39.   the mast, or "trinchetto," stepped about amidships; small lateen mizzen, and two headsails. Sometimes a square topsail or a topmast was carried over the large main.

PARDO   A vessel used in the 17th and 18th centuries in the China Seas, both for trade and war. It was not so large as a "junk," but was similar, except that its sails were slackly laced by one side to the masts instead of being suspended by a yard.

PATACHE   A southern European vessel, popular previous to the 19th cen-
Illustration on page 59.   tury. It resembled the "brigantine." The mainmast was a pole, without a topmast, rigged with a large fore-and-aft sail without a boom. The foremast consisted of three sections, each with its square sail. Liberal staysails were carried in addition to the jib and jib staysail. The hulls were generally

cumbersome, with a stern pierced with small cabin windows. They were used in the coasting trade.

PATANI — A Malay craft with a two-masted Chinese lug rig; sharp bow and stern, with overhanging counter and curved stem.

PATTAMAR — A large two- or three-masted dhow of India. The hull is sharp
Illustration on page 65. forward, the long stem severely raking in the "dhow" manner, the stern is square without a poop deck. There is generous sheer. The "pattamar" is distinguished by the red paint, the black gunwales, and the globe painted on the stern transom. While the basic rig is that of the lateen with bowsprit and jib, there are many variations. The lengths vary, but do not exceed about 75 feet.

PAYANG — A native fishing craft of the east coast of the Malay Peninsula.
Illustration on page 69. The hull has rounded sections, bow and stern alike, some sheer, shallow draft, hardwood frames and planking, and is carvel-built. The keel is V-shaped in section and is parallel longitudinally to the gunwale. The stem and sternpost are wide, flat boards which project two to three feet above the gunwale, and are carved to a point at the upper end. The decking consists of loose planking, with a seat at the stem and stern. The steering is done with a long oar, kept in position at the inner end by a strap and line made fast to an inclined timber. Two masts are usually used, the shorter stepped in the bow and the mainmast about one-third the length of the hull from the stem. The hooked mainmast is boused down with fore-and-aft stays, but with no shrouds. The lug rig is used, the head and foot set obliquely, and reefing is done by rolling the sails around the booms. The sails are of black cloth and the leeches of the sails are made very baggy. A typical length is about 50 feet, with one-seventh the beam, and a moulded depth of about 3 feet. On this size "payang" a crew of 20 is carried, 18 oarsmen, a steersman, and a lookout, or "pawang" (wizard). The latter uses a small canoe cruising about to locate shoals of fish, which he does by diving under water to catch the peculiar sound made by a shoal. An elongated purse seine, 125 feet by 16 feet in breadth, is then shot around the shoal of fish. The hulls are painted in various color schemes.

PEA POD — An open, double-ended, clinker-built boat used in general fisheries off the coast of Maine; 15 feet long with 4½ feet beam; good sheer; cat-rigged, with single sail. Built at Jonesport, Maine.

PEDIWAK — A decked, keel sailing craft of the northern Celebes. It is 30 to 35 feet long, wide and deep. The bow is hollow and sharp and is much lower than the main part of the hull. Raking curved stern. Sharp aft with

[165]

large square, vertical stern. High poop. A wide lugsail, with a yard on the foot, and a jib to a bowsprit are carried.

PENCHALANG   A craft used for transportation purposes at Johore, average size 30 to 35 feet long, 7 to 7½ feet beam; a mast 15 to 18 feet high above gunwale is stepped in the forward thwart and carries a lugsail with a yard on the foot; sharp, hollow bow and stern; raking, curved stem and sternpost; four or five thwarts; no sheer; steered with a paddle.

PENJAJAP   A Malay trading vessel, rigged with two sails which are a
Illustration on page 69.   combination of the square sail and dipping lug, common on native Malay craft. The hull is low, sharp, long, of small beam, of generous sheer, and has a raised overhanging poop. A lattice platform projects forward from the bow instead of a bowsprit, but no headsails are carried. There is generally a grating, or lattice, forming a raised floor just below the top of the gunwale, upon which the crew is accommodated. A bundle of bamboos is sometimes placed under each gunwale for stability.

PENTECONTER   An early galley, having 25 oars to a side.
Illustration on page 51.

PENZANCE   Lug-rigged fishing boats out of and registered in Penzance,
LUGGER   England. See "Mousehole" and "Mount's Bay" luggers, both illustrated on page 33.

PERIGA   A small lateen-rigged vessel of the Mediterranean.

PETER BOAT   A small, sturdy, beamy, open fishing boat. Double-ended,
Illustration on page 35.   rounded stem and stern alike, very shallow keel, clinker-built, with outboard rudder. Decked over fore and aft, with a well amidships, the hinged cover forming a seat. Single spritsail and jib carried. This type was used on the lower Thames in England for centuries and was descended from the Vikings. The last ones were used in 1890 in the smelt fishery at Chiswick, England.

PICAROON   Corsairs' or pirates' craft. A term used usually in the Caribbean.

PICKET BOAT   An outpost scouting or guard boat.

PILOT BOAT   The American pilot boats were fast schooner-rigged vessels
Illustrations on page 167.   used by pilots to put them on incoming ships. Of prime con-

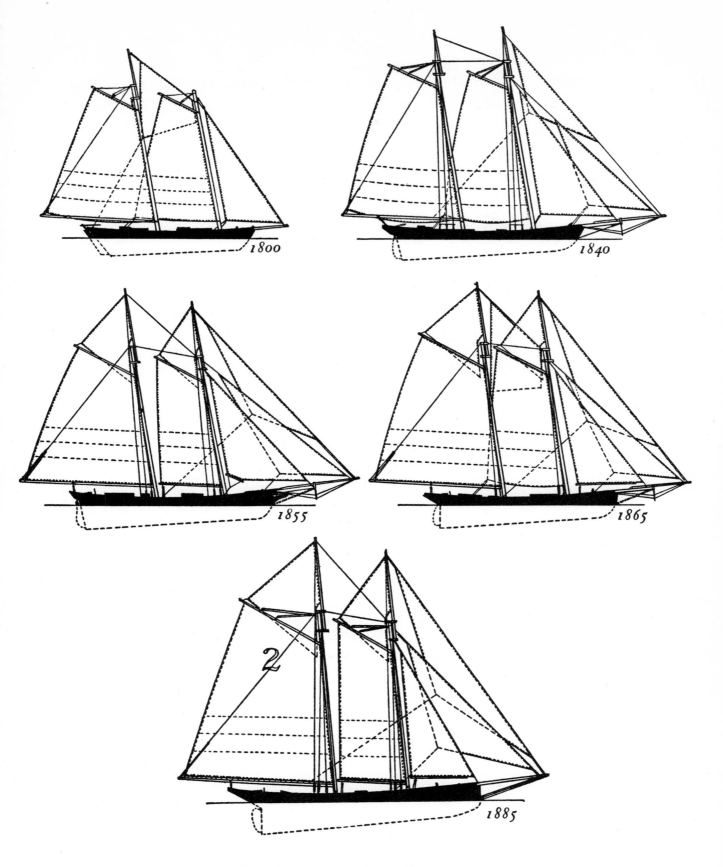

SOME EXAMPLES OF PILOT SCHOONERS

sideration in pilot-boat design were speed and sail-carrying capacity, seaworthiness and the ability to roll easily in a seaway. The pilot schooners of the last quarter of the 18th century closely approximated the "Virginia model"—the forerunner of the "Baltimore clipper"—according to H. I. Chapelle, who has made a thorough study of the subject. They ranged from 45 to 60 feet long, with raking masts, great dead rise, deep drag, low freeboard and raking ends. The hulls were quite shallow.

After 1800 the pilot boats became larger and deeper and the usual rig for the next 35 or 40 years was a lofty fore- and mainsail, the former boomless and overlapping the main, a loose-footed mainsail with boom, large headsail, and "fisherman," the latter two set flying. There was usually no standing rigging, which necessitated masts of large diameter. The topmasts were short.

About the middle of the century the pilot boats were given a finer hollow entrance, making for a faster hull, and a V-shaped stern. Some had a clipper bow—which was favored in Boston—but the cutter bow with a straight vertical stem above the water line and curved forefoot became popular. The full schooner rig with jib boom, jib, and jib topsail was in use, as well as the variation mentioned above, the hoist of which was cut down and with higher topmasts. A shallower, beamier type of hull was tried out, but, while fast, it lacked the seaworthy qualities necessary in the pilot service. This was replaced by a deeper model with less beam, having low inside ballast and raking, V-shaped stern. It had great dead rise, long lean run, graceful sheer, varied rake to sternpost, heavy drag, long sharp bow usually with the cutter stem and greatest beam about amidships. This model, combining the required essentials, persisted with little change until steam took the place of sail.

Up to the last, the pilot-schooner retained certain characteristics of the Baltimore clipper. The famous schooner yacht *America* was a specialized pilot-boat model. It might be added that the pilot boat had a marked influence on yacht design of the period. See also "Havre pilot boat," "Hvalor-baad," "lodsbaad."

PILOT CUTTER   A cutter-rigged vessel used in the pilot service on the Bristol Channel before steam was employed about 1912. A fast and able ship, easy in a seaway, with cutter bow, short counter, and long keel with deep drag. The mast was set well back from the bow and supported by three shrouds, and no bobstay was used.

PINK   A term applied to different types of hulls and rigs. The "pink"
Illustration on page 59.   is characterized by the upper part of the stern, which is narrowed and projects beyond the hull proper, the planking underneath curving sharply to the sternpost. This is called "pink" stern.

The Mediterranean "pink" is a lateen-rigged merchant craft, with two and sometimes three masts, having the "galley" form of masthead. It resembles the "xebec" (illustrated on page 61), but the hull is fuller with a "pink" stern, and no oars are used.

The term "pink" is also applied to the "dum," a fishing boat of Scheveningen, Holland. See "dum," illustrated on page 43.

PINKY
Illustration on page 19.
A pink-sterned, schooner-rigged vessel used extensively in the cod and mackerel fisheries of New England from 1820 until the middle of the century, although until recently a few could be found here and there on the Maine coast. The "pinky" succeeded the "chebacco boat" (illustrated on page 19), from which it differed only in size, being larger, and in that it carried a bowsprit and jib. The bow was full and rounding, with raking sternpost, curved stem with gammon knee, low round bilge, straight sides, short run, heavy sheer, and the overhanging "pink" stern. Some carried topmasts. They were noted for their seaworthiness and sailing qualities. Their maximum length was about 53 feet.

PINNACE
Illustration on page 53.
A light sailing vessel used from the 16th to the 18th centuries, generally rigged with a single square sail on the foremast, a course and square topsail on a high mainmast, and a small lateen sail on the mizzen. "Pinnaces" were used in the battle between the English fleet and the Spanish Armada. Also a small boat used as a tender to larger ships.

PIRAGUA
Another form of "pirogue." Also, a "periagua." The piragua is used mainly by the Carib Indians of British Guiana, South America. It is made by hollowing out the section of a tree trunk until the sides are thin. The open ends are each filled in with a V-shaped piece, then shape is given to the canoe by spreading the sides apart by means of sticks placed athwartships and lashed to the gunwales. These piraguas are crude affairs, but they are made to comparatively large sizes.

PIROGUE
Illustration on page 87.
The old West Indian name for a dugout canoe. There is a type of "pirogue" used in the bayous of Louisiana. See "Louisiana pirogue," illustrated on page 87.

PLAT
A small, flat-bottomed, square-sterned rowboat, about 5 feet long, used as a dinghy by Breton fishermen.

POJAMA
A Swedish galley-type, armed naval vessel of the 19th century, with two heavy guns at each end. It was two-masted, with a fore-and-aft mizzen and square-rigged on the mainmast. The hull was built much heavier than that of the galley. There were ports for sweeps.

[169]

POLACRE

Illustration on page 59.

A sharp-bowed Mediterranean vessel. This type still exists. It usually carried three pole masts without crosstrees or caps, and a one-piece bowsprit. Cleats were put on the masts as stops for the shrouds and stays. The upper yards could be dropped close to each other and the men stood on the under one when furling sail, thereby eliminating footropes. It was square-rigged, and in earlier times a lateen sail was used on the mizzenmast. Rope ladders were fixed from the mastheads to the lower rigging.

POLACRE-
SETTEE

Illustration on page 59.

Similar to a "polacre," but with the mainmast square-rigged and lateen-rigged on the fore- and mizzenmasts. Also called a "polacre corvette."

PONTO

A Roman vessel circa 200 A.D., rigged with square mainsail and a small artemon, the latter being supported by shrouds. The yard and sail were kept stowed until required.

POOKHAUN

A double-ended, Scandinavian yawl-type, lug-rigged craft of Galway, Ireland.

POPO

Illustration on page 83.

The "flying proa" or outrigger sailing canoe used for sea voyages and interisland travel in the Caroline Islands. The "popo" is not to be confused with the "flying proa" (illustrated on page 83) of the Marianas Islands, although it is of the same general form, except that the "popo" has a cantilevered lee platform for carrying supplies and, secondly, that the outrigger connection is more complex. Like most of the Micronesian sea-going canoes, this canoe has the flattened side of the hull. The latter is usually built of planking above a dugout base. The ends are elongated and carved to represent the head of a bird. The hulls are painted in varying designs of red, black, and white. The Oceanic lateen rig is used and the steering is done with a quarter rudder or a paddle. The "popo" is still in existence. See "flying proa."

PORTPATRICK
LINE BOAT

A two-masted, open fishing skiff about 16 feet long, 7 feet beam, used in the "long-line" cod fishery at Portpatrick, Scotland. The foremast is set well up in the bow and the aftermast stepped amidships. The features of this boat are a full bow and quarters and its breadth of beam.

POST-SHIP

In the British Navy, ships carrying less than 24 and more than 18 guns. They were the lowest class of ships a captain could command.

PRAAM   A Norwegian sailing lighter.

PRAHU *or* **PRAU**   The Malay term for "boat." A Malay pirate "prahu," known
Illustration on page 69.   by sailors as "flying prau," was a type of rowing and sailing
                         vessel of the East Indies, formerly used by Malay pirates to
attack merchant vessels when becalmed. A carvel-built, keel vessel, with sharp,
hollow bow and stern; raking, curved stem, with a long, oddly shaped head; straight
raking sternpost and high square stern; easy run. A poop deck extended abaft and
and beyond each side of the hull; strong sheer. The rail was open forward of the
poop for oars. Two rattan square sails were generally carried on slim bamboo masts,
which could be lowered. Armed with swivel guns or small cannon. The hull proper
(between perpendiculars) ranged from 35 to 45 feet long and 12 to 15 feet longer
over-all; 11 or 12 tons' burden. The hull was above the water line and was painted
with red, yellow, and green stripes, with a design on the upper one.

Another important type of "prahu" was the Malay pirate vessel of the East Indian Archipelago. It was similar to, but larger by 15 feet or so and more heavily
armed, than the previous type of Malay pirate craft. A small bowsprit often extended
beyond the bow, but no sail was set to it. The natives of Sooloo, which island was the
chief center of the pirates in the 18th century, and those of the south side of Mindanao Island had "prahus" of even larger size, ranging up to 30 tons, and were better
fitted.

The Malay pirates only operated when the sea was calm and generally in flotillas
of from 5 to 20 "prahus." It is estimated that in the 18th century over 10,000 Malays
of Sooloo and Mindanao Islands alone were engaged in the business of pirating at one
time, operating over 250 vessels. They infested the Straits of Macassar, the Sooloo
Sea and the Celebes Sea. When pursued by naval ships, they easily escaped by going
over a bar at a river mouth and then turning up one of the innumerable creeks.

Still another type of "prahu" is a Malay canoe, having long ends, high poop, and
double rudders. The rig is diversified, generally two-masted, often with a spar forestay. Some of these "prahus" have adopted a fore-and-aft rig, but the usual sails are
triangular in shape, with gaff and yard, and made of matting.

PRAHU PELET   A Malay lug-rigged pilot boat.

PRAU BUGIS   A two-masted cargo boat of the East Indies. The hull is of
Illustration on page 75.   ancient model, not unlike that of a "junk," having an overhang-
                         ing poop roofed over with matting supported by bamboo poles.
Usually built of teak. The bow is cut away above the deck some distance from the
stem, bulkheaded, leaving the stem exposed. Above the long spike bowsprit is a
bamboo grating supported by side planks on which fish are dried.

The steering is done by two rudders, or steering oars, which can be raised and lowered, and are slung from the quarters. They are held in position by rattan straps and the tillers lead athwartships to the center. The helmsman stands under the poop deck, an open hatch over his head and a square opening in the hull on either side of him. Raking stem and sternpost, considerable sheer rising to the stern, and moderate dead rise.

The rig is that of a ketch, with tripod lower masts, topmasts, fixed gaffs, a bamboo boom on the mizzensail and none on the mainsail. A wide-footed fore staysail, two or three jibs, and main and mizzen topsails are carried. Average size about 60 feet by 16 feet by 8 feet 6 inches. Two dugout canoes are usually carried on deck.

PRAU NADI   A keelless dugout used by the natives of Johore, Malay States, with V-shaped raking ends. The floor rises sharply and there is a sharp turn to the bilges; no sheer. It is sometimes partially covered with a deck of bamboo. Average lengths 20 to 25 feet, with a beam about one-fifth.

PRAWNER   A small sailing craft engaged in trawling for "prawns" (pink shrimp) off the English coast. A beam trawl is used, the beam being about 20 feet long. Trawl irons, weighing about 30 pounds each, at either end lift the mouth of the bag-shaped net about two feet above the ground, while between the irons a horizontal chain of oak bobbins, 6 to 10 inches in diameter, is stretched. The trawl is attached to the boat by a line and bridles, and is dragged over sea bottom. The prawns and other fish are boiled in a large copper kettle on the boat.

The "prawners" of Morecambe Bay are fine little cutters, ranging from 25 to 35 feet in length, and are excellent sea boats. Nowadays they are motor-powered, using only a small mainsail and jib.

PRIVATEER   A privately owned vessel, armed and manned at the owner's expense, which was used for capturing enemy merchant craft in time of war. A commission or "letter of marque" was obtained from the government under whose flag it sailed. Without this, it was considered a pirate. The owner, officers and crew held shares in a privateering enterprise. At the beginning of each war it was customary to fit out merchant craft as privateers, though fast sailers were naturally preferred, and carried only enough guns to overawe lightly armed merchantmen and make them surrender. Though the ship, brig, and brigantine rigs were used as privateers, the topsail schooner was the favorite rig. The largest American privateers did not exceed 120 feet in length. The size of the American privateer was fixed by the difficulty in obtaining large crews. The French, however, built privateers comparable in size to naval frigates. Privateering was at its height during the period beginning with the Revolutionary War and ending with the War of 1812.

PROA   A narrow, double-ended dugout sailing canoe of the Microne-
                sian Islands and the Malay Archipelago. The outstanding fea-
ture of this type is the flattened lee side of the hull. The weather, or outrigger, side is
curved in the normal manner. The flattened lee side compensates for the pull to
weather by the outrigger. The number of outrigger booms, the method of attaching
them to the float, and the design of the latter varies with the locality, as does the exact
shape of the hull. Another feature of the "proa" is the method of stepping the
pivoted mast amidships, thereby permitting the canoe to sail in either direction.
When coming about, the stern becomes the bow and vice versa. The rig consists of an
Oceanic lateen sail on a raking mast. See "flying proa," "popo," "wa lap," and others
illustrated on page 83.

PROSUMIA   A Roman vessel circa 200 A.D. similar to the "ponto."

PU HOE   An outrigger, dugout, paddling canoe of the Society Islands.
                 On the larger sizes a washstrake is usually added. The un-
decked hull ranges in size from 15 to 28 feet long, 16 to 20 inches wide, 12 to 18
inches deep, and has a rounded bottom (transversely), a vertical, slightly concave
stem, pointed stern, and a rail or moulding around the gunwales. The long outrigger
float is on the port side and is connected with the hull by two asymmetric booms.
The fore boom is reversely curved and projects beyond the hull on the off side. The
fore attachment is composed of paired "V" connectives and sennit braces. This may
vary, however. The after boom, arched outboard, is connected directly to the float
near the end. The booms are spaced widely apart. The "pu hoe" has remained unchanged through the years and is in use at the present time.

PULWAR   A native sailing craft of Bengal, India, similar to a "malar
Illustration on page 65.   panshi" with a larger single square sail.

PUMPKIN SEED   A dinghy of wide beam.

PUNGY   A two-masted keel schooner which was employed extensively
Illustration on page 17.   in the dredging of oysters in Chesapeake Bay. It is built on the
                 lines of a Baltimore clipper and is, in fact, the last true model of
this type of fast schooner. The hull is carvel-built, with a moderately flaring bow
and a strongly raking, curved stem. The square stern is shallow with a raking sternpost. The runs are long. It has a typical schooner rig and is fast and quick in stays.
The masts are tall and raking in the Baltimore manner, the bowsprit is long and the
sails high and narrow. The average size is 65 to 70 feet long by 20 to 22 feet beam.
The heyday of the pungy was from about 1845 to 1900, but there may be some
around the Bay at the present time. It is purely a local type.

PUNT   A small, flat-bottomed, open boat for rowing or sculling. A
              term used at sea for a broad beamy dinghy. Also, a large type
of deep-ballasted, half-decked boat of Falmouth, England.

PUNTER   A small pleasure craft of the Netherlands—a combination of
              the "hoogaar" (illustrated on page 43) and the dory of New
England. There is a narrow transom at the stern, and the bow has the long raking
stem of the latter. The sides flare out somewhat, with tumble home above the main
sheer line. Usually has a leg-of-mutton mainsail and a jib to a short bowsprit.

QUAICHE   The French term for "ketch."

QUARTER BOAT Boats swung from davits at the quarters of a vessel.

QUAY PUNT   A sailing craft of Falmouth, England, used for fishing, carrying
              stores to ships, pleasure boating, etc. This type of boat has a
deep keel, a straight stem, transom stern, a large open cockpit, and is high-sided and
deep-hulled. The length is 20 to 22 feet, with a beam of about one-fifth. The summer
rig consists of a gaff mainsail, standing lug mizzen, forestaysail set to a short iron
boomkin, and a jib to a running bowsprit, which is removed in winter along with the
jib. A smaller mainsail and a jib-headed mizzen are used with the shorter rig. They
are fine sea boats. Lately motors are employed with a very small spread of canvas.

QUECHE   The Portuguese term for "ketch."

QUINQUEREME   A term sometimes applied to a galley having five banks of
              oars, but more correctly designating the number of men per
oar—in this case, five men to an oar. The term was also applied to war vessels of the
Romans and contemporary peoples, regardless of whether they were biremes (illustrated on page 49) or triremes (illustrated on page 51).

QUODDY   A type of open keel boat used in the fisheries off the coast of
Illustration on page 17.   Maine. It was sloop- or cat-rigged and 20 to 35 feet long. A
              cuddy was placed just aft of the mast. The stem and sternpost
raked and the rudder was hung outside.

RADEAU   A square-ended scow, fitted with deep bulwarks, sweeps, gun
Illustration on page 11.   ports, and rigged as a schooner, brig, ketch, or even a ship;
              40 to 95 feet long. They were very fast running before the

wind. They were used for harbor defense in the Revolutionary War. The British used a large ketch-rigged "radeau" on Lake Champlain against Arnold's squadron.

RAKIT

A "Malacca catamaran." A crude, primitive raft used in the shallow waters of the Malay Peninsula. Average size about 40 feet long.

RAM'S-HEAD BOAT

A large "chebacco boat," a characteristic feature of which was a high stem, generally painted red, around which the mooring hawser was put. Illustration of "chebacco boat" on page 19.

RAM SCHOONER

A schooner carrying no topmasts, but tall pole masts.

RANGOON LIGHTER
Illustration on page 67.

A cargo vessel of India, with a sharp-sterned hull, having high freeboard and built entirely of teak. The rig consists of a square-headed lugsail on the foremast, stepped well forward, and a smaller leg-of-mutton mizzen. No shrouds are used and the sheets are single lines with no purchase.

RAZEE

In the American Navy a "razee" was a very heavy frigate which had been cut down from a ship-of-the-line. The *Independence* was a "razee" and was 188 feet long, which was larger than the *President* type. The 1830's and 1840's was the period of this type of warship.

REACH BOAT

A clinker-built, open, keel boat employed in the fisheries off the coast of Maine. It is from 14 to 22 feet long, has a curved stem; straight sternpost, both ends sharp; cat-rigged, with single spritsail and one pair of oars. The name is derived from "Moose-a-bec Reach" (Jonesport), Maine.

REDNING-SKOÏTE

A sailing lifeboat used on the west coast of Norway. It was carvel-built, with extremely heavy hull and gear; yawl- or ketch-rigged. The hull resembled the old "Hvalor-baad" (illustrated on page 45), but had a heavy iron keel.

REVENUE CUTTERS
Illustration on page 21.

Fast, heavily-built, armed sailing vessels used by the governments of various nations in the revenue service before the advent of steam in combating smugglers and pirates, and in preventing crime on the high seas; also used in life-saving. The "cutter" was a favorite type with the British and French, while the American Government used schooners almost entirely. The average size of the cutters was about 50 feet long, 18 to 21 feet beam, while the American schooners ranged from 48 to 100 feet on deck. The heyday of the sailing "revenue cutter" was from 1750 to 1850. See illustration for "cutter" type on page 55.

RICE BOAT
Illustration on page 67.
A distinctive type of craft used for carrying rice on the Irrawadi and other Burmese rivers. Owing to the prevailing southerly wind blowing upstream, these boats are rigged with a huge square sail for running only, never beating to windward. Against the wind they are punted. A long standing yard (bow-shaped with the ends up) is supported by numerous halyards from a mast formed by two spars set about one-third the length of the hull abaft the bow. The sail and its topsails are brailed to the mast when furled and are hauled out along the yard when set. The hull is canoe-shaped, usually with a clipper bow and rounded up ends, shallow draft, the heel and forefoot often out of water. There is good sheer, with an overhanging stern higher than the bow, on which is the steersman's seat, often lavishly carved. The steering oar is slung on the after quarter.

RUA
The Siamese word for boat. A prefix on all Siamese boat names.

RUA CHALOM
A Gulf of Siam type, the name being applied to all sailing craft with high stem and sternpost, without distinction of rig. One large standing lugsail is carried on a mast which rakes extremely aft. Double quarter rudders are used. This type is favored by the Chinese fishermen of the Gulf of Siam.

RUA PET
Illustration on page 67.
A craft typical to the Gulf of Siam. The deep hull has a high overhanging "spoon" bow and pointed stern. The mainmast is set well forward of amidships and carries a standing lugsail. A small lug foresail is set on a light mast stepped in the bow. There is no standing rigging on the foremast. The deck is roofed over aft of the mainmast with palm leaves and bamboo laths.

RUA TA
Illustration on page 67.
A Gulf of Siam type, somewhat resembling a "junk." The crude hull has an overhanging stern gallery and has an eye painted on the bow. It is lug-rigged, with a tall mainmast, shorter foremast set well forward, and a tiny mizzen at the stern.

SAÏQUE *or* SAÏC
Illustration on page 59.
A small vessel of the Near East and the Levant, popular previous to the 19th century. The mainmast was square-rigged, with three capped topmasts. The mizzenmast was lateen-rigged and

a spritsail was carried on the bowsprit. The hull had considerable sheer, with a flat stern.

SALMON BOAT An open, double-ended model used in the salmon gill-net industry near the mouth of the Columbia River, Oregon. It was carvel-built, had nearly vertical stem and sternpost; washboards along the sides; short deck at either end; four thwarts; cat-rigged, with single spritsail; 25 feet 9 inches long by 6 feet 9 inches beam. First built in 1869.

SAMBUK A small "dhow" of 18 to 20 tons used in the Red Sea.
Illustration on page 67.

SAMOAN CANOES The canoes of Samoa may be classified as follows:

"*Paopao*"—The smallest of the Samoan outrigger, dugout, paddling canoes. It is used in the quiet lagoons and holds but one occupant. Two straight booms support the outrigger float, each with two V-type connectives and sennit brace. The hull is a simple dugout, with no decking, washboards or thwarts. Pointed clipper bow and raking curved stern. In use at present.

"*Soatau*"—A larger dugout canoe with multi-bottom outrigger. Used along the coast. Three and five booms are commonest. V-type connectives. Paddled and occasionly sailed. Illustration on page 77.

"*Va'a alo*"—A small outrigger canoe with sewed plank hull, used in the bonito fishery. Clipper bow, curved raking stern, decked at the ends, two-boomed outrigger with "V" connectives, ends are very sharp. This type is the most graceful of all Polynesian canoes.

"*Taumualua*"—A double-ended, sewed-plank canoe without outrigger, on the order of a whaleboat. Paddled and occasionally sailed. Now extinct.

"*Fautasi*"—A large double-ended canoe of nailed planks, without outrigger, similar to a whaleboat. In use at the present time.

"*Va'a tele*"—A seagoing double canoe, with large platform between the hulls. Formerly used for cargo-carrying. Now extinct.

"*Alia*"—A large, seagoing, sailing double canoe. It is similar to the Fijian "ndrua."

SAMPAN A general term applied to all small, open or half-decked boats
Illustrations on pages 71 of Chinese build, used on the coasts of China, Japan, Siam, and
and 73. other near-by Asiatic countries. The largest size is about 30 feet in length, with the beam about one-fourth of the length. These are two-masted, the foremast with a very forward rake and the mainmast raked aft, and are rigged with battened lugsails.

The two-masted "sampans" of Hongkong, which ply the harbor for hire, are smart-looking craft, with a shelter for passengers aft and the helmsman sits abaft the shelter.

However, the "sampans" are usually one-masted, and the best known type is the two-tailed boat. This type is open, flat-bottomed, with rounded, sloping sides, the widest beam aft; fine entrance, good sheer, deep rudders, and a battened lugsail. The stem and sternpost are extremely raked.

The smaller "sampans" are of innumerable varieties and vary in design with locality, but the usual rig is the standing lugsail of cotton, with upper and lower yards of bamboo.

The hulls of the "sampans" of China are usually oiled, finished bright, with an eye painted on each bow, while those of Singapore, Bangkok, Penang, and other harbors of the lower countries are gaily painted.

SAMPAN PANJANG	A half-decked, keel sailing craft used at Johore, Malay States.

SAMPAN PANJANG
Illustration on page 69.

A half-decked, keel sailing craft used at Johore, Malay States. It has a long, sharp, hollow bow with a concave stem; long, sharp stern; practically no sheer; hollow rising floor; rudder hung outside. A lugsail is set from a vertical mast stepped about one-fourth the length aft the bow.

SAND-BAGGER
Illustration on page 219.

A sloop- or cat-rigged racing boat, 18 to 28 feet long, popular in New York and New England waters as early as 1855. The hull was quite flat and shallow, with little freeboard, and shifting ballast was used. A centerboard and an outboard rudder were carried and the transom was very broad. An extremely long bowsprit was used, if sloop-rigged, and a very long boom was on the mainsail. The main sheet was trimmed by means of an outrigger, or boomkin, extending beyond the stern of the boat. Racing crews of the 28-foot boats numbered as many as 17, most of whom were engaged in handling the ballast. The "sand-bagger" was extraordinarily fast in smooth water. The flaring topsides permitted the ballast to be carried farther out from the center line than a boat having topsides more nearly vertical.

SARDINIER, *or* **SARDINE BOAT**
Illustration on page 47.

The early type of boat used in the sardine fishery of Brittany, France, was a two-masted, lug-rigged, open boat, very beamy, with straight stem and vertical sternpost, long straight keel, outboard rudder, the foremast stepped in the bow and the mainmast amidships. This type has been extinct for many years. Later the hulls underwent a change, being built with a tremendous rake to the transom stern, short keel, and straight raking stem. These, too, have disappeared.

Following this type, the Breton builders went back to the straight, vertical stem, the sterns raking and varying in shape. The beam was great and the rig was the two-

[178]

masted dipping lug, the foremast set in the bow. The larger ones were decked. The nets (dyed blue) were stowed in a chest, or locker, built in the stern.

Some "sardiniers" are cutter-rigged, with mainsail, topsail, and two jibs, a long bowsprit, roller-reefing on the mainsail being employed.

The Breton "sardine boats" are painted white, blue, gray, or black above the water line, working sails are dyed brown and light sails often a sky blue.

SAYKE   An old type of Turkish ketch. See "saique," illustrated on page 59.

SCAITH   A Scotch lugger. See "skaffie," illustrated on page 33.

SCHOKKER   A yacht of the Netherlands, not unlike the "botter" (illustrated on page 43), but having a fuller stern and the stem is straight and rakes at 60 degrees with the water line. The "schokker" is the largest of the Dutch pleasure craft and may be rigged as a yawl, ketch or cutter.

SCHOONER   A two- or more masted vessel, fore-and-aft rigged. The essen-
Illustrations on pages 11, 17, tials of the schooner rig are two fore-and-aft sails and a head-
19, 21, 47, 89, 134 and 219. sail (jib), any other sails being incidental.

This type of rig was not known until the last quarter of the 17th century, although boats similar to the schooner, but without a headsail, are supposed to have been used in Holland as early as 1630. The early schooners had square topsails on the foremast and sometimes on the mainmast as well. The former were known as "topsail schooners" and the latter as "maintopsail schooners." In certain parts of the world this practice continued until recent years.

Schooners were first mentioned in American colonial records about 1716, and their popularity spread rapidly, not only in this country, but in Canada, Europe, South and Central America, and elsewhere. A great portion of the foreign trade of the United States has been carried by schooners. This was especially true during the period of the Baltimore clippers. The schooners built to the "Virginia model" in the 18th century were the forerunners of the famous Baltimore clipper schooners.

Through the years there had been a gradual sharpening of the hull lines, in response to the ever-increasing demand for speed. In the lines of traffic where a fast ship was a vital necessity, the clipper schooner filled the bill most satisfactorily. Hence, they were employed extensively in privateering, the slave trade and other illicit enterprises, as naval vessels and revenue cutters, pilot boats, market and off-shore fishermen, and in the fruit trade.

The majority of the early yachts were schooners and the contestants for the *America's* Cup were schooner-rigged until the middle 1870's. The *America* herself was a modified pilot schooner. To-day it is the favored rig for cruising yachts. The

[179]

schooner is, without doubt, the most important of all American sailing craft. Since the War of the Revolution its numbers have exceeded those of any other type of commercial sailing vessel, including the "ship."

While the period of development of the three-masted schooner was in the 1820's, '30's, and '40's, several were built at an earlier date. The three-master *Flying Fish* was built in Baltimore just after the turn of the century and Carl C. Cutler states that the *Success* was reported in 1801, the *Urania* in 1804, and in 1806 three others were in service. After 1870 the three-masted schooner really came into its own as a coasting vessel. It was also popular on the Great Lakes, as was the two-master.

The four-masted schooner was introduced about 1880 and the five- and six-masters came in somewhat later. But one seven-master was ever built, the *Thomas Lawson*, which was too unwieldy to be a successful vessel.

SCHOUW A small, shallow-draft, open pleasure craft of Holland and, to a lesser extent, of Belgium. The hull is flat-bottomed and has pronounced sheer fore and aft. Both bow and stern have a wide transom, the former raking and the latter vertical. The sides might be called semi-hexagonal, the upper planks having some tumble home. It is sloop-rigged, with a jib extended to a short bowsprit and a loose-footed mainsail having the usual short curved gaff of the Dutch boats. There are no shrouds. The rudder is outboard and there are leeboards. The average size is 21 feet length over-all, 18 feet water line, 6 feet beam, and 18 inches draft with the leeboards up.

SCHUYT A contemporary small Dutch sail boat. The hull is sturdily built
Illustration on page 41. rotund and shallow, with outboard rudder and the usual leeboards. It is sloop-rigged, with one or two headsails and the mainsail has the short curved gaff.

The "schuyt" of the 17th century was rigged differently. The mainmast, stepped just forward of amidships, had a square course and square topsail, a forestaysail, and a jib to a bowsprit. A diminutive mizzenmast was set just forward of the tiller and carried a single square sail. The hull was built in the Dutch manner, with outboard rudder and leeboards.

SCOW A large, flat-bottomed, flat-decked vessel having broad square ends and straight sides.

SCOW *or* BILGE A flat-hulled sailing craft, usually sloop-rigged, used for racing
BOARD SCOW or pleasure sailing. The typical scow has a very flat floor and
Illustration on page 219. sections that are generally parallel throughout and is of ex-
tremely shallow draft. The hull may have square ends or a pointed bow and square stern. A "bilge board" is built on each side of the bottom,

in lieu of a keel or centerboard. Double rudders, too, are employed, so that one will always be in the water when heeled over. It is conceded that the scow-type sloop is one of the fastest boats ever developed and in a strong breeze on smooth water speeds of 15 or 16 knots have been made. Scows are popular on Lake St. Louis of the St. Lawrence River above Montreal, Barnegat Bay, New Jersey, and the inland lakes of Minnesota and Wisconsin, where boats of shallow draft are a necessity.

The fast scow-type racing sloops which came into being in 1895 were an outgrowth of a loose interpretation of the Seawanhaka rule of measurement. While this rule was designed to favor the deep, or "compromise" type of hull, it eventually worked out in just the opposite manner, unforeseen by the rule makers. A freakish hull was developed, with short water-line length, long overhangs, flat floor, light displacement, and with large sail area. Often there were transoms at the bow and stern, and on some models the cross-section was dish-shaped.

The idea behind the scow design was to obtain a long water line when heeled over, while the actual water line as measured was short. Most of the earlier scows had centerboards, but soon they were built with bilge boards or fin keels. The crew was used as shifting ballast. The scow type went out of favor with the adoption of the more conservative universal rule in 1901–03, with the exception, of course, of those used on inland lakes.

The largest scow-type sloop ever built was the fast, but cranky, *Independence*, an unsuccessful *America's* Cup defense candidate in 1901. She was 140 feet 10½ inches length over-all, 90 feet water line, 23 feet 11½ inches beam, 20 feet draft and had a sail area of over 14,300 square feet.

SCOW
  SCHOONER
A flat-bottomed, square-ended vessel of the scow type, with the rig of a two-masted coasting schooner, used in former days in the vicinity of San Francisco, California.

SCOW SLOOP
A New England scow, 50 to 60 feet long, used for carrying ice, cordwood, and stone in the coastwide trade and on the larger rivers. The hull was that of the ordinary sand scow seen today and was equipped with either a centerboard or a large leeboard on the port side. It was sloop-rigged and was fast under favorable conditions.

SEILSJEGTE
A clinker-built open skiff used by fishermen on the southern coast of Norway, 18 to 20 feet long and rigged with one or two spritsails.

SELSEY GALLEY
A long, narrow, double-ended, clinker-built rowboat used by the coast guard at Selsey, England, up to the time of the

Great War. It was about 40 feet in length and carried twenty-two men who pulled eleven pairs of oars.

SETTEE   A long, sharp vessel formerly used on the Mediterranean, rigged and navigated similarly to a galley (illustrated on pages 49 and 51) or xebec (illustrated on page 61), but fitted with "settee" sails instead of lateens. A settee sail is quadrilateral with a short luff, whereas the lateen is triangular.

SEXERN   A six-oared, open, double-ended, clinker-built boat from 20 to 23 feet long, used in the Shetland Islands off the coast of Scotland. The stem and sternpost are raking and it is rigged with a single square lugsail. The single sail has been abandoned, to a great extent, however, in favor of a standing lugsail and jib. The "sexern" is similar to an ordinary lifeboat in appearance and is a survival of the old Viking "long ship" (illustrated on page 51). It is used for inshore fishing and ferrying, but is rapidly becoming obsolete.

SHALLOP   The American "shallop" was a nondescript type of small sailing boat, open or half-decked, of various sizes. It was used in early Colonial times for fishing, etc. See "French shallop," illustrated on page 55.

SHARPIE   A small flat-bottomed boat with centerboard, usually cat-
Illustration on page 19. schooner rigged with leg-of-mutton sails having horizontal spirits to extend the clews. The hull is open, carvel-built, and has a long sharp bow, slightly flaring sides, a square stern, and good sheer. The after part of the bottom is flared up to form the run. The average size is 35 feet long by 11 feet beam. The "sharpie" was originated in the Connecticut oyster fishery and it became popular, as a good load of fish could be carried in shallow water. They were most favored in southern New England and North Carolina, although they were found along the Atlantic coast as far south as Florida, and even on the Gulf of Mexico side of the latter state. Their numbers are now depleted, due to the inroads made by the power boats.

The "pound boats," formerly used on the Great Lakes in the pound net fisheries, were of the "sharpie" model, as they not only could carry an adequate load of fish, but the net could be lifted without upsetting the boat.

SHARPSHOOTER A small sailing boat of the Bahamas. The average size is about 24 feet long, 9 feet beam, 4 feet 4 inches draft, 20 feet long on the keel. The hull has a long run, with a short hollow entrance. The greatest beam is well forward and there is drag to the keel. The stem and sternpost are straight and raking. A mast, which rakes aft, is set in the bow and is rigged with a leg-of-mutton sail. No jib is carried. The hull is decked over, with one or two cabin houses and a cockpit. An outside rudder is slung on the sternpost.

SHARPSHOOTER See "Gloucester fisherman," illustrated on page 134.

SHEBEK The Russian "shebek" of the latter part of the 18th century
Illustration on page 55. was probably an adaptation of the Mediterranean "xebec," although it was more clumsily and heavily built. While retaining the lateen rig on the raking foremast, the remainder was a mixture—square-rigged on the mainmast, a square topsail and a fore-and-aft gaff driver, or spanker, on the mizzenmast. The hull had little sheer, a raking stem, prolonged into a head, and a raking sternpost with an overhanging counter. There were ports for guns and sweeps.

SHELL A long, light, extremely narrow rowing craft employed only for racing or rowing exercise. The largest shell accommodates eight oarsmen and the smallest but one. Owing to the small width, the fulcrum of the oars is supported by an outrigger.

SHIP Among seamen, a "ship" is a sailing vessel with a bowsprit and three masts—foremast, mainmast, and mizzenmast, and, rarely, with a fourth mast—each composed of a lower mast, a topmast, and a topgallantmast, and, sometimes, higher masts (royal mast and skysail mast), on all of which square sails are set.

As used in general, any large seagoing vessel is a "ship"; any vessel, sail or power, especially one not propelled by oars, paddles, sculls, etc.

SHIPENTINE A four-masted sailing vessel with three square-rigged masts like a "ship" and the after mast fore-and-aft rigged. The ship *Great Republic*, built in 1853, was an example of a "shipentine."

SHIP-OF-THE- A sailing warship of three or more decks, carrying 70 to 140
LINE guns (cannon), and usually ship-rigged. These huge vessels
Illustration on page 13. were the largest ships of the battle fleet and corresponded to the heavy battleships of the present time. U.S.S. *Pennsylvania* and H.M.S. *Victory* were examples of "ships-of-the-line." (Note—*Victory* is still in existence, being laid up in England.)

SHIP-SLOOP A ship-rigged naval vessel of 18 or 20 guns. *Ranger*, which was
Illustration on page 27. commanded by John Paul Jones in the American Revolution, was a "ship-sloop" as was *Peacock* in the War of 1812.

[183]

SHIPS

SHIP OF THE FIRST CENTURY
Illustration on page 185.

The illustration on page 185 may give an idea of the appearance of a Mediterranean cargo vessel of 1900 years ago. It was heavily built, blunt-bowed and flat-floored, with rounding sides, which were probably strengthened by means of skids and girdles of ropes. The rig consisted of a mainmast, stepped amidships, on which was a square sail, with a divided triangular topsail above, and an artemon on a sharply raking mast or bowsprit in the bow.

The ship on which St. Paul and his fellow apostles started for Rome in 60 A D. and were shipwrecked was, no doubt, a vessel of this type.

SHIP OF THE THIRTEENTH CENTURY
Illustration on page 185.

Little is known about this early Venetian vessel, but it is thought that the Venetians were the first to use a combination of the lateen and square rigs.

SHIP OF THE LATE FIFTEENTH CENTURY

See "nao" and "nef" (illustrated on page 185), and "merchant ships of the 15th century" (illustrated on page 53).

SHIP OF THE EARLY SIXTEENTH CENTURY
Illustration on page 185.

A capital ship of this period, such as the *Henri Grâce à Dieu,* was a sumptuous affair of about 1,000 tons, and perhaps 165 feet long. The waist was three decks high above the water and the sheer rose to a high, narrow stern. There was a forecastle and a long, double-decked poop, while the bow terminated in a long decorated beak. Along the upper rail and the castles were rows of shields, or "pavese." In form these vessels resembled a carrack (illustrated on page 53) and the masts were four in number, square-rigged on the fore, main, and mizzen, with a lateen sail on a short bonaventure. A sharply steeved bowsprit carried a spritsail. It is said that the sails of the above-mentioned vessel were made of cloth of gold and long pennants swung from all the tops and yardarms. The hull was dotted with cannon and the narrow after part of the poop was studded with Gothic windows.

SHIP OF THE LATE SIXTEENTH CENTURY
Illustration on page 185.

A Tudor ship, such as Francis Drake used on his famous voyage of discovery, loot and circumnavigation of the globe in 1577–80, had the high, narrow stern with two-decked poop and a raised forecastle common to the ships of the period. The bow terminated in a long, curved beak. The sheer was heavy and rose gracefully to the stern. The fore- and mainmasts each carried course and topsail, there was a spritsail on the steeved bowsprit, and the mizzen was lateen-rigged. Nearly all seagoing ships of that time were armed. It was in the *Golden Hind* (form-

Ship of 1st Century

13th Century Venetian Ship

Nao 15th Century Ship

Nef 15th Century Ship

Capital Ship of 16th Century "Henri Grâce à Dieu"

Late 16th Century Ship "Golden Hind"

Late 18th Century Ship "Bounty"

Square-rigged Steamer
"City of Savannah" 1818

French Transport (Indiaman) 1779
"Bon Homme Richard"

Steam Screw Sloop of War 1861 "Hartford"

1900 YEARS OF SHIPS

erly *Pelican*) that Drake stopped off on the California coast for overhaul in 1579. This remarkable vessel was not over 90 feet long with a beam of 23 feet.

A FRENCH SHIP OF THE EIGHTEENTH CENTURY
Illustration on page 185.

The vessel pictured on page 185 was of the class used in the French Navy as a transport and in the East India service. It was not unlike the medium-sized armed ship of the period, except that the broad stern was typically French in character, with quarter-galleries rounding into the hull proper. There were two rows of square windows, piercing the stern. The bow was low, with beak head and rails, above which rose a bowsprit. The rig was that of a "ship."

It was on a vessel of this type, namely, the *Bon Homme Richard* (formerly *Duc de Duras*) that John Paul Jones won his remarkable combat against the British 44-gun frigate *Serapis* off Flamborough Head, September 23, 1779. This ship mounted twenty-eight 12-pounders on the gun deck, six 18-pounders in the gun room on the lower deck, and eight 9-pounders on the forecastle and quarter-deck. She had a crew of approximately 375 officers and men, of whom only perhaps 150 were Americans.

SHIP OF THE LATE EIGHTEENTH CENTURY
Illustration on page 185.

A good example of a small ship of this period is H.M.S. *Bounty*, on which Captain Bligh and his crew had so many difficulties, resulting finally in the mutiny. This ship-rigged vessel was only 85 feet 1 ½ inches long on the lower deck, 24 feet 3 inches beam and 11 feet 4 inches depth of hold. She was built in Hull, England, in 1783 and sold to the Admiralty in 1787, in which year Bligh left on his memorable cruise.

EARLY SQUARE-RIGGED STEAMSHIP
Illustration on page 185.

While the steam-driven vessel has not been discussed in this book, nevertheless a word about the square-rigged, paddle-wheel steamer *City of Savannah* should have a place herein, inasmuch as it is credited with being the first steamship to cross the Atlantic. However, her engines were used for eight hours only, as her coal supply became exhausted and she made the balance of the trip under sail alone. This ship-rigged vessel had been designed as a sailing packet ship and the engine was mounted after her launching, which may account for the lack of success as a steamer. Upon the return to America the vessel was sold and the new owners promptly removed the power plant. She was 100 feet long and 26 feet beam.

STEAM-DRIVEN WARSHIP
Illustration on page 185.

Again we touch on the subject of power-driven sailing ships and use a particular example for illustration. The steam screw sloop-of-war *Hartford*, Admiral Farragut's famous flagship in the battles of Vicksburg and Mobile Bay in the Civil War, was (and is) an unarmored, wooden, ship-rigged vessel, with auxiliary power. Her armament consisted of 24 smooth-bore cannon and two 20-pounder rifles, all placed on the upper deck. She is 225 feet long, 44 feet beam, with a displacement of 2,900 tons, and at the start of the war was listed as a first-class sloop-of-war, one of five. The *Hartford* is now laid up at Washington, D. C.

SHOTTER
A sailing craft used in the British mackerel fisheries in the middle 19th century. They ranged in tonnage from 6 to 25. The rigs varied.

SINGORA
LAKE BOAT
Illustration on page 69.
A crude, shallow-draft, sailing craft of Singora Lake in Malaya, though it is more Siamese than Malayan in character. The hull is a dugout, with a rough plank superstructure. The top strakes are extended aft over the stern, forming the sides of an overhanging platform, while the forward ends are turned up a little abaft the bow. Bulkheads are placed near the ends of the dugout to keep out the water. The one or two sails are high-peaked standing lugs of light matting.

SKAFFIE
Illustration on page 33.
A type of Scotch lugger; double-ended; stem and sternpost raked; short, deep keel; a lug rig similar to that of the "fifie," but with no jib. Some carried three masts. A "skaffie" was not so good beating to windward as a "fifie" and it differed mainly from the latter in that it had a flatter bottom, with a deeper keel, and had more bluffness to the bow and quarters, causing the boat to labor harder in heavy weather and to slam in a head sea. The stem of the "skaffie" was usually curved and the foresail was longer along the foot than that of the "fifie." The latter feature was necessary in order to keep the boat to the wind owing to the shortness of the keel. Some "skaffies" of 50 or 60 years ago used a spar bow line to set the luff of the sails taut when on the wind. The Scotch fishermen called this spar a "wand" or "set." This type of boat has been supplanted by the "zulu" (illustrated on page 33) and none has been built for many years.

SKEID
A large Viking long ship (illustrated on page 49), with no figurehead.

SKIFF
A light, open boat, usually for rowing, but sometimes equipped for sailing. Generally double-ended.
Among the eastern villages of Banffshire, Scotland, the larger "baldies" of 25 feet on the keel and upwards are known as "skiffs."

SKIPJACK
Illustration on page 19.
A V-bottomed sloop, carrying leg-of-mutton mainsail and jib, generally clipper-bowed. A centerboard was used. Popular on Chesapeake Bay.

SKOFFNAR	A lower Burmese coasting craft, with a combination of schooner and ketch rig of from 80 to 100 tons. Some carry topsails, and the sails are stowed up and down the mast with brails. Very often the masts are of the same height. A single jib is generally carried, and sometimes a Chinese lug is used on the raked foremast and a fore-and-aft sail on the aftermast.

SKOVSHOVED
HERRING
BOAT
Illustration on page 45.

A Danish double-ended, spritsail-rigged, open boat used in the herring fishery. The peak of the spritsail is lower than the throat, and the foot shorter than the head. Two headsails and a jib-headed topsail are carried. The average length is about 24 feet over-all by 9 feet beam by 3 feet 6 inches draft. The mast is stepped about 8 or 9 feet from the bow and is a heavy spar standing 20 to 24 feet from the deck. The stem and sternpost are curved and raking. The topsail is hoisted on a long spar, and in fine weather a large jib is set on a light, running bowsprit.

SKUTA	A small, but very fast Viking ship.

SLAVER *or*
SLAVE SHIP
Illustration on page 21.

A vessel used for transporting slaves from the west coast of Africa to Brazil, Cuba, and illicitly to the southern coasts of the United States until the Civil War. A favorite type of ship used in this trade was the fast Baltimore clipper, but many were especially designed, speed being the main requisite. Brig, brigantine and topsail-schooner rigs were the most popular. The armament on most "slavers" consisted of a single carronade or a long-gun on a pivot. They were lightly armed, as the slavers depended on speed to escape pursuing ships, for they could not hold their own against a heavily armed man-of-war. The slave ships were comparatively small for ocean-going vessels, the average size being about 75 or 80 feet long on deck. Large ships were difficult to conceal when loading and, if captured, the loss was too great. Also, a large ship was more expensive to operate, and it was found that vessels between 60 and 100 feet in length paid out best.

On a slave ship the miserable, usually naked, captives were manacled together and confined between decks. Owing to the low headroom, they could only sit or lie prone. About 12 square feet were allotted to each person. The filth and stench were nauseating. Pestilence usually broke out en route and many died. If a government cruiser was seen by the officers of a slaver and escape was impossible, the captives were unceremoniously dumped overboard in order to destroy the evidence.

SLOEP
Illustration on page 55.

A small, shallow-draft Dutch sailing craft, originally rigged with a sprit mainsail, but now sloop-rigged. It is equipped with leeboards and outboard rudder. The "sloep" was originated in

Holland, probably in the 17th century, for the navigation of their canals and shallow coastal harbors.

SLOOP
Illustration on page 11.
A craft with a single mast and fore-and-aft rig—in its simplest form a mainsail and jib. The sloop rig was introduced into America from England in the latter 17th century.

SLOOP-OF-WAR
A war vessel armed on a single deck and sometimes on the quarter-deck, rigged as a ship, brig, brigantine, etc. In the American Navy, while the term was rather elastic, it was usually applied to ship-rigged vessels of less than 24 guns. In the British Navy, a "sloop-of-war" carried 18 guns or less.

SMACK
A general term for a fore-and-aft rigged sailing vessel, used chiefly in the fishing and coasting trades. The only use of the term "smack" in the fisheries of the east coast of the United States is for a vessel with salt water wells for bringing in fish alive.
Also, a local term for a "Brixham trawler" (illustrated on page 31).

SMACKEE
Illustration on page 17.
A welled fishing boat of Key West, Florida. A typical size is about 24 feet long by one-third the beam. It is a carvel-built, keel boat, with good sheer; long run; V-shaped raking stern; cuddy hatch forward; a fish well amidships; cockpit aft. Sloop-rigged with leg-of-mutton mainsail and jib to a bowsprit; mast stepped well forward.

SMAK
A Dutch fishing schooner or sloop.

SNAEKKA
A Norwegian clinker-built skiff. Often equipped for sailing with a sprit mainsail and jib.

SNEAK BOX
Illustration on page 223.
A sailing punt used for duck hunting along the New Jersey coast. It was introduced about a century ago at Barnegat Bay.
The boats have a draft of but a few inches with centerboard up to enable them to enter the shallow marshes. They are decked, except for a cockpit which can be hatched over; freeboard 6 or 7 inches, rounded sides meeting a dish-shaped bottom; the broad stern square and plumb; the bow round in plan, with a full under-bow overhanging about 1 foot. The early models were 12 to 15 feet long and 4 to 5 feet beam. Steered by an outboard rudder or oar. Formerly the cat spritsail or leg-of-mutton rigs were employed. About 30 years ago, 20-footers were built for racing, with gaff sails and sand-bag ballast. These were the forerunners of the fast

marconi-rigged, "scow"-type sneak boxes brought out in Barnegat Bay in 1924. Boats of the old hunting type are still in use.

SNEKKJA — An early Norse ship of the 12th and 13th centuries. Similar to the Viking ship, but having a raised platform, or deck, fore and aft. A single mast was carried, with a standing yard, to which a square sail was bent. Above the yard was a fighting top.

SNOW
Illustration on page 11.
A "snow" of the early 19th century was similar to a "brig," except that an extra mast was carried close abaft the mainmast, which mast carried the spanker or driver. It terminated at the main top and was fixed in a wood step on deck. "Snows" were usually larger vessels than the "brig" or "brigantine."

SÖNDFJORD
YAWL
Illustration on page 45.
A west coast Norwegian open herring boat, double-ended, with rounded stem and sternpost; deep hull, and is a fine sea boat. Clinker-built, with wide planking. Single square sail used for sailing on a short mast stepped a little forward of amidships.

SÖNDMÖERSK
YAWL
Illustration on page 45.
A small, open fishing craft of the west coast of Norway, not unlike the old Viking long boat (illustrated on page 51) in line of hull, which is double-ended, with heavy, rounded, ornamental stem and sternpost. Wide planking is used, with a peculiar construction of timbering. The mast rakes aft and is stepped about amidships; rigged with a single lugsail, with a very short yard and odd cut.

SOUND BOAT
Illustration on page 47.
A Danish cutter-rigged fishing boat employed in the fisheries of the Strait of Kattegat and Oresmund Sound. These boats are known locally as "sound boats." They are double-ended, decked, sharp at the bow and stern with raking curved stem and sternpost, and have a deep keel. There is a cabin house amidships and a cockpit aft. Clinker-built with oak frames and planking. The average length is 25 feet, with a beam of about 9 feet and a depth of around 4 feet 8 inches.

SPONGE-
FISHING
SCHOONER
A type of schooner used in the Bahama Islands in gathering sponges from the reefs. Men from the schooner go out in small boats and take in the sponges, while the larger vessel cruises about. This type resembles the "Baltimore clipper" schooners (illustrated on page 21) of 100 years ago, and no doubt the "sponge schooner" originated in Chesapeake Bay. Average length between 50 and 60 feet over-all, beam 14 to 15 feet; carvel-built, with keel; a sharp bow, with a moderate flare above the water line; raking, curved stem, with long head; sharp floor; long, lean run; wide

V-shaped stern, with slightly raking sternpost; medium sheer; low bulwarks; large cabin trunk; two or more boats are stored on deck. Two-masted, with a loose-footed foresail and a jib on the foremast; gaff and boom mainsail, and a long bowsprit.

SPLOSHER   A "coble" (illustrated on page 35) local to Staithes, Yorkshire, England, used in the herring fishery. About 25 feet long on the keel, 30 feet over-all, beam about 10 feet; square-sterned, with a rake of 3½ feet.

STONE SLOOP   A sloop-rigged craft, with various types of hull, used in the stone trade of New England.

STORNOWAY YAWL   A Scottish open skiff, with a lug rig, the sails being broad and low. The hull is clinker-built; raked stem and sternpost; broad in the beam, and 25 to 30 feet long.

STUMPY   A "Thames barge" (illustrated on pages 31 and 35) with no topmasts.

SUEZ SHORE-BOAT
Illustration on page 63.   An Arabian boat of Suez, with a long, sharp, overhanging bow, with sharp sections, the hull having great beam amidships to carry the mast and sail weight. A raking transom stern is used and an outboard rudder. The lateen sail is of Arab cut, with a few feet of luff below the lower end of the yard. The yard, which is set on the starboard side, is kept standing, the sail being hauled out with an out-haul from the mast where it is furled. A small jib is carried on the larger craft.

SWEDISH FISH-ING BOAT
Illustration on page 45.   A husky, flush-decked, clinker-built ketch or yawl-rigged vessel, used in the mackerel fishery of Sweden. The hull has an enormous beam, three-quarters of the length. It is double-ended, with curved, very raking stem and sternpost; hollow floor and deep keel; very strongly built; sprit mizzen, mainsail, topsail, and two head sails. The topmast is of the sliding gunter type and it carries a bowsprit and boomkin. It is a fine sea boat.

TAHITIAN CANOES   The outrigger and double canoes of Tahiti may be classified as follows, according to James Hornell:
     "*Va'a motu*" (illustrated on page 77).—A large outrigger dugout, square upturned stern, for sailing and making distant voyages. Crab-claw sail.
     "*Pu hoe*"—A small dugout canoe with outrigger, used at the present time for lagoon fishing. Paddled only. See "pu hoe."

[191]

"Pahi"—A large, keeled, plank-built double canoe used for voyaging to distant islands. Two-masted, with sails. See "pahi."

"Tira"—A double fishing canoe, dugout, with square upturned stern. Formerly employed in the albacore fishery. Paddled.

"Maeha'a"—A small double canoe, equal sized dugouts, stem and stern sharp, paddled.

"Tipaitua"—A larger form of "tira" with higher elevation to the stern and a thatched cabin on a platform between the canoes.

"Va'a ti'i"—A sacred double canoe, highly carved and ornamented with feathers, usually with a shrine erected on each canoe. Of the same type as the war canoe.

War canoe—Largest type of double canoe, capable of accommodating 40 to 50 men and used for fighting purposes only. The ends were upturned, the stern higher than the bow.

TARADA   An open flat-bottomed boat used by Arab sheiks in the marshes of Southern Iraq. The gunwales curve up at the ends to a high peak and the stem and stern rise gracefully from the bottom to meet the sheer line. The inside is decorated with hundreds of brass-headed nails. The outside is painted with bitumen to make it water-tight. The "tarada" is usually punted, the sheik sitting amidships.

TARTANE   A term generally applied to medium-sized vessels used on the
Illustration on page 61.   Mediterranean, having a tall mainmast, with square sails, and a shorter mizzenmast, carrying either a square sail or lateen. However, some types carry but one mast and a bowsprit. A single large jib is used. When the wind is aft, a square sail is used on the main, but when the wind is from other quarters this is sometimes replaced by a lateen mainsail.

The present-day "tartane" illustrated on page 57, or coasting trader, of the Riviera coast carries a single mast, with a lateen mainsail, bowsprit and one or more jibs. A topmast is sometimes carried, on which a jib-headed topsail is set.

TCHEKTIRMÉ   A Turkish coasting vessel. Hull is low in the waist; round
Illustration on page 57.   bilged and high of stern. The low waist is sometimes protected by a canvas strake or weather cloth. Outboard rudder. Leg-of-mutton rig is generally used, with two or three jibs on a long bowsprit.

TEA CLIPPER   A large, fast, square-rigged "clipper ship" employed in the
Illustration on page 5.   China tea trade. The period of the American tea clipper was from 1847 to 1860, and that of the British tea clipper from 1850 to 1875. While other vessels were engaged in transporting tea, the "clipper" was designed to carry a maximum cargo at maximum speed. Therefore, they had great

sail-carrying capacity. The China tea trade (and the California gold rush) was responsible for bringing the square-rigged ship to its highest point of development, and were the prime reasons for the boom in shipbuilding during the periods mentioned. Until the expiration of its charter in 1834, the China tea trade was entirely controlled by the British East India Company. From that year until the early 1840's the trade in tea was small, but after 1843 new Chinese treaty ports[6] were opened, tea became more plentiful, and a demand was created for larger and faster ships.

Beginning with the *Rainbow*, the first extreme clippers to engage in the China tea trade were of American build. The *Rainbow*, of 750 tons' registry, was launched early in 1845 and is famous as the first of the great American clipper ships. She was built with hollow, concave bow lines, a long, thin entrance, instead of the old-fashioned barrel-shaped bow, with projecting cutwater, and had much dead rise to her bottom. Her second voyage was the fastest, making the trip from New York to Canton, China, in 92 days, the return trip taking 88 days.

The success of the *Rainbow* caused her owners to build the celebrated *Sea Witch* in 1846, and she was an exceptionally fast vessel, making the voyage from Canton to New York in 78 days on her second trip in 1847.

After gold was discovered in California in 1848, the American clippers stopped at San Francisco to unload passengers and supplies, and then proceeded to China to load tea for home. The gold rush made tremendous additional profits for the vessels' owners, some of them nearly paying for their cost in a single voyage. The demand for speed made some builders sacrifice other essentials at first. Donald McKay, William Webb, and other reputable builders, however, made every effort to combine strength with speed. Then followed a long list of famous ships, such as *Staghound*, *Flying Cloud* (the latter being perhaps the most notable, only one vessel, the *Andrew Jackson*, ever equaling her record of 89 days, plus, from New York to San Francisco), *Flying Fish*, *Challenge*, *Sovereign of the Seas*, *Witchcraft*, and many others. *Flying Cloud's* best run, made in 1851, was 374 knots, or 427.5 statute miles, in a corrected day of 24 hours 19 minutes, making the 17,597 statute miles at an average of 10 miles per hour.

After the repeal of the British navigation laws in 1849, American clippers entered the British tea trade. The first American vessel to unload tea in England was the *Oriental* and her appearance there in 1851 caused a sensation, and she was immediately chartered at $30 per ton, while the slower British ships waited for cargoes of tea at less than two-thirds of this figure. British builders busied themselves at once in turning out ships modeled on the lines of the *Oriental*, the Admiralty even having her lines taken off while in dry dock.

The British ships were less powerful in heavy weather than the big American "clippers," as they were built with less beam in proportion to their length and had little bearing forward. In light winds, however, they were faster.

Owing to the improvement in British vessels, American ships in the English-Chinese tea trade became scarce after 1855.

In 1856 a premium was offered of $5 per ton on the freight for the first tea ship arriving in London. As a consequence, a great race was made by the "clippers," the British *Vision* having the honor and reward of being the first ship home.

These tea races were held each year until 1878, when tea freights dropped to such an extent that even fast ships like *Cutty Sark* and *Thermopylae* had great difficulty in getting a cargo. The late 1860's and 1870's saw many famous British tea clippers launched, among these being *Ariel* and her sister-ship *Sir Launcelot* in 1865; *Leander* in 1867; *Thermopylae*, the masterpiece, in 1868; the great *Cutty Sark* in 1869; *Black Adder* in 1870, etc., etc.

Perhaps the two most outstanding clippers flying the British flag were the *Thermopylae* and *Cutty Sark*. In comparing these two ships, the former was at her best in light to moderate winds, being a great drifter in just a whisper of air, although she was an exceptional ship in any weather. *Cutty Sark*, on the other hand, was superior in a strong breeze and rough water. She is still in existence in England, but has been sailed but once since Captain Dowman, her owner, reconditioned her in 1922. The generous captain died about three years ago, so her fate is uncertain.

The last out-and-out British tea clipper to be built was the *Lothair* in 1872.

A number of clippers were built in the United States (and Canada) for British firms. Donald McKay turned out four of his finest creations for James Baines—*Lightning*, *Champion of the Seas*, *James Baines* and *Donald McKay*.

A comparison of the American and British tea clippers shows that the latter had less sheer and narrower beam in proportion to their length than those of American build. The American ships were usually built of soft wood, the British of hard wood.

The British ships were considerably smaller than the American "clippers," although the larger British "clippers" could load nearly one and one-quarter million pounds of tea. The drawings on page 5, showing an American clipper and a British clipper of average sizes are drawn to scale and give an idea of the difference between the two vessels.

Using two crack clippers of the two nations as examples, *Flying Cloud* registered 1,783 tons, measured 225 feet long on deck, 40 feet 8 inches beam, depth of hold 21 feet 6 inches, mainmast 200 feet, step to truck, while *Thermopylae* registered 991 tons, was 210 feet long, 36 feet beam, 21 feet depth of hold. The dimensions of *Cutty Sark*, were: length 212 feet 5 inches; beam 36 feet; depth 21 feet; mainmast 145 feet 9 inches, deck to truck.

TEPUKEI
Illustration on page 79.

The sailing, outrigger, dugout canoe of Matema Islands of the Santa Cruz group, which are located north of the New Hebrides and east of the Solomon Islands. The Santa Cruz canoes are different from any others, in that the opening of the pointed, hollowed log is extremely narrow, being only a few inches wide. The outrigger arrangement is rather complicated. Two main central booms with connective sticks are used and fore and aft of these is a curved boom secured directly to the float near each end. The booms support two platforms, one of which is inclined and extends beyond the hull on the off side. On the larger seagoing canoes two floats were often employed on the same side. A hut of leaves and sticks is sometimes built over the platform on the outrigger side. The float is short and heavy. The rig is a large "crab-claw" Oceanic lateen sail, set from a short raking mast stepped on the center boom of the off platform close to the hull.

TERN SCHOONER   A three-masted schooner, "tern" meaning a series of three. The Nova Scotiamen use the term to denote any type of three-masted schooner—fisherman or coaster—but it is not commonly used in the United States, although the term seems to have been employed here in the 1850's.

TERRA-NEUVA .   A large, auxiliary, barkentine-rigged vessel of St. Malo, St. Servan, and other ports in Brittany, France, engaged in the cod fishery off Newfoundland. They range in size from 200 to 400 tons. Each "terra-neuva" carries 12 dories in nests, from which the actual fishing for cod is done (with a hand line), as in the case of the American Gloucester fishing vessels. The steam trawler is gradually displacing the "terra-neuva."

THAMAKAU   A large, finely built, outrigger dugout canoe of the Fiji Islands
Illustration on page 77.   used for inter-island travel. It is the finest type of sailing outrigger canoe known. In former times lengths of 100 feet were known. Transversely the hull is ovate in section. A washboard is added to each side. The outrigger or weather side of the hull is straight from stem to stern, while the lee side is bowed in the regular manner. A quarter of the length at each end is covered with removable hatches. Thirteen poles cross the central third of the hull, projecting about 2 feet on the off side and to varying lengths on the outrigger side. The two end and the central poles, or booms, are connected to the heavy float with two pairs of "V" connectives on each. Five poles are lashed fore and aft on the outrigger frame, three near the hull, and over the canoe is built a platform. A diagonal strut runs from the bow and stern to the lee corners of the platform.

A mast, stepped amidships, is supported by two weather shrouds and a fore-and-aft stay. The sail is large and triangular in shape, with a boom and yard on the long vertical sides. These spars are lashed together at the bottom. The sail is made of finely pleated lauhala. When the sail is set, the heel of the yard rests in a step on the bow and is held down with a short line. A sheet is bent to the boom one-quarter the distance in from the outer end. As the outrigger must always be kept to windward to prevent overturning, the bow becomes the stern, and vice versa, when tacking and the sail has to be reset in the opposite end of the canoe. The experienced Fiji sailors are able to complete this maneuver in less than a minute. When not sailing, the Fijian canoes are sculled. The influence of the "thamakau" is Micronesian rather than Polynesian or Melanesian.

THAMES BARGE   A sailing barge used on the Thames River and near-by waters,
Illustration on page 31.   rigged as a ketch or yawl, with a large loose-footed boomless mainsail. It is fitted with brails and a topsail is carried. The sails are invariably tanned with a preparation of red ochre and oil to prevent weathering, for the main and topsail are never covered up. On the old time barges the mizzen-mast was stepped to the rudder head. The newer craft, especially seagoing types, have the mizzen mast stepped well inboard and have increased the size of the mizzensail, which, along with the addition of a bowsprit, make the rig that of a huge ketch. The peak of the mainsail is controlled by vangs. A flying-jib, called by the bargemen a "spinnaker," is set in light weather. Deep leeboards are used when on the wind in the open sea. The present-day types have a straight stem and sternpost, the former replacing the flat, overhanging Dutch bow of many years ago. The stern is built with a broad transom, onto which is slung a huge outboard rudder. The larger seagoing barges run up to 70, 80, and even 95 feet in length, 14 to 23 feet beam, 2 feet draft light, 6 to 9 feet draft loaded, leeboards drop 8 to 10 feet below the bottom, 100 to 175 tons' carrying capacity, hound of topmast 55 to 70 feet above the deck, 3,500 to 5,000 square feet of sail.

In spite of their apparent clumsiness, the "Thames barge" is fast to windward, good in any wind, handy in every point of sailing, and quick in stays. The crew generally consists of two men, or a man and his wife or boy, and they are noted for their excellent seamanship. This most distinctive type of English vessel is an ubiquitous craft, bobbing up in any port or creek from the Lizard to Lowestoft, and cross channel to Bruges and Calais. Illustration of "hay barge" on page 35.

THONNIER *or*   A modern yawl-rigged fishing boat used on the west coast of
TUNNY   Brittany, about 50 to 60 feet long, with beam about one-third
FISHERMAN   water-line length. Fore-and-aft, loose-footed main and boomless
Illustration on page 37.   mizzen sheeted to a long boomkin. Two headsails and topsails are carried and a large balloon jib is used in favorable weather. Long fishing rods are hinged on either side of the mainmast near the deck which are triced up to the masthead when not in use. The hull is painted in various colors and the working canvas is of various shades of tan, while the light sails are blue or white. Tunny is the same fish as the American tuna.

TILT-BOAT
Illustration on page 35.

A sailing ferry boat formerly used for transporting passengers between London and ports on the east coast of England, such as Margate and Gravesend. The name came from the awning, or "tilt," over a portion of the deck for the protection of the passengers. The later types were shoal-draft, double-ended, clinker-built sloops, with gaff mainsail, fore-topsail, and jib. "Tilt-boats" were displaced by steamers about a century ago.

TJALK

A small Dutch sailing vessel of about 60 tons used for sea and river navigation; usually with but one mast. The hull is rotund in the manner of the Dutch boats and there has scarcely been any change in three centuries, except in rig, which is now fore and aft. Leeboards are used.

TJOTTER

A beamy, round-bottomed, cat-rigged pleasure boat of Holland. The hull is on the order of the "boeier" (illustrated on page 43) and just as rotund, but having a more pronounced bilge. The beam is apt to be one-half the length. For centuries the Dutch have used leeboards in place of a keel or centerboard to reduce side drift or leeway—but do they?

TONGKANG
Illustration on page 69.

A large, open, Chinese ketch-rigged sailing lighter used mainly for carrying cargoes of logs from the Dutch East Indies, Johore, and other near-by places to Singapore. The hull has a sharp high bow with raking stem; vertical sternpost; straight keel; little dead rise; sharp buttocks; flaring sides (in order that the logs will be thrown clear when unloading); wide transom stern; low freeboard, when loaded, necessitating the use of washboards. The sheer line turns up strongly at the bow. There is a short deck fore and aft, and a cabin beneath the after deck. An overhanging platform projects beyond the stern, and there is also one beneath the long, sharply steeved bowsprit extending the whole outboard length, on which the two or three headsails are stowed when furled. The vessel is steered by a huge rectangular rudder with a long tiller. The main- and mizzensails are set on standing gaffs, sliding down on rings when brailed. The sails are of tanned canvas and the mainsail is boomless.

Another class of sailing lighter in Singapore uses a large main lugsail.

TONY
Illustration on page 65.

A curious, open, sailing dugout canoe used for fishing at Bombay, India. It is long, narrow, and double-ended, and is made of Malabar teak. The ends are strongly raking and sharp, rising abruptly to form a high stem and sternpost, carved on top. The rudder is attached to stern by rope beckets. A single settee sail is carried on a mast raking forward, the clew of the sail trimming ahead of amidships. Oars are also used. Average size about 31 feet long by 4 feet 6 inches beam.

TOPO
Illustration on page 39.

A small fishing boat of Venice. It has a flat bottomed, double-ended hull of light draft. A lugsail of vari-colored patterns is carried on a mast stepped aft of the center.

TOPSAIL SCHOONER
Illustration on page 21.

A fore-and-aft-rigged schooner, with one or two square sails above the foresail on the foremast, and sometimes on the main-mast.

TRABACOLA
Illustration on page 39.

An Italian two-masted, lug-rigged vessel of the Adriatic, the general use of which is that of a coasting trader. The hull is double-ended with curved stem and sternpost. A heavy out-board rudder is slung from the latter. There is moderate sheer. The rig consists of a balanced lugsail on each mast and one or two jibs to a bowsprit. As in most of the lug-rigged Italian craft, the tack purchase is brought to the deck, abreast of the mast some distance away. A better purchase to flatten the sails is obtained by this method.

TRABACOTO
Illustration on page 57.

A small southern European fishing boat which was popular in the 17th century, but which has remained in use until quite recently. It was two-masted with gayly colored lateen or set-tee sails. The mainmast was vertical and the foremast raked forward. The "traba-coto" was probably an off-shoot of the galley.

TRAWLER

A fishing vessel which tows a large net, called a "trawl," as the "Brixham trawler" (illustrated on page 31). Power-driven vessels have supplanted the sailing trawlers almost entirely.

TRIREME
Illustration on page 51.

(Quadrareme, pentereme, etc.) As applied to early Greek and Roman galleys, the consensus is that the terms are used to denote the number of men pulling on each oar. The older idea applied these terms to galleys with three, four, or five superimposed banks of oars. This application has been found to have been impracticable, if not impossible, to row owing to the great length required of the upper oars in order to clear those of the lower banks. "Triremes," etc., were in use up to the late 15th century.

TROW

A type of barge found in various forms in various British localities.

TSUKPIN
Illustration on page 83.

An outrigger sailing canoe of Yap Island, which lies at the western end of the Caroline Islands. It is employed by the natives in the catching of flying fish. Unlike the other sailing canoes of the Carolines, the hull is symmetrical transversely and it is beamier. In these respects and in the crescentic keel it is not unlike the Palau "kaep" (illustrated on page 83), but the outrigger, lee platform, and rig resemble the "popo" (illustrated on page 83). The ends, which terminate in a swan-like head, are alike.

TUCK BOAT — A 19th century rowing boat of Cornwall, England. It was about 20 feet long and carried a "stop-net." It was carvel-built, with a sharp bow and square-transomed stern. Six-oared. Used for pilchard fishing.

TUCKER — A small English craft of the middle 19th century of about 3 tons' burden, used for plaice fishing out of Brighton.

TUINGUTU — An outrigger dugout canoe of the Tongan Archipelago. Two or three outrigger booms with U-type or paired connectives to float. A washboard is sewed on to each side of hull. Decked at each end with boards. Round bottom with tumble-home sides. This canoe is in use at the present time.

TUREMA — A Swedish armed craft of the latter 18th century. A combination of the galley and man-of-war. Armed with 26 guns, with sweeps in pairs between the guns. Three-masted; square-rigged.

TULE GRASS BALSA — A grass boat made of bundles of tule grass lashed together, tapering on the ends. Used by the Indians on Pyramid Lake, Nevada.
Illustration on page 87.

TWAKOW — A Chinese craft of Singapore, used for general cargo carrying. The hull is flat-bottomed with flaring sides—a combination junk and sampan design, with a flat, rounded, V-shaped bow and a wide transom stern, both raking. The ends are rather high, with good sheer, but there is little freeboard amidships when the vessel is loaded. Rocker keel. There is a cabin aft beneath the deck. A huge rudder, with a long tiller, is slung from the stern. One or two masted, the mainmast being stepped well forward, with the foremast right in the bow carrying a severe forward rake. The rig is that of the Chinese battened lug, with a large mainsail and a small foresail. Each batten is kept to the mast by means of a parrel. The sails are of tanned canvas. "Twakows" without sails are sculled. They vary in size, but the beam runs from 35 to 40 per cent of the length, the greatest breadth being about two-thirds the length aft the bow. The crew consists of three men. Great numbers of these vessels may be seen around Singapore.
Illustration on page 69.

TYNE KEEL — A coal-carrying "keel" used on the Tyne River in England. This type is similar to the "Mersey lighter" (illustrated on page 35) and is about 42 feet long, 19 feet beam, and 4 feet 6 inches draft. See "keel" and "Mersey lighter."

UCHE
Illustration on page 81.
The native name for "dugout canoe" in the Hermit Islands, a small group which lies west of the Admiralty Islands in the Bismarck Archipelago. The last specimen of the large two-masted dugout sailing canoes reposes in the Berlin Museum. Above a huge dugout are several rows of planks which form the sides of the hull. The stem and sternpost are extended upwards and curve inboard. The whole hull is highly decorated. The outrigger float is supported by four heavy booms, on which a platform rests. On the off side of the hull is a sloping platform. The masts are stayed and each is further supported by a curved transverse spar secured to an outrigger boom. The sails are oblong, with upper and lower yards, and are slung obliquely in the manner of a standing lug. This craft could carry about four dozen people.

UDEMA
Illustration on page 55.
A Swedish armed naval vessel of the 18th century, mounting nine heavy-caliber guns on the center line of the ship. It was three-masted, square-rigged on the main and foremast, a fore-and-aft sail on the mizzenmast, and three head sails. There were small ports for oars under the gun ports and a convenient distance above the water.

UBÁ
A dugout canoe used by the Brazilian native and Samaracás Indians of French Guiana on the Oyapook region of the Amazon River delta. See "montaria."

UMIAK *or* OOMIAK
Illustration on page 87.
An open skin boat used by the Eskimos of Greenland, Northern Canada, and Alaska. It is made by stretching unhaired walrus or seal skins over a light wooden frame and lashed with thongs. Though there are forms and differences in structure, it is usually flat-bottomed with flaring sides having thwarts between, and sharp-ended. The usual means of propulsion are oars and paddles, although a square sail made of matting or skins is sometimes used. On some types, the gunwales are extended to a point, fore and aft. Average lengths 20 to 30 feet, beam about one-third. In the Hudson Bay region they are 11 to 27 feet. See also "bidarra."

UNA BOAT
An English sail boat similar to the American cat boat.

VAKA
A dugout canoe with single outrigger of the Marquesas Islands. The modern "vakas" are simple in design, being 12 to 18 feet

in length and 12 to 18 inches wide and deep, with a narrow washboard nailed to each side of the dugout. The two outrigger booms are secured to the long cylindrical pole floats near either end with crude slat connectives. The early Marquesan canoes were highly ornamented and carved affairs, with long, pointed ends and rounded underbodies. The sails were similar to those used on the Hawaiian canoes.

VAKA
Illustration on page 79.

An outrigger sailing dugout canoe of Rennel Island (or Moava Island) (latitude 11° south, longitude 160° east). Sailing canoes are used only on the inland lake on the southeast portion of the island and not on the seashore. The hull is a very narrow dugout, pointed and sharply raked at each end. The outrigger float has pointed, raked ends, and is nearly the length of the hull. On the larger canoes the float is supported by three booms, which sometimes support a platform, while the smaller canoes have but two booms. Two kinds of sails are used. One type is pear-shaped, the foot ending in a point, and is lashed to a curved spar on either side. One sail spar is supported by a short spar, which is braced by a single stay. The other type of sail is very long and narrow, the lower edge straight and the upper curved. It is hung from an inverted U-shaped mast, stepped on the forward outrigger boom. The sails are made of pandanus leaf matting. Most of the natives of this Melanesian island are pure Polynesians.

VAKA POTI

A Marquesan outrigger dugout canoe, of larger size than the "vaka" from these islands. Some have a dugout underbody with a wide washboard nailed above either side. In others the dugout portion is just a strip, which forms the backbone, to which a few ribs, a stem, and sternpost are bolted. The sides are clinker-built planking and a short deck is often built at each end. In form this canoe resembles a narrow double-ended rowboat. It is 20 to 26 feet in length, with a beam of 2 to 3 feet. Two straight outrigger booms are employed and each is secured to the long pole float with a stave connective. The booms rest across the gunwales close to the ends of the canoe. Contrary to the practice in other Polynesian islands, the outrigger is always carried on the starboard side. Both oars and paddles are used for propulsion and a leg-of-mutton sail is sometimes used. The Marquesan natives always sail before the wind, as they do not seem to understand tacking. The population of the Marquesas Islands has dwindled to a mere handful of natives, consequently very few "vakas" remain to-day.

VANAGI
Illustration on page 85.

An outrigger dugout canoe of Port Moresby, Papua (British New Guinea). The hull is quite narrow, tapering towards the ends. These terminate in a point and curve up from the bottom in a sharp rake. A mangrove pole lies above each gunwale, rising at the ends. A weather screen, made of coconut cloth, is made by stretching this cloth over the pole and down to each side of the gunwales, where it is secured by means of bamboo strips. On some canoes the weather cloth is omitted at the bow to lessen the free-board when fishing. Five, six, or seven outrigger booms pass between the poles and the gunwales, and project beyond the off side on which projection one or two planks are laid. Another plank platform or deck is laid across the booms on the outrigger side adjacent the hull. A pointed float, shorter than the canoe, is secured to the booms by connectives, each of which consists of two crossed sticks and a third one set obliquely. If the canoe is equipped for sailing, the rig consists of one or two sails, in shape that of an inverted truncated triangle, supported between two nearly vertical mangrove spars. These are set on the bottom and stayed fore and aft and to the outrigger. The leeward side of the sail is controlled by a sheet. The craft can sail in either direction, the sails being adjusted accordingly. They are usually paddled.

VĀRAGAM ORU   A narrow dugout sailing canoe of Ceylon, with outrigger. The transverse section is round and the overhanging ends rake strongly. It is 25 to 30 feet long, with about one-tenth the beam. In some sections of the island a square sail hung on a double V-shaped mast is used. Two curved booms are connected directly to a long float. Washboards with pointed ends are sewed on to the dugout proper. This canoe is also known as the "monsoon canoe."

VELOCERA   A large three-masted coasting ship of Italy. Square-rigged on
Illustration on page 39.   the foremast; boomless fore-and-aft sail on the main; and la-teen-rigged on the mizzen. A bowsprit is carried, as well as a topmast on the main. The latter is only used occasionally.

VIGILENGA   A "canoa" of the Amazon delta having the town of Vigia as a base. See "canoa," illustrated on page 89.

VIKING SHIP   An early Norse "long ship," propelled mainly by oars, but
Illustrations on pages 49 and 51.   also carrying a single demountable mast with a square sail hung from a horizontal yard. These vessels were clinker-built and sharp-ended, with long easy sheer rising sharply at the ends and a rather flat bilge. The rounding stem and sternpost were elongated vertically and usually terminated in a dragon's head, scroll, or some such carving. There were no decks, except at the bow and stern, and the oarsmen sat in the open, their shields hung along the gunwales. Small ports just beneath the gunwales received the oars. The oar ports could be closed by shutters fastened on the inside. Fore-and-aft stays, as well as shrouds, supported the mast when in its vertical position. At night the mast could be lowered, set into crutches, and used as a ridge pole for a tent (usually the sail) to afford protection from the elements.

The rudder was always rigged on the starboard (steerboard) side and a trans-verse tiller was set in the upper end of the rudder post.

The Viking ships ranged in size from the "skuta" of fifteen oars to a side, through

[202]

the "skeid" with thirty oars to a side and a crew capacity of about 220, up to the even larger dragon ships, or "dreki."

The first record of a Norse "long ship" dates back to the latter part of the 8th century, A.D., when three Viking pirate ships looted a port on the southwestern coast of England. For the subsequent century and a half Europe was harried by a succession of cruel piratical raids by the people of the northland, which inflicted great suffering on the populace. Nearly all of the monasteries in Western Scotland were destroyed.

While the British Isles and Northern France, especially Normandy, are commonly associated with Viking invasion and settlement, the fierce Norsemen plundered as far south as Italy and the north African coast, established themselves in Iceland, Russia, and Germany, and legend tells us that they later even reached the coast of North America. In spite of their propensity for cruelty and ruthlessness, when not engaged in their warlike pursuits they displayed an unbelievable capacity for organization and, strangely enough, were a law-abiding people.

Certain authorities claim that the Viking ships owe their origin to the Roman galleys, which seems quite plausible as the Romans spent considerable time in Western Europe. The double-ended, clinker-built boat has remained a distinctive Scandinavian type for well over eleven centuries.

Among the early Viking vessels unearthed is one known as the "Gokstad ship," found near Sandefjord, Norway, in 1880, now in the Royal Frederiks University in Oslo. This model is 78 feet long, 16 feet 7 inches beam, and 5 feet 9 inches deep, with sixteen oars to a side. An exact replica is now in Lincoln Park, Chicago.

VINCO *Illustration on page 61.*	A three-masted vessel of Italy, with a high foremast, polacre-rigged, and the main and mizzen lateen-rigged.
VINTA	A Philippine outrigger canoe.
VIRGINIA MODEL	This type of vessel was developed on Chesapeake Bay about 1750 and was characterized by a very sharp hull. It was closely related to the "Baltimore clipper" (illustrated on page 21),

which followed it, and from which it was developed.

WA *Illustration on page 81.*	A sailing, outrigger dugout canoe of the Ninigo Islands, which lie west of the Admiralty Islands in the Bismarck Archipelago.

This type is individual in that the sides of the narrow hull are straight and the bottom flat. The ends sheer up somewhat. The hull is decorated with simple native designs. One (sometimes two) short raking mast carries a long, narrow pandanus leaf sail stretched between two parallel yards and set almost vertically. The sail is controlled by sheets leading from the upper end of the yards. A model of a "wa" is in the Cologne Museum, Germany. This particular model is two-masted and a platform is built on the outrigger booms.

WA'A

Illustration on page 77.

A Hawaiian outrigger dugout canoe. The keelless bottom of the hull is semi-circular and the sides are straight, with a thin plank washboard 6 or 8 inches high above. In former times this was sewed to the hull, but nailing is the modern method. At the ends the bottom rounds up in an easy curve and narrows laterally, terminating in a point, above which the washboards join, the extremities forming a short upturned edge, spatulate when viewed head on. The gunwale formed by the washboard has a gentle sheer, the dugout itself having none. The single outrigger float (always on the port side) is a square or round pole, upturned at the ends, the after extremity being brought to a point, and the one forward to a thin carved head. The float is connected with the hull by two slightly arched booms, which rest across the gunwales, each secured with a lashing. No connectives are employed, the booms being lashed directly to the float. In addition to the gunwale lashing, the booms are bound to a "V"- or "U"-shaped fitting or spreader, which is inserted and secured inside the hull at the point of crossing. This is done to relieve the washboards of some of the strain.

The "wa'a" is very light in weight, one of average size (25 feet long, 1 foot wide and 1 foot deep), weighing not much over 50 pounds. In Captain Cook's time, some of the canoes were fitted for sailing with an Oceanic "crab-claw" spritsail of matting, the mast being stepped on the inboard part of the forward boom. When sailing, the outrigger was always to port, whether to windward or leeward, and the canoe was not brought "about" in the regular manner. A century or so ago a European spritsail of cloth was introduced. At that time there were thousands of canoes in the Hawaiian Islands, but now they are becoming scarce.

WA'A KAULUA

A double Hawaiian dugout canoe. The hulls were similar to the "wa'a," although larger, and were connected a short distance apart with three of four slightly arched booms. A platform, made of a few poles or a plank, was usually laid on the booms between the hulls to carry passengers or cargo. The double canoes were always equipped with a sail, similar to that of the "wa'a." The Hawaiian canoes were paddled. The paddles consisted of an ovate pointed blade secured to a shaft. The double canoes have vanished, the schooner having replaced the sailing "wa'a kaulua."

WAGA

Illustration on page 85.

The outrigger dugout canoe illustrated is typical to the Daui district in Papua, extending from Mullens Harbor to Suau Island. The ends of the canoe are prolonged to blunt points cut down obliquely. In elevation the ends rise from the bottom in an easy raking "S."

[204]

There is some sheer and there might be tumble home. Ten booms, common to the district, support the float by means of double inverted-V connectives. The float is the length of the canoe. A platform of thin planks is laid over the booms between the hull and the connectives. A rectangular sail, made of plaited coconut leaves, is set obliquely from a mast stepped amidships. The mast is supported by a transverse shore below and by two stays above. A yard is on each long side of the sail, which is controlled by one or two sheets from the lower yard and a vang from the foot of the upper yard. There are variations of the "wagas" in the areas near the Daui district.

WAKA *or* **VAKA**
Illustration on page 79.

The dugout sailing canoe of the Taku[7] (or Tauu) atoll group, which lies north of the Solomon Islands. The hull is a fairly wide, heavy dugout, often with planks sewed on above to form a washstrake. The ends are usually drawn to a point and were carved on the older canoes. The outrigger float is supported by three transverse booms. An Oceanic lateen sail is set from a mast stepped amidships. The Taku natives are fine sailors.

WAKA KORARI *or* **WAKA PUHARI**

A woven punt-shaped boat raft formerly used by the Moriori of Chatham Islands, which lie eastward of New Zealand. Having no trees for making canoes, the natives used the stalks of ferns, pieces of wood from shrubs and any other available vegetation to fashion their craft. It was rectangular in plan, with straight sides, a "grab" bow, steeply sloped transom stern and ranged in size from 9 feet long by 20 inches wide, to 50 feet long by 8 feet wide by 5 feet deep. There were thwarts across and oars were used for propulsion. This craft was never sailed. Kelp bladders were employed on the larger boats to increase the buoyancy.

WAKA TAUA
Illustration on page 77.

A Maori war canoe of New Zealand. This was a very large type of dugout, of an average length of 60 to 70 feet, with the freeboard increased by means of a washstrake, sewed to the hull. An exquisitely carved figurehead, which also served as a breakwater, ornamented the bow and on the after end was a very high upstanding stern piece. This, too, was richly carved and its dimensions were, 10 to 18 feet high, about 18 inches wide, and 2 inches thick. The transverse section of the hull was that of a wide "V" with curved sides. A floor grating of light rods lashed to crossbars was laid a little distance above the bottom. There was little or no sheer. The canoe was usually paddled, but at times a V-shaped Maori sail of matting was employed. It was laced along the two long sides to a mast and boom and the apex of the triangle was stepped on the floor of the dugout. The sail was stayed to the thwarts fore and aft. The war canoes of the Maoris were exceptionally well constructed and a great amount of time was spent on the ornamentation.

WAKU-AMI-
  BUNE   An open rowboat used in the pound-net herring fishery off the
             coast of Hokkaido, Japan. A bag-net is suspended under the
             boat to receive the fish from the pound-net. The boat is flat-
bottomed, with raking stem projecting above the bow; square raking stern. The
bottom curves up aft.

WA LAP   An outrigger sailing canoe of the Marshall Islands in the west-
  Illustration on page 83.   ern Pacific. In many respects it resembles the "popo" of the
             Carolines. The main difference is in the outrigger, which is
made up of two main straight booms flanked by three curved booms on each side.
The latter are lashed directly to the long float, while each straight boom is connected
with a short stanchion. There is a lee and weather platform. The Oceanic lateen rig
is employed and the mast is braced by several shrouds to the main outrigger booms.
The present-day canoes are about 20 feet long by 30 inches wide. Schooners are also
built by the Marshall Islanders, who have always been adept at boat building and
navigation. The native-constructed schooners have taken the place of the large seagoing canoes of the "wa lap" type, which could accommodate as many as fifty
people. See "popo."

WA-RIRIK   An outrigger canoe of the Gilbert Islands. See "baurua."

WEST   A ship engaged in the West Indian trade.
  INDIAMAN

WHALEBOAT   A double-ended, single-banked rowing boat. It is very sea-
             worthy and is sometimes called a "whaler." Whaleboats were
28 to 30 feet long, beam about 6 feet 6 inches; sharp-ended; round, easy bilge; raking,
curved stem and sternpost; good sheer; open; with five thwarts. They were noted
for their lightness, strength, and buoyancy. A completely equipped whaleboat carried a mast, with mainsail and jib, harpoons, lances, oars, long steering sweep, boat
spade, boat hook, line bucket, buckets, etc.

WHALER   A vessel used in the hunting of whales. The term "whaler"
  Illustration on page 25.   goes back many centuries, as the English sought the Greenland
             whale through the 16th century, and the Dutch were especially
active in the industry as early as 1600. The early Nantucket and New Bedford whalers were broad-bottomed, sturdy little vessels, carrying square topsails, which were
trimmed by braces leading forward to cleats on the bowsprit. They were sometimes
sloop-rigged and were usually manned by thirteen men, two crews of six men each
for the boats and a cook, the latter taking care of the ship while the boats were away.
    In those early days the whales pursued were those found close to shore, and after

they were killed, were towed ashore, and then cut up and the blubber boiled to extract the oil. Later, as the ships worked farther from shore, the blubber was stored in casks and then taken ashore.

As whaling operations were extended farther out to sea, larger vessels were built, and it became necessary to build "try-works" on board in which to boil the blubber. The industry was at a standstill during the Revolutionary War, but after peace was declared it got under way again and the "whalers" began to cruise around Cape Horn to the Pacific Ocean. It was there that the greatest activity in the whaling industry took place. A whaling voyage lasted from one to four years.

After the War of 1812 the whaling business entered its palmy days, continuing for over 50 years. The ships were stout, heavily-built, and had distinctive hull and deck designs. The average lengths of "whalers" were from 115 to 130 feet long, about one-fifth the beam, built with raking, convexly curved stem; bow moderately full above the water; straight vertical sternpost; heavy, square stern, often ornamented with scroll work; slight sheer, and long run. It was necessary to have an "easy cutting-in ship," one that was not too wide and flat on the floor, so that the ship would not pull too hard at the "cutting-in tackles" when a whale was being cut up for its blubber in a seaway.

A cabin on either side of the stern, with a covered passageway running between, served for the storage of whaling gear. The helmsman stood underneath the covered opening. The whaleboats, usually five in number (but two on the starboard side) were slung from wooden davits along the rail, and at the masthead, generally on the mainmast, was a crow's-nest, from which the lookout scanned the sea. At the mainmast head, two heavy blocks were slung, for the tackle used in supporting the whale when it was being cut up alongside the vessel. The cutting stage was located between the fore and after whaleboats on the starboard side.

A boat's crew consisted of six men—the officer of the boat, who was one of the mates, carried the title of "boat header"; the harpooner, a petty officer, whose rank was next to that of a mate and known as a "boat steerer," and four oarsmen. The "boat steerer" struck the whale with the harpoon and the officer usually killed it.

The "bark" rig was the favorite, although there were brigs, ships, etc.

Three kinds of whales were hunted—the deep-sea "sperm" whale, the oil from which was of a superior grade, and it also furnished spermaceti, from which candles were made. The second was the "right" whale, which yielded a cheaper oil, called train-oil, and whalebone. The latter forms a sieve, or strainer, in the mouth of the whale for the minute marine creatures on which it lives, its throat being very small. The third was the "bowhead," or Greenland right whale, found in Arctic waters, which also gave oil and whalebone.

On a successful voyage, a whaler of the size stated above would bring back between 5,000 and 6,000 barrels of whale oil, over 150 barrels of sperm oil, and over

60,000 pounds of whalebone. The *Charles W. Morgan*[8] earned $2,000,000 in thirty-seven voyages. Nowadays the "whalers" are steamers or fast motor boats and the whales are harpooned with machine guns.

WHERRY

Illustration on page 31.

The "wherry" of Norfolk, England, is a light-draft, sailing cargo carrier, about 50 feet long and 13 feet beam. The greatest beam is well forward; bow short and hollow; low freeboard, and the stern sharp with a fine run aft. The 40-foot spar is set in the bow and a single halyard acts for throat and peak. The single fore-and-aft sail is high-peaked, with a 30-foot gaff and no boom. For reefing a bonnet is used.

Also, a long, light English rowboat.

WOOL CLIPPER A large, square-rigged "ship" or "bark" of the clipper type engaged in the Australian-British trade from about 1866 until the 1890's, carrying passengers and supplies from England to Australia and returning with a cargo of wool. This type was usually built especially for the wool trade.

Most of the "wool clippers" were built of iron and many had a long, rounded poop. The earlier ships had tremendous, lofty sail plans, a sail area of 35,000 square yards being common. This yardage included headsails, staysails, spanker, and spencer, as well as the square sails. However, with all this sail-carrying capacity, they were not so fast as the smaller "tea clippers" of a decade earlier.

A first-class "wool clipper" was capable of loading 8,000 to 10,000 bales of wool, worth up to $650,000, and the cargo represented a wool clip from nearly 1,000,000 sheep. Some ships made as many as twenty trips before the steamship made inroads on their commerce, so the financial returns were indeed very satisfactory.

The 1870's saw the rapid development of trade between England, her Colonies, India, and America. There were such large amounts of wool, grain, and other commodities waiting for shipment in British colonial ports that the small ships previously built could not take care of them, and there was a great demand for larger ships. Wire rigging and iron plates had come into use,[9] which solved the difficulties of staying huge masts and yards, and of building unwieldy hulls of wood. It was soon found that three-masted, full-rigged ships of over 1,500 tons were uneconomical to run, owing to the necessity of large crews. As a result the four-masted "ship" and "bark" were evolved, with a shorter sail plan, and they became popular. They were nearly as fast as the "ship" and required fewer men to handle them.

The British "wool clippers" were, on the whole, carefully built, finely proportioned ships, and were well sailed. This may be attested to by the fact that many were in fine condition and carrying cargoes in the first quarter of the 20th century.

The last two British ships built for the Australian wool trade were the steel-hulled *Mount Stewart* and her sister-ship, *Cromdale*, in 1891. These two ships registered 1,900 tons each, were 271 feet 6 inches long, 40 feet 1 inch beam, 23 feet 4 inches depth, with a freeboard amidships of 5 feet 3 inches loaded, and carried seven sails on the mainmast. Their lines were not so fine as their predecessors, being designed to carry large cargoes. Yet they were not slow ships as they could be depended upon to do 300 miles in 24 hours with a favorable breeze.

XEBEC
Illustration on page 61.

A Mediterranean and Oriental three-masted, narrow-hulled vessel. The hull generally terminated forward with a sharp beak, and aft with an outer platform comprised of two wings. It was usually lateen-rigged and the foremast raked forward. The mizzenmast was added to the "xebec" in the late 18th century in order to better balance the boat. This mast was fitted with a topmast, top, etc. There was no bowsprit. Instead, a sort of a boomkin was lashed or confined to the bow in a horizontal position, to which led the bow lines. The shrouds were set up to toggles, fixed to the sides of the ship, similar to the runners on English cutters. These shrouds were easily shifted when coming about. The lateen sails were each bent to a yard on the longest side and were confined to the mast by a parrel about one-third the length of the yard from the lower end. The yards were worked at the lower ends by bow lines and the sail was controlled by a sheet at the clew. The upper lee yardarm was worked by a brace.

When the wind was favorable a "xebec" sometimes carried square sails, and in heavy weather the lateen sails could be reefed. Lateen-rigged vessels could sail about a point closer to the wind than the square-rigged.

French "xebecs" were sometimes rigged similarly to a "polacre" (illustrated on page 59), but the primitive rigs were better sailers.

YACHT
Illustration on page 47.

Any vessel used for pleasure purposes, whether sail or power. Chatterton tells us that the word "yacht" is derived from the early Dutch "jaght-schip" of the 17th century; the term came into use in England about 1660. Although the Europeans had their pleasure craft and vessels were built for the same purpose in America as early as 1816, since the building of the 90-foot, water line schooner *Onkahye* in 1840 (which vessel was a distinct departure from the then accepted hull form for fast sailing craft), a "yacht" has usually been considered a type of craft quite distinct in hull, rig and finish from commercial or naval vessels (Chapelle). See "Pleasure Craft" and "A Short History of the *America's* Cup Defenders" in this volume.

YARMOUTH YAWL
Illustration on page 33.

A long, narrow, double-ended, clinker-built boat used in England on the Norfolk coast, rigged with three lugsails and a jib. In the middle of the 19th century these "yawls" were built up to 70 feet in length, and 50-footers with 10 or 11 feet beam were common. A 69-foot "yawl" was said to have sailed 16 knots on a reach in the 1850's. This type was a true yawl as derived from the Scandinavian model.

YAWL
Illustration on page 219.

The true "yawl" is the Yarmouth yawl and is descended from the Scandinavian "yol."

The modern "yawl" is a fore-and-aft rigged boat, with the mainmast stepped forward and a small mizzenmast stepped in the stern aft of the helmsman. The mizzen sail sheets to a boomkin. There is a jib forward. A yawl gets its name from the rig described above. The yawl rig is used to a great extent on pleasure craft.

YAWL BOAT

An open boat used by coasting vessels, carried on the stern from davits. It also was used by fishing vessels previously to the 1870's, before the dory was adopted. It is a carvel-built keel boat, with a sharp flaring bow, a curved stem and a wide, heart-shaped, square stern. It has four or five thwarts and a stern seat. The lengths are from 18 to 20 feet, beam about 30 per cent. It is rowed.

YOL
Illustration on page 45.

Norwegian for "yawl," meaning a double-ended boat. The Scandinavian "yol" is a light, open, double-ended, clinker-built boat, stem and stern alike, for rowing or sailing. The usual rig is a single lugsail.

YULOH *or* **FORMOSAN CATAMARAN**

A type of catamaran used at Takow, Formosa (Taiwan), Japan, for getting through the heavy surf to vessels lying in the open roadstead. They are 30 to 35 feet long, 7 to 10 feet wide at the stern, the bow narrower and sharply curving upward. Made up of 12 to 14 bamboo logs bound to several cross pieces on top with rattan lacings and a bamboo gunwale runs along either side, to which oarlocks are fastened. A single mast is stepped just forward of amidships, on which a single matting Chinese sail is carried. Steered with an oar. Two leeboards are carried on the lee side and one inserted between the logs in the center. Passengers are carried in a large tub lashed down near the stern. The crew consists of three men. It is the only type that can get through the extremely heavy surf over the bar in this vicinity.

ZABRA

A small sailing ship of the 16th century.

ZARUG
Illustration on page 57.

A small, lateen-rigged craft of the "dhow" family, used mainly by Arabs for fishing in the Red Sea. "Zarugs" are also often used clandestinely by the Arabs in smuggling and in the slave traffic (now greatly repressed), carrying slaves from the African to the Arabian shore. It is a narrow, sometimes crudely built, double-ended, open boat, with raking stem and sternpost, varying sheer, outboard rudder, steered with a tiller. It is 15 to 40 feet long; carvel-built. Often a deck, made of slats and sticks laid on the thwarts, is used to conceal contraband. A short single, demountable mast is stepped somewhat ahead of amidships and has a severe forward rake. The tack of the lateen sail leads to the head of the stem post, which projects somewhat above the gunwale.

ZULU

Illustration on page 33.

A double-ended, lug-rigged Scotch fishing boat, which is a compromise of the "fifie" and "skaffie" (illustrated on page 33), dating from the late 1870's. The straight stem and bow of the "fifie" was retained—with a deeper forefoot—while the stern was modeled after the "skaffie" with more rake to the sternpost. The deeper forefoot improved the windward sailing qualities. A high-peaked dipping lugsail is used and while the "zulu" is primarily a one-sail boat, many of the larger ones, which run up to a top size of about 80 feet over-all, carry a mizzen and a small jib extended to a boomkin and bowsprit. This type of boat superseded the "fifie" and "skaffie," but its numbers in turn have been greatly diminished by motor-driven craft.

PLEASURE
CRAFT

Introduction

UP TO A comparatively few years ago, yachting and pleasure boating were considered a rich man's sport. Nowadays there are thousands upon thousands of water craft of all sizes and description used solely for recreational purposes. Age or wealth do not enter into the enjoyment of boating—the six-year old gets as much kick out of skimming over the cool, blue water as do the twenty-, forty-, and seventy-year olds. This applies to the person of small means as well as the tycoon.

The first American yacht was the brigantine *Cleopatra's Barge*, built in Salem, Massachusetts, in 1816. Although yachting had been in vogue in the countries of Western Europe, it was not until after 1816 that out-and-out pleasure craft were built in America. About that time certain wealthy men of New York and other coastal cities turned toward the sea for their sport and relaxation. In 1844 the New York Yacht Club was organized (the first one in this country) and the next year its initial regatta was staged.

Before the building of the experimental *Onkayhe* in 1840, all of the vessels constructed for pleasure purposes had been modeled after contemporary commercial craft, mainly, the schooner-rigged pilot boats.

The success of the *America* in British waters and the publicity given the clipper ships were probable factors in the stimulation of the sport. As stated in another chapter, the contests for the *America's* Cup were the classic events of the yachting world and also helped bring boating to the attention of the general public. Small-boat racing became increasingly popular, and by the turn of the century yacht clubs dotted the coasts.

As boats of different sizes raced against each other, handicapping became necessary. While methods differed with various clubs, the New York Yacht Club first gave time allowance on the basis of displacement—so many seconds per ton. The rules were changed frequently during the next few years, but for eleven years, or until 1870, yachts were rated on water-line length and beam. This rule brought forth the shoal, "skimming-dish" type of hull. The British rule, on the other hand, had tended toward the cutter type—extremely narrow and deep. Cutters became quite the rage in eastern yachting circles and their popularity lasted for fifteen years or more after their introduction in 1870.

The measurement rules were again altered a number of times, but in 1882 the Seawanhaka Yacht Club introduced a rule which combined the water-line length and sail area in an effort to make a more normal hull. This is known as the Seawanhaka rule.

However, as it turned out, the new rule eventually produced a craft as freakish as before, with a short water line, long over-all length, and large sail area—the scow type, which still survives on the inland lakes. The extreme Seawanhaka types fell into disfavor in the early 1900's and boats for racing were built to the new "universal" rule, and the popular classes were the P, Q, and R, or 30, 25, and 20 raters. This rule, while expected to produce an ideal type of racing boat, again fell short of the desired results. The sharp overhangs make a wet, uncomfortable sea boat and the full mid-section produced a none too fast hull.

Late in the 1890's, N. G. Herreshoff conceived the idea of the "one-design" class —several yachts of one kind built exactly alike in every respect, usually sponsored by a single club. This put a premium on the skill of the skipper and crew, rather than on the boat itself, and the boats were not apt to be outbuilt so quickly. Among the first one-design classes were the famous New York Yacht Club's "30's," which were brought out in 1905. Some years later the New York Yacht Club's "40's" and "50's" and the Larchmont "O" class were developed, but these yachts were expensive to build and operate, and were out of reach of the average enthusiast.

In the meantime, the classes of smaller boats, such as sailing canoes, sneak boxes, cat boats, dinghies, scows, knockabouts, etc., were gaining in popularity and numbers. It should be mentioned here that as early as 1860 a class of small, speedy sloops and cat-rigged boats was popular for racing on the east and south coasts, as well as on the Great Lakes. They were known as "sand-baggers" and are described elsewhere in this volume. Because of their dangerous character, they fell into disrepute and died out in the '80's.

Early in the 1920's European designers brought out the 6-meter boat, built to the "International" rule of measurement. This type found immediate favor on Long Island Sound, and international 6-meter races became an annual affair. The "sixes" were followed by the 8-, 10-, and 12-meter classes, and to-day yachts built to the International rule are favored types for course racing.

The snappy "star" class should not be overlooked. The "stars" have grown by leaps and bounds since they were first introduced in 1911. Each fleet of star boats holds its annual elimination races and the winner is sent to compete in the international championship series, which is held on the waters of the club having won the title the previous year. "Stars" from halfway around the world are sent to compete in this event. These Marconi-rigged sloops are 15 feet 6 inches long on the water, 22 feet 7 ½ inches over-all, 5 feet 8 ¼ inches beam, and have a sail area of 281 ½ square feet. Other types that are having a flare are the Chesapeake Bay "bugeye" and, for racing, the "30 square meter" sloop, with its narrow inboard rig.

After the World War, the schooner, and to a lesser extent, the ketch, became increasingly popular. With the introduction of the staysail and "wishbone" rigs, some of their handicap over the sloops was eliminated, at least in weather work. The "motor-sailer," a modified power boat with sails, has come into favor with those craving comfort.

While the prevailing measurement rule determined the design of racing yachts, cruising craft have no such limitations and are built according to intended use or whim. Sailing can be done with a greater degree of comfort on these huskier models. They are usually equipped with a motor and may be rigged as a schooner, yawl, ketch, cutter, etc. Among the more important races for cruising yachts are the New York-Bermuda, San Francisco-Honolulu, Transatlantic race and the Mackinac races on Lakes Michigan and Huron.

Pictured on the ensuing pages are some examples of the many varieties of pleasure craft.

Pleasure Craft

On the opposite page are illustrated several types of pleasure craft of the past and present, from the "sand-bagger" of the 1860's and '70's to the modern staysail-rigged schooner of to-day.

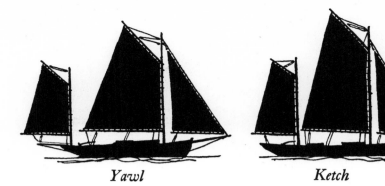

Yawl   *Ketch*

Cat Boat   *Scow*   *Sand-Bagger*

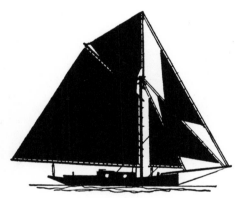
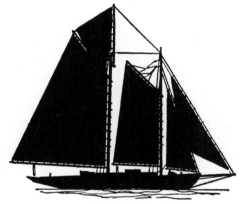

Sloop 1880   *Schooner*

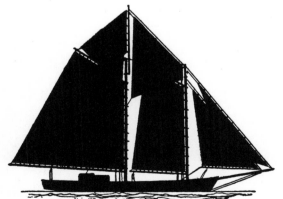
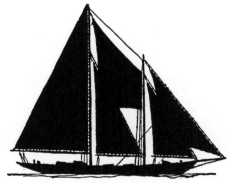

Biloxi, Miss., Centerboard Schooner   *Modern Staysail Schooner*

Miscellaneous Pleasure Craft

Here are six types of sailing craft used in pleasure pursuit. The ketch is shown with the new-fangled wishbone rig, while the Chesapeake Bay log canoe and bugeye are modern prototypes of boats that have long been popular in the waters of Maryland.

Ketch, Wishbone Rig

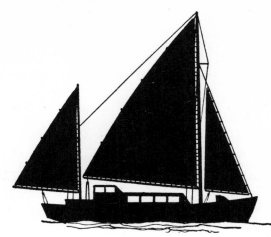

Motor Sailer

30' Navy Whale Boat

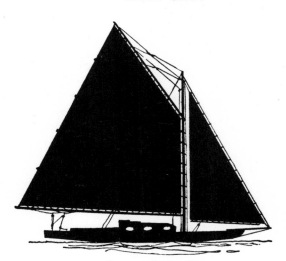

Seawanhaka Sloop

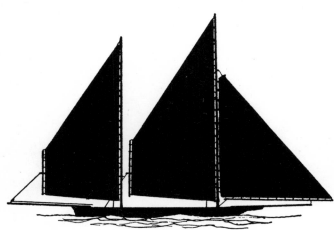

Chesapeake Bay Log Canoe

Chesapeake Bay Bugeye

Small Racing and
Pleasure Craft

These little boats are popular for afternoon racing
with youngsters and oldsters.

Racing Canoe

Open Canoe, Lateen Sail

Knockabout

Moth

Star

Snipe

Comet

Sneak Box

Dinghy

Dory

Some Racing Sloops and a Modern Cutter

The modern single-stickers are sharp-hulled and their rigs are narrow and high—everything inboard—which makes it easier for the crew to set sail in a blow. The cutter is a modern adaptation of an old-time model introduced here from England seventy years ago.

Cruising Cutter

30 Square Meter

Class R Sloop

Class Q Sloop

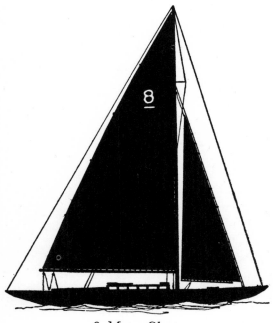

8 Meter Sloop

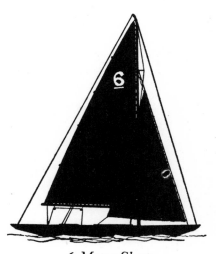

6 Meter Sloop

Some Club One-Design Classes

Here are a few examples of "one-design" class sloops which are sponsored by yacht clubs here and there about the land. The type shown is the fourth New York Yacht Club one-design class yacht, the former ones being the famous "30's," "40's," and "50's."

International One-Design

New York Y. C.

American Y. C. Bulldog

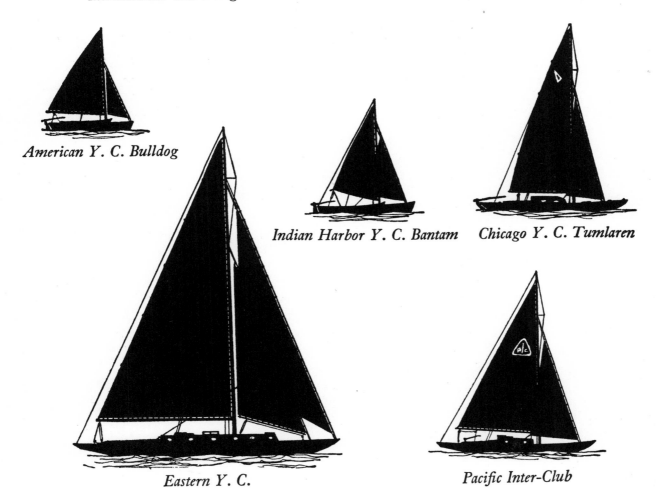

Indian Harbor Y. C. Bantam   Chicago Y. C. Tumlaren

Eastern Y. C.

Pacific Inter-Club

America's Cup
DEFENDERS

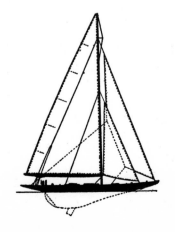

Introduction

EVER SINCE that memorable day at Cowes in August, 1851, when the schooner
yacht *America* threw consternation into the ranks of British yachtsmen, the
races for the *America's* Cup have been the outstanding spectacle of the yachting world, if not of the entire field of sport.

Many millions of dollars have been expended in the sixteen attempts to recapture
and retain the pewter mug. In the face of this fact alone the contests assume prime
importance. The great yachts that have contested through the years are the creations
of the finest talent in the field of naval architecture. With international honor at
stake, rivalry has been intense. Because some of the results appear to be one sided,
it does not mean that the runner-up was not fighting every inch of the way around
the course. He was!

Great credit must be given Sir Thomas Lipton, T. O. M. Sopwith, and the other
yachtsmen of Britain who tried so valiantly to take the cup back to their own
country.

Getting back to the *America*. She was built on the lines of a modified keel pilot
boat, no doubt because this was a more wholesome type in which to cross the
Atlantic. Also, her designer, George Steers, had some fast pilot boats to his credit.
In spite of *America* whaling the tar out of the British fleet, the subsequent trend in
yacht design was away from the keel pilot boat model and toward the shoal-draft
centerboard type, especially around New York. The following two *America's* Cup
winners were centerboarders, namely, *Magic* and *Columbia*. The schooner rig persisted on the defenders until 1881, however, when the sloop-rigged *Mischief* was
selected. Since then all of the yachts defending the Cup have been sloops. *Resolute*
was the last to use the old style gaff rig, in 1920, which gave way to the Marconi or
jib-headed rig on *Enterprise* in 1930. Incidentally, *Enterprise* came out with a lot of
labor-saving gadgets, a light duralumin mast and a new type of boom, flat on top
with an adjustable track for the foot of the mainsail.

The writer of this volume believes it will be of general interest to include drawings and data regarding the history and dimensions of the *America* and the subsequent defending yachts. The line drawings have been made to approximate scale,
enabling the reader to note the comparative sizes of the yachts, as well as showing
the changes in design and rig that have taken place down through the years.

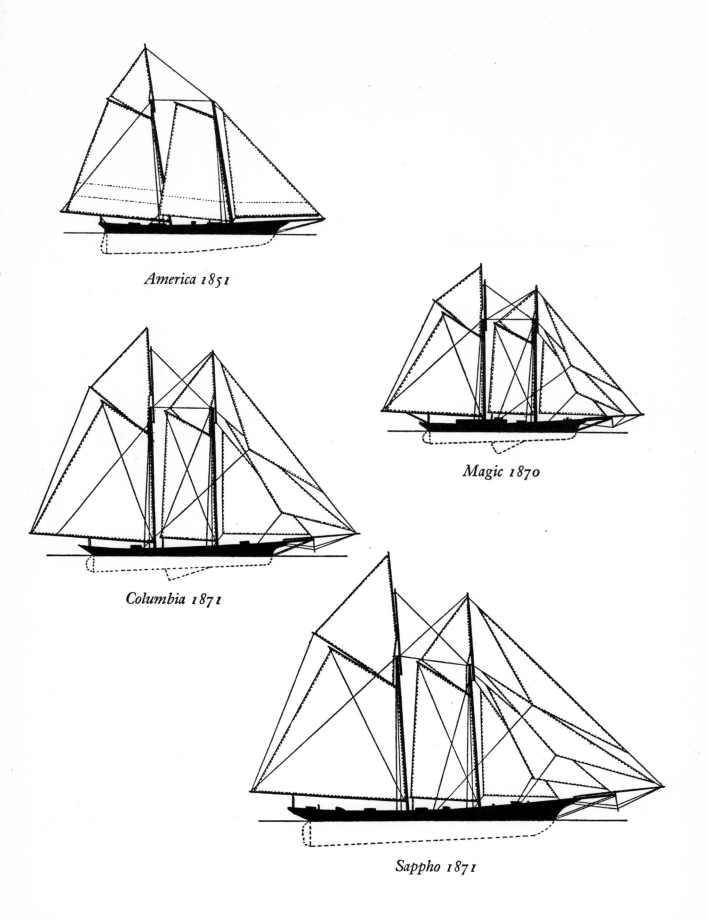

America 1851

Magic 1870

Columbia 1871

Sappho 1871

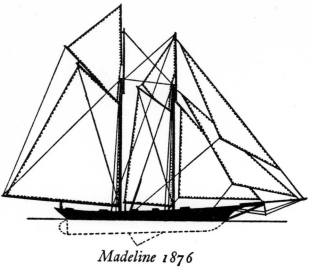

Madeline 1876

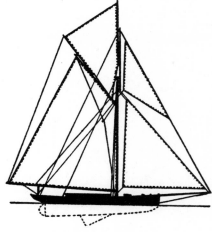

Mischief 1881

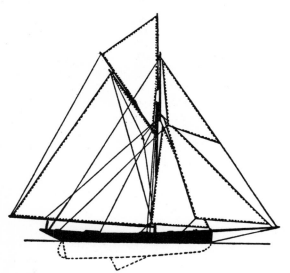

Puritan 1885

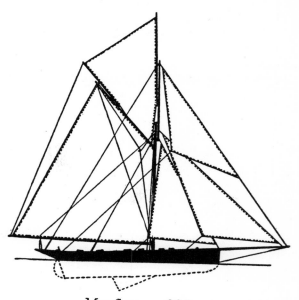

Mayflower 1886

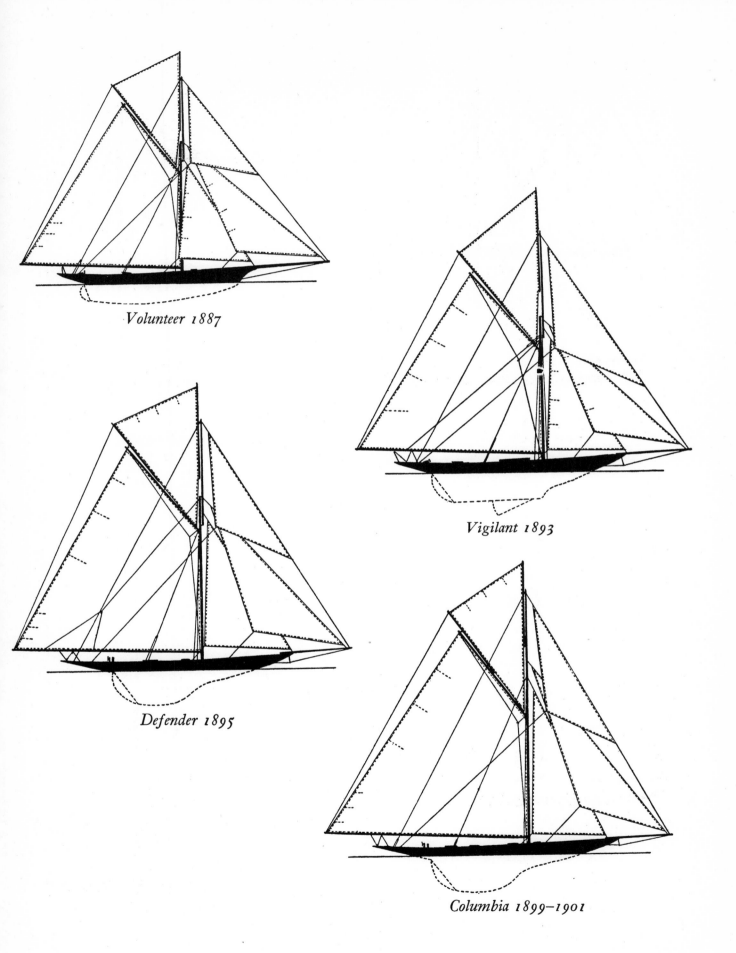

Volunteer 1887

Vigilant 1893

Defender 1895

Columbia 1899–1901

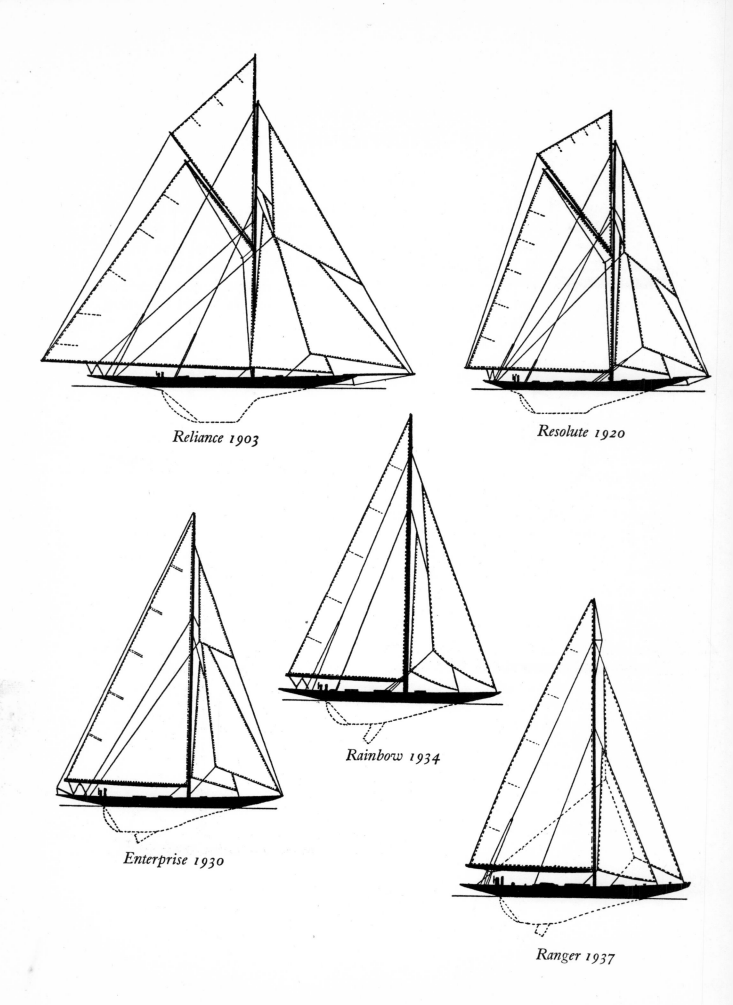

Reliance 1903

Resolute 1920

Rainbow 1934

Enterprise 1930

Ranger 1937

Their Histories in Brief

AMERICA

On August 22, 1851, the schooner-yacht *America* defeated a fleet of seventeen British schooners and cutters, ranging from 47 to 392 tons, in a 53-mile race from Cowes around the Isle of Wight, England. The trophy was called the "100 Guinea Cup," put up by the Royal Yacht Squadron. The cup has since been known as the *America's* Cup. The *Aurora* was second, the difference in finishing times of the two yachts being reported as eight minutes by some and eighteen minutes by others. *Bacchante* was third, *Eclipse* fourth, and *Brilliant* fifth.

The *America* is 101 feet long over-all, 90 feet 3 inches water-line length, 23 feet beam, 11 feet draft, with a sail area of 5,263 square feet. The length of the mainmast is 99 feet from deck to topsail halyard block. The greatest breadth is abaft the center of the length, the bow sharp with a hollow entrance and the dead rise great. The rig was that of the pilot boat of the time, with strongly raking masts, boomless foresail, mainsail with a boom, but loose-footed. She was the masterpiece of her designer, George Steers, who had brought the pilot boat to such a high state of perfection, and was built at the yard of William Brown, at the foot of East 12th Street, New York City, in 1851. The *America* was sailed by Commodore Stevens of the New York Yacht Club, which had been organized seven years previously.

After the Cowes race, the yacht was sold in England to Lord John de Blaquiere, who in turn sold her to Viscount Templeton in 1853. In 1859 she was renamed *Camilla*. Two years later a southerner of the United States purchased her and during the early years of the Civil War she was used as a Confederate blockade runner, finally being sunk in the St. John River, Florida, in 1862. The Union government salvaged her and used the yacht as a naval vessel for a few years. In 1870, *America* was one of the fleet that raced against the British contender for the *America's* Cup, *Cambria*, and finished fourth. Three years later she was purchased by General B. F. Butler, who rebuilt her. In 1917 the famous old yacht was bought by C. H. W. Foster, and was presented to the United States Naval Academy in 1921, where she now lies at a dock at Annapolis, Maryland. *America* was the only Cup Defender that returned a profit to the owners, a net return of $1,700 being divided after the sale of the yacht in 1851.

MAGIC

The second race for the *America's* Cup was sailed on August 8, 1870, from New York Upper Bay, through the Narrows, around Sandy Hook Light Vessel and return, a total distance of 38 miles. The British challenger, *Cambria*, was required to sail against the entire New York Yacht Club fleet, numbering twenty-three schooners and finished tenth, the schooner *Magic* winning the race in 4 hours 7 minutes 54 seconds. *Cambria* was 27 minutes 3 seconds behind *Magic*. *Idler* was second, *Silvie* third, and *America* fourth.

Magic was 79 feet long water line; 86 feet over-all; beam 20 feet 9 inches; draft 7 feet 2 inches; sail area about 5,000 square feet. The mainmast was 76 feet long, deck to topsail halyard block. She was built in 1857 as a centerboard sloop, changed to a schooner in 1859, and was completely rebuilt in 1869 at City Island, New York. She was designed by Richard F. Loper.

After *Magic's* racing career was ended, she served as a dispatch boat during the Spanish-American War. Later she was used as a pilot boat off Key West, Florida, and afterwards as a supply ship for a sponging fleet for many years. *Magic* was sunk in Key West during the hurricane of 1926, lay on the bottom until 1930, when she was towed out in the Gulf of Mexico and sunk.

COLUMBIA AND SAPPHO

The schooner *Columbia* defeated *Livonia*, the British challenger, in two out of three races in October, 1871, the series consisting of the best four out of seven races, *Columbia* being chosen for the first three races because of light winds, and *Sappho* for the fourth and fifth races. The latter defeated *Livonia*, a big 264-ton schooner, in both races, the fresh, reefing breeze being to *Sappho's* liking. The series ended in Mr. Ashbury, the owner of the *Livonia*, going home in a huff, claiming he had been treated unfairly as he had to sail against the whole fleet with his *Cambria* in 1870 and because of a disallowed protest when *Livonia* rounded a mark in the wrong direction. The course was 40 miles long off Sandy Hook.

Columbia was of the "skimming-dish" type and one of the fastest centerboard schooners ever built. She was designed by J. B. Van Deusen and built at Chester, Pennsylvania, in 1871. She was 112 feet long over-all, 98 feet 6 inches water-line length, 25 feet 6 inches beam, 5 feet 10 inches draft, with a sail area of 12,000 square feet. The mainmast was 107 feet 6 inches high, deck to topsail halyard block. After passing through many hands *Columbia* was dismantled in 1908 and lay on the stocks until 1911, when she was rebuilt and rerigged and was used as a house boat on Chesapeake Bay for about nine years. In 1920 she was sold to some fishermen, and to-day her whereabouts and fate are unknown.

Sappho was designed by William Townsend and was built in 1867 by C. and R. Poillon on speculation and was sent to England to be sold. As no purchaser was found, the big schooner was brought back to America, and after some alterations was considered the fastest keel yacht in America; also the largest. *Sappho* was 138 feet long over-all, 121 feet water-line length, 27 feet beam, 12 feet 10 inches draft, sail area about 15,000 square feet. Mainmast 121 feet 6 inches high, deck to topsail halyard block. She was broken up at Cowes, England, in 1887.

MADELEINE

The third challenge was made by Major Charles Gifford, whose centerboard schooner *Countess of Dufferin* sailed under the flag of the Royal Canadian Yacht Club. She was defeated by the *Madeleine*, which won the first two of three races easily. The series was sailed in August, 1876, over the Sandy Hook Light Ship course.

The *Madeleine* was 106 feet over-all, 91 feet on the water line, 24 feet beam, 7 feet 6 inches draft, with a sail area of 9,844 square feet. The mainmast was 106 feet, deck to topsail halyard block. She was built in 1869 as a sloop by David Kirby, of Rye, New York, and designed by J. B. Voorhis. She was changed to a schooner and her hull was altered in 1870, and again in 1871, after which she became one of the fastest centerboard schooners in the country. *Madeleine's* racing career ended in 1900 and she became a freight boat out of Tampa, Florida. After this she sank to the ignominious position as a supply boat for a sponge fishing fleet, as did her contemporary *Magic*. In 1907 she was stripped of her metal and usable parts, and finally went to pieces on a bank of the Hillsborough River in Florida.

MISCHIEF

The series of 1881 saw the end of the schooner in the races for the *America's* Cup. The Canadians again challenged, and the iron sloop *Mischief* was selected to defend the cup against the Canadian sloop *Atalanta*, owned by Captain Cuthbert and sailed by him. *Mischief* defeated the challenger easily in the first two races of a series of three. The first race was over the N. Y. Y. C. course; the second 16 miles to leeward from Buoy 5 and return.

Mischief was 67 feet 5 inches long over-all, 61 feet water-line length, 19 feet 10 inches beam, draft 5 feet, with a sail area of 6,953 square feet. Mast 99 feet, deck to top sail halyard block. Designed by A. Cary Smith and built in 1879 by Harlan and Hollingsworth, at Wilmington, Delaware. She was the second iron yacht to be built in this country and was narrower and deeper than the sloops of the time. Her rig resembled that of the English cutter. *Mischief* went off the yacht registry in 1909 and was used commercially for twenty years. On May 26th, 1929, she was towed out in the ocean and sunk off Boston Harbor.

In 1882 the deed of gift of the *America's* Cup was altered, barring any yacht club from challenging that was not located on salt water, requiring a challenger to sail on her own bottom to the port where the contest was to take place, and also that the holding club must defend the cup with but one vessel in all the races of a contest.

PURITAN

In the first race in the series of 1885 the cutter *Puritan* fouled the British cutter *Genesta* in the first race for the Cup, but the latter's owner sportingly refused to disqualify *Puritan*, and the race was sailed over on September 14th, the American vessel winning by 16 minutes 19 seconds corrected time. She also won the second contest by the close margin of 1 minute 38 seconds.

The *Puritan* was designed by Edward Burgess and was a compromise cutter. She was 94 feet long over-all, 81 feet 1½ inches long on the water line, beam 22 feet 7 inches, draft 8 feet 8 inches, with a sail area of 7,982 square feet. Mast 98 feet 6 inches, deck to topsail halyard block.

After the Cup races, *Puritan* was sold at auction and was raced continuously until 1890. In 1896 she was changed to a schooner, and in 1902 was sold, going to Marblehead, Massachusetts, where she remained until 1905. *Puritan* was broken up in 1925 at New Bedford, Massachusetts, after a commercial career of twenty years at this port.

MAYFLOWER

The sixth challenge was made by Lieutenant William Henn, Royal Navy, with his *Galatea*, sailing under the flag of the Royal Yacht Squadron. The American defender *Mayflower*, then the largest sloop in the country, defeated the *Galatea* in two races in September, 1886, the first by 12 minutes 2 seconds, and the second by 29 minutes 9 seconds.

The *Mayflower* was 100 feet long over-all, 85 feet 7 inches water-line length, beam 23 feet 6½ inches, draft 10 feet, sail area 8,634 square feet. Mast 105 feet 6 inches, deck to topsail halyard block. She was designed by Edward Burgess.

Mayflower was raced continuously until August, 1900, in the latter years with indifferent success. In 1889 she was changed to a schooner, and in 1894 was sold to William A. Gardner, of Boston, Massachusetts. She was flagship of the Eastern Yacht Club for three years. Her last owner had a motor installed in 1905, the only cup defender to have power.

In 1908 the *Mayflower* was chartered for a treasure hunt to the Bahamas and on this trip she was dismasted and abandoned.

VOLUNTEER

In 1887 the Scottish challenger *Thistle* was easily defeated by the *Volunteer* in two races. The *Volunteer* was 106 feet 3 inches long over-all, 85 feet 10 inches length water line, beam 23 feet 2 inches, draft 10 feet, with a sail area of 9,271 square feet. Mast 105 feet 6 inches, deck to topsail halyard block. Designed by Edward Burgess. The sloop *Thistle* sailed under the flag of the Royal Clyde Yacht Club.

Besides winning the *America's* Cup, *Volunteer* captured the Goelet Cup three times, Morgan, Boston *Herald*, Providence, and Newport cups, three squadron runs and a single trial race with the *Mayflower* during the period up to 1890. In 1891 Burgess lengthened her and made a schooner of her. Her final victory was on August 15, 1893, and her last race was in the Goelet cup race of August 2, 1895. During the next twelve years she was in commission only occasionally, and in 1909 Charles Barr, the old skipper, took her to New York from New London and she was broken up.

VIGILANT

The *Vigilant* was victorious in the 1893 series, defeating the challenger *Valkyrie II* of the Royal Yacht Squadron in three races, the first two easily, but the third was a hard-fought contest, sailed in a gale. The *Valkyrie II* was two minutes in the lead at the mark after a hard beat to windward, but while setting the huge spinnaker at the mark the sail was torn to ribbons in the heavy wind. *Vigilant* shook out her reefs, and setting a spinnaker in stops was able to overtake the Britisher near the finish line, and won the race by 40 seconds, corrected time. The first and third races were 15 miles to windward, and return, while the second race was over a 30-mile triangle.

Vigilant was 126 feet long over-all, 85 feet 4 inches water-line length, 26 feet beam, 13 feet 6 inches draft, with a sail area of 11,272 square feet. Mast 127 feet 6 inches, deck to topsail halyard block. She was designed by Nathaniel Herreshoff and was a deep centerboarder with a bronze hull.

Vigilant was in commission eleven seasons after defeating the *Valkyrie II*, during which time she started in 89 races, winning only 36. In 1894 she was sailed to England and her showing there was disappointing, for *Brittania* defeated her in 12 out of 17 races. On July 30, 1895, *Vigilant* established a speed record for major American sailing yachts, logging an average of 13¾ knots for 64 miles. She sailed the last race on August 13, 1909, from Rockland, Maine, to Bar Harbor, and was sold to a wrecking company in New London, Connecticut, in 1910 and broken up.

In 1887 a new deed of gift was drawn up, requiring the challenger to give ten months' notice, giving at that time the name, rig, and dimensions of the challenging yacht.

DEFENDER

Lord Dunraven's *Valkyrie III* was the tenth challenger in 1895 and was defeated by *Defender*, the series being sailed over the 30-mile course off Sandy Hook. At the start of the second race *Valkyrie III* fouled the *Defender* and was disqualified, both yachts sailing the course, the latter being beaten by 2 minutes 18 seconds actual time. Dunraven refused to sail the third race and *Defender* merely sailed around the course and won on default.

The American sloop was Herreshoff designed, 124 feet 2 inches long over-all, 88 feet 5 inches water-line length, 23 feet 3 inches beam, 19 feet draft, with a sail area of 12,602 square feet. Mast 127 feet 6 inches from deck to topsail halyard block. Her frame was steel, bottom bronze, and topsides aluminum. She was broken up in City Island, New York, in 1901.

COLUMBIA

Sir Thomas Lipton made the eleventh challenge for the Cup in 1899 with the *Shamrock*, designed by Fife. She was beaten by *Columbia*, a fine Herreshoff-designed sloop in three straight races. In the second race, however, *Shamrock's* club topsail gave way during a close fight and she was forced to withdraw.

Columbia was 131 feet 8 inches over-all, 89 feet 8 inches water-line length, 24 feet 2 inches beam, 19 feet 6 inches draft, with a sail area of 13,135 square feet. Mast 139 feet 6 inches, deck to topsail halyard block. She had a fin keel.

In 1901 *Columbia* was again the defender against Lipton's *Shamrock II*, defeating the challenger in three closely contested races, the finishes being the closest of any Cup series. *Columbia* won the first race by 1 minute 20 seconds, the second by 3 minutes 35 seconds, and the third by 41 seconds.

Columbia was on stocks for many years at City Island, New York, and was finally scrapped in 1913.

RELIANCE

In 1903 Lipton made his third try for the *America's* Cup with *Shamrock III*. The huge, extreme, bronze *Reliance* was the victor in three straight races over a windward and leeward, and a triangular course of 30 miles off Sandy Hook, the *Shamrock III* missing the finish line in a fog in the last race and so did not finish.

The *Reliance* was 143 feet long over-all, 84 feet 6 inches water-line length, 25 feet 10 inches beam, 19 feet 9 inches draft, with a sail area of 15,780 square feet. Mast 154 feet, deck to topsail halyard block. She carried 2,000 square feet more of sail than the *Shamrock III* and had to allow the latter 1 minute 57 seconds in time. The mainsail of the *Reliance* was the largest ever spread by any vessel. She was the most costly of all the Cup defenders.

During the 146-day period, from the time she was launched until the day after the 1903 series was over, *Reliance* started in 23 races, winning 20, being beaten in two on time allowance by the *Constitution*, and withdrawing in a third with a broken topmast. She was broken up in 1913 at South Brooklyn, New York.

After the 1903 series, the measurement rule was changed from the "water line-sail area" rule to the present "universal rule," in order to produce a less extreme and more wholesome type of hull.

RESOLUTE

In 1920 the *Resolute* was selected to defend the Cup after trial races with *Vanitie*, a Gardner-designed boat, and *Defiance*, turned out by George Owen. Sir Thomas Lipton made his fourth challenge with the *Shamrock IV*, which came closer to winning the *America's* Cup than any foreign yacht thus far. She did not conform to the "universal rule," being more of a Seawanhaka type, but was measured under the former. The *Shamrock IV* took the first two races, the first one after *Resolute* withdrew with a parted throat halyard. This was the first time an American yacht failed to finish. *Resolute* lived up to her name, however, and took the next three races by the following corrected times: 7 minutes 1 second; 9 minutes 58 seconds; and 19 minutes 45 seconds.

Resolute was designed by Francis Herreshoff and sailed by Charles Francis Adams. She is 106 feet 1½ inches long over-all, 75 feet water-line length, 21 feet 1½ inches beam, 13 feet 8½ inches draft, with a sail area of 8,775 square feet. Mast 129 feet ½ inch, deck to topsail halyard block. Her original rig was that of a gaff-rigged sloop, under which she sailed in the Cup series. She was changed to a staysail schooner in 1926, and in 1920 to 1931 she sailed as a Marconi-rigged cutter.

Resolute is now laid up at Herreshoff's yard at Bristol, Rhode Island.

ENTERPRISE

Enterprise was the first Marconi-rigged sloop to defend the *America's* Cup. She was selected after a series of trial races with *Whirlwind*, *Weetamoe*, and *Yankee*, as she was a fine, light-weather boat, as was the challenger *Shamrock V*, and the best of the four in beating to windward.

In the four races against Lipton's *Shamrock V*, held over 30-mile courses off Newport, Rhode Island, in 1930, *Enterprise*, sailed by Harold Vanderbilt, was victorious. She was 120 feet 9 inches long over-all, 80 feet water-line length, 22 feet 1 inch beam, 14 feet 6 inches draft, with a sail area of 7,583 square feet. Mast 152 feet 6 inches, deck to topsail halyard block.

Her racing career was only three months long, in which time she won 18 races and lost 9, including the four with the *Shamrock V*. A few days after the Cup series she was laid up at Herreshoff's yard at Bristol and was broken up in 1935. She was designed by Starling Burgess, built by Herreshoff Manufacturing Company, and launched April 14, 1930. In the final race of the series *Enterprise* broke the record established by *Columbia* in the *America's* Cup race of 1901, sailing the 30-mile course in 3 hours 10 minutes 13 seconds, at an average speed of 9.45 knots.

RAINBOW

Mr. T. O. M. Sopwith challenged in 1934 with his *Endeavour*, a beautiful, steel, Marconi-rigged sloop, designed by Charles Nicholson. She was sailed by her owner under the colors of the Royal Yacht Squadron. *Rainbow* was selected after trial races with *Weetamoe* and *Yankee*.

Six races were sailed beginning September 17, 1934, off Newport, Rhode Island, three over a windward and leeward course, and three over a triangular course, both being 30 miles. *Endeavour* took the first two races, the first by a margin of 2 minutes 9 seconds, and the second by 51 seconds, both sloops breaking the Cup race record established by *Enterprise* four years before. *Endeavour's* time was 3 hours 9 minutes 1 second, which was 1 minute 12 seconds better than the old record. However, *Rainbow* came through magnificently, under the superb handling of Harold Vanderbilt, and his after guard, and won the next four contests, winning the third race by 3 minutes 26 seconds; the fourth by 1 minute 15 seconds; the fifth by 4 minutes 1 second; and the sixth and last race by 55 seconds.

The 1934 series was the longest and one of the bitterest in the history of *America's* Cup racing. *Endeavour* was conceded to be the faster boat, but the *Rainbow* won by superior headwork on the part of her skipper and by errors in judgment and handling on board the *Endeavour*.

Rainbow was designed by W. Starling Burgess and built by the Herreshoff Manufacturing Company, at Bristol, Rhode Island. She is 126.57 feet over-all, 82 feet water-line length; 20.92 feet beam; 14.93 feet draft; 7,655 square feet of sail area, and of 138.7 tons' displacement. *Endeavour* is somewhat larger than her rival, being 130 feet long over-all; 83 feet water-line length; 22 feet beam; 15 feet draft, with a sail area of 7,550 square feet and a displacement of 143 tons, the minimum weight allowed for a Class "J" vessel of 83 feet water line.

During the fourteen weeks of *Rainbow's* competitive racing, she started in 36 races, won 19 and lost 15, failing to finish in 2, the lowest percentage ever made by a Cup defender. In 1935 Mr. Vanderbilt purchased *Rainbow* from the syndicate, then sold her to Commodore Chandler Hovey of the Eastern Yacht Club, who sailed her in the trial races of 1937 against *Yankee* and *Ranger*, the latter being selected to defend the Cup.

There were two radical changes in rules in 1934. First, the boats had to have cabin accommodations, with no gear below decks, and, second, the mast could not be below a minimum weight, center of gravity, and width of cross section. The "universal rule" still held.

RANGER

Mr. Sopwith again challenged in 1937 with his *Endeavour II*. Harold Vanderbilt's *Ranger* was selected over *Rainbow* and *Yankee* to defend the Cup and came through with four, straight, decisive victories over the British yacht. *Ranger's* margin of time in the first race on July 31st over the 30-mile windward and leeward course, off Newport, Rhode Island, was 17 minutes 5 seconds.

In the second race, over a triangular course, *Endeavour II* was beaten even more severely, *Ranger* coming in 18 minutes 32 seconds ahead.

The third race, windward and leeward, was closer, *Ranger* nosing out her rival by the less embarrassing margin of 4 minutes 27 seconds, setting a new *America's* Cup record by sailing the fastest 15-mile windward leg in 2 hours 3 minutes 55 seconds. The fourth and last race was the closest, *Ranger* winning by 3 minutes 37 seconds and setting a new course record, bettering the previous record for the 30-mile triangular course set by *Endeavour I* in 1934 by 1 minute 12 seconds. Her elapsed time was 3 hours 7 minutes 49 seconds.

The clean sweep of the 1937 series and the winning of the last four races in 1934 gave Mr. Vanderbilt eight straight victories over Mr. Sopwith, and he also had the distinction of being the first amateur yachtsman to defend the *America's* Cup successfully three times.

Ranger is the largest Class "J" yacht ever built, exceeding *Endeavour II* somewhat in over-all length and displacement. At this writing *Ranger's* complete dimensions are not available, but it is known that her water-line length is 87 feet, the maximum for Class "J" yachts, while she is 135 feet long over-all, 15 feet draft, centerboard up, beam 20 feet plus. She was designed by W. Starling Burgess, assisted by Sparkman and Stephens.

THE RACES SUMMARIZED

Year	Yacht	Rig	Yacht Club	Result	Challenger
1851	*America*	Schooner	New York	Won against 14 British yachts at Cowes, England.	
1870	*Magic*	Schooner	New York	First	
	Cambria	Schooner	Royal Thames	Tenth	James Asbury
1871	*Columbia*	Schooner	New York	Won 2	
	Sappho	Schooner	New York	Won 2	
	Livonia	Schooner	Royal Harwich	Won 1	James Asbury
1876	*Madeleine*	Schooner	New York	Won 2	
	Countess of Dufferin	Schooner	Royal Canadian		Major Chas. Gifford
1881	*Mischief*	Sloop	New York	Won 2	
	Atalanta	Sloop	Bay of Quinte		Captain Cuthbert
1885	*Puritan*	Sloop	New York	Won 2	
	Genesta	Cutter	Royal Yacht Squadron		Sir Richard Sutton
1886	*Mayflower*	Sloop	New York	Won 2	
	Galatea	Cutter	Royal Northern		Lieutenant Wm. Renn, R.N.
1887	*Volunteer*	Sloop	New York	Won 2	
	Thistle	Cutter	Royal Clyde		James Bell
1893	*Vigilant*	Sloop	New York	Won 3	
	Valkyrie II	Cutter	Royal Yacht Squadron		Lord Dunraven
1895	*Defender*	Sloop	New York	Won 3	
	Valkyrie III	Cutter	Royal Yacht Squadron	Withdrew 3d race	Lord Dunraven
1899	*Columbia*	Sloop	New York	Won 3	
	Shamrock	Cutter	Royal Ulster		Sir Thomas Lipton
1901	*Columbia*	Sloop	New York	Won 3	
	Shamrock II	Cutter	Royal Ulster		Sir Thomas Lipton
1903	*Reliance*	Sloop	New York	Won 3	
	Shamrock III	Cutter	Royal Ulster		Sir Thomas Lipton
1920	*Resolute*	Sloop	New York	Won 3	
	Shamrock IV	Cutter	Royal Ulster	Won 2	Sir Thomas Lipton
1930	*Enterprise*	Sloop	New York	Won 4	
	Shamrock V	Cutter	Royal Ulster		Sir Thomas Lipton
1934	*Rainbow*	Sloop	New York	Won 4	
	Endeavour	Sloop	Royal Yacht Squadron	Won 2	T. O. M. Sopwith
1937	*Ranger*	Sloop	New York	Won 4	
	Endeavour II	Sloop	Royal Yacht Squadron		T. O. M. Sopwith

SAILS
and
RIGGING

Introduction

WHEN THE SAIL first came into use is unknown, but we do know, from carvings and wall decorations on ancient tombs and temples, that over 4,000 years ago the Egyptians were using a simple square sail, with a yard along the top and bottom, to propel their craft before the wind. If the breeze came from an unfavorable quarter oars or sweeps supplanted the sail.

The Phoenicians were excellent sailors and they, too, employed the single square sail as auxiliary motive power, dispensing with the lower yard, however. The Greeks and Romans learned from the Phoenicians and improved the rig by adding a triangular topsail, not unlike the "raffee" of the present day, reefed by means of a "bonnet"; and also employed a raking spar similar to the bowsprit from which was hung an "artemon." From this latter innovation the later spritsail was descended. Furling was done by means of vertical brails and this method has continued in use on square-rigged ships up to the present with a few minor changes and additions. The Romans also employed lanyards reeved through deadeyes for setting up the shrouds. This, too, has remained through the centuries. For several hundreds of years after the disintegration of the Roman Empire in the third and fourth centuries, with the attendant loss of the marine, sail-making and boat-building were at somewhat of a standstill in Western Europe. True, the hardy Norsemen were making voyages across the North Atlantic and the seas of Northern Scandinavia, but they contributed little to the betterment of sails, though they certainly knew their naval architecture when it came to hull design. In the meantime, however, the seafaring peoples of the Mediterranean had been developing the lateen sail and it probably was in general use on this inland sea by the 12th century. The Moors are supposed to have introduced this rig to the mariners of Northwestern Europe. A combination of square and lateen sails is known to have been used by the Venetians as early as the 13th century.

About the middle of the 15th century things began to happen. Ships became larger and with bigger hulls more driving power was needed. As a single sail of sufficient area to do the work was too unwieldy, additional masts and topmasts were added, each carrying smaller pieces of canvas. On most of the commercial vessels sail alone was relied upon for propulsion, but the oars had been retained by the galleys and galleasses of the Mediterranean.

The bowsprit and spritsail again came into use, the latter enduring until well into the 19th century. Even the clipper ships of the 1850's and '60's often carried a "Jamie Green," which was in reality a spritsail. Early in the 16th century the triangular jib came into being. It was probably invented by the Dutch, who were also responsible for the fore-and-aft mainsail. The peak of this sail was extended by a diagonal sprit. This spar eventually was raised and shortened, laced to the head of the sail and became the gaff. Hence, the sloop rig. The adoption of the fore-and-aft sail was gradual, even though it was found that it enabled a vessel to point closer into the wind.

For three centuries square-rigged ships carried a lateen sail on the mizzenmast. The forward portion of this mizzen sail was gradually cut down until it became a fore-and-aft sail. For some reason, the fore end of the lateen yard was still retained until about 1765 when it gave way to the gaff. This sail was known as a driver, mizzen course, and finally as a spanker.

The square rig reached its highest development during the American and British clipper-ship era. The big demand at that time was for speed and the sail plans became loftier and loftier, reaching dizzy heights. In the 18th century "stuns'ls" came into being to increase the sail area when running before the wind.

Early in the 18th century an additional mast was added to the sloop and the American schooner was born. Toward the end of this century experiments were made with a three-masted schooner and in two decades or so they became quite popular. As time went on longer hulls of greater capacity were needed and more masts were added to the schooner. The ketch rig was developed in Europe considerably earlier than the schooner. It was used to quite an extent in the navies of the western European nations, but was never really popular commercially in America. Other combinations of square and fore-and-aft sails were made to form such rigs as the brig, brigantine, hermaphrodite brig, topsail schooner, bark, barkentine, etc.

The lugsail was introduced in Western Europe some time during the 16th century, probably in the latter half. It was fast and efficient, and was used extensively on fishing boats of England and France until replaced by power. It is still to be seen here and there in European waters, however. The battened lugsail of the Chinese has been in use by these people since time immemorial and it was probably brought to the western countries in a modified form by the early explorers and voyagers.

The invention of chain about 1820 and of wire rope some years later was a boon to the sailor, as it eliminated the continual back-breaking work of setting up stretched stays and shrouds.

The present "Marconi" or jib-headed sail, the forerunner of which was the Bermuda rig, is the highest and most efficient development of the sloop. It was evolved for and is used almost exclusively on sailing yachts.

In spite of the old-time sailor's antipathy for change and improvement, the last 450 years have seen greater achievement in the science of sailing than in all the centuries before. The evolution of sail was an extremely slow process. While very brief and sketchy, the foregoing history may give the reader a general idea of what has transpired in the development of the sail. The drawings on the ensuing pages will give a detailed picture of the sails and rigs used on the various types of vessels illustrated and described elsewhere in this volume.

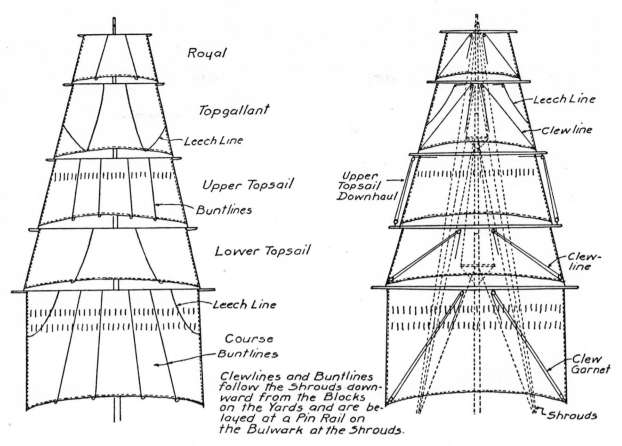

Royal

Topgallant

Leech Line

Upper Topsail

Buntlines

Lower Topsail

Leech Line

Course
Buntlines

Clewlines and Buntlines
follow the Shrouds down-
ward from the Blocks
on the Yards and are be-
layed at a Pin Rail on
the Bulwark at the Shrouds.

*The Forward Side of the Sails Showing
Buntlines and Leech Lines*

Leech Line

Clewline

Upper
Topsail
Downhaul

Clew-
line

Clew
Garnet

Shrouds

*The After Side of the Sails Showing
Clewlines and Downhaul*

The Square Sails of a Ship *(after 1855)*

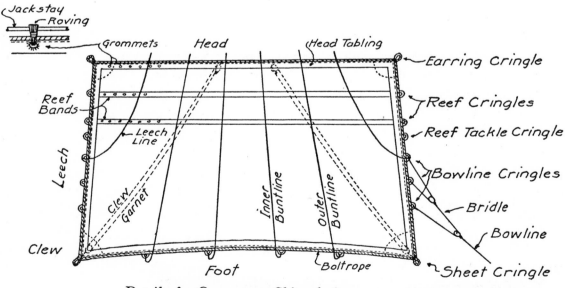

Jackstay

Roving

Grommets

Head

Head Tabling

Earring Cringle

Reef
Bands

Leech
Line

Reef Cringles

Reef Tackle Cringle

Bowline Cringles

Leech

Clew
Garnet

Inner
Buntline

Outer
Buntline

Bridle

Bowline

Clew

Foot

Boltrope

Sheet Cringle

Detail of a Course on a Ship of 1800

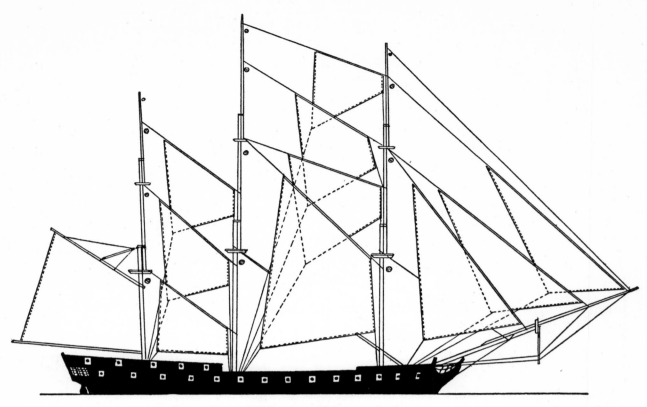

Staysails and Jibs on a Frigate of 1800

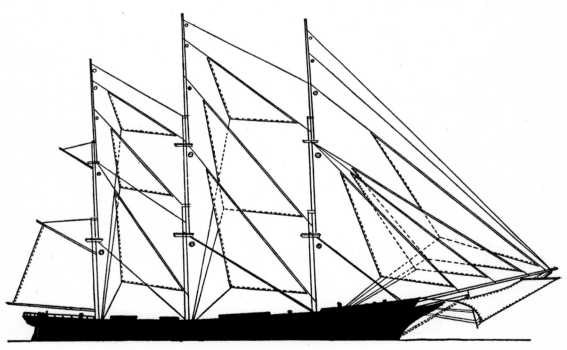

*Staysails, Jibs and "Jamie Green" on a
Clipper of 1853*

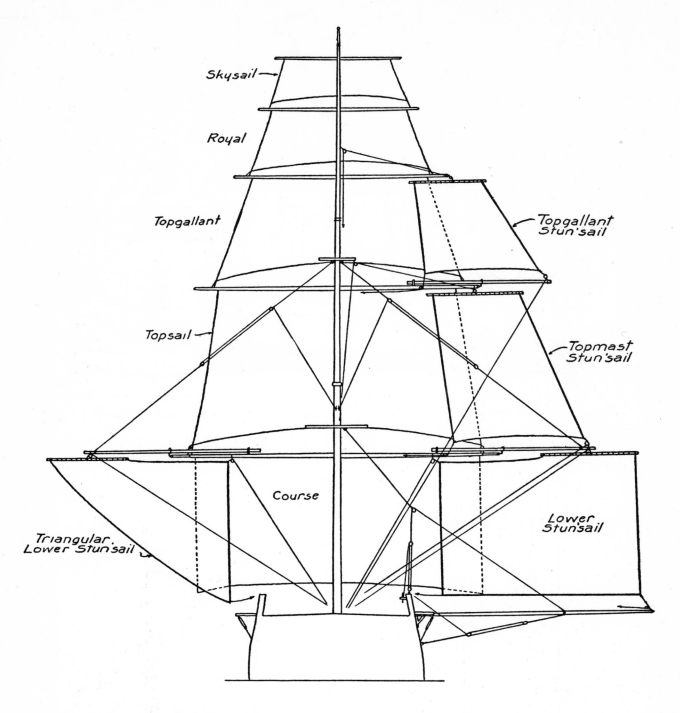

*Diagram Showing Studding Sails (Stun'sails) and
Their Rigging (Looking Forward)*

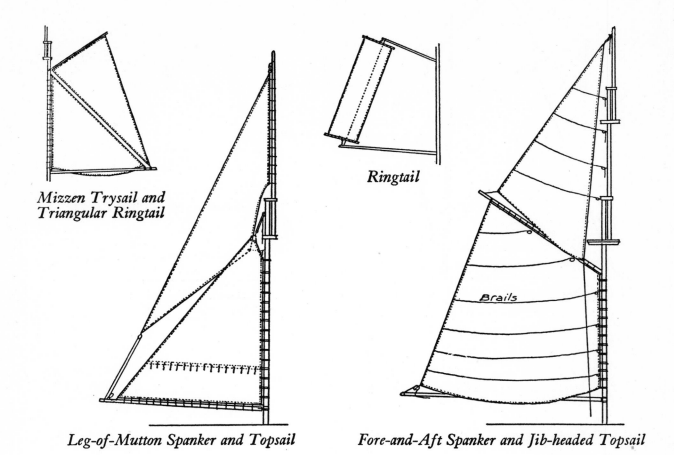

*Mizzen Trysail and
Triangular Ringtail*

Ringtail

Leg-of-Mutton Spanker and Topsail

Fore-and-Aft Spanker and Jib-headed Topsail

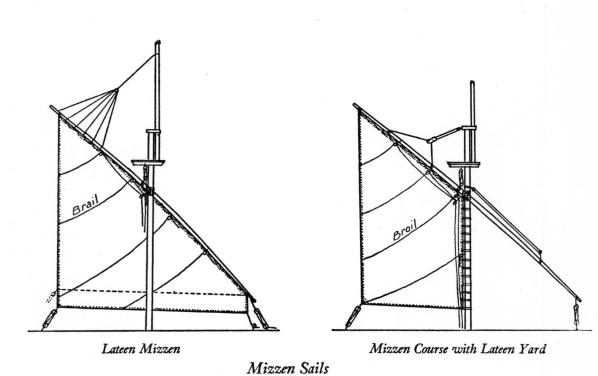

Lateen Mizzen

Mizzen Course with Lateen Yard

Mizzen Sails

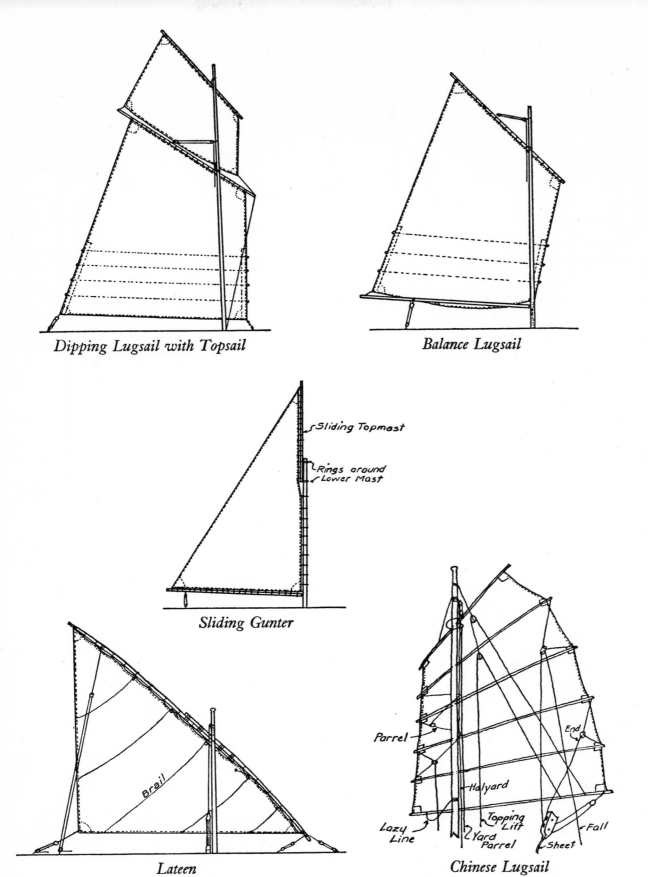

Dipping Lugsail with Topsail

Balance Lugsail

Sliding Topmast

Rings around
Lower Mast

Sliding Gunter

Brail

Lateen

Parrel

End

Halyard

Topping
Lift

Lazy
Line

Yard
Parrel

Sheet

Fall

Chinese Lugsail

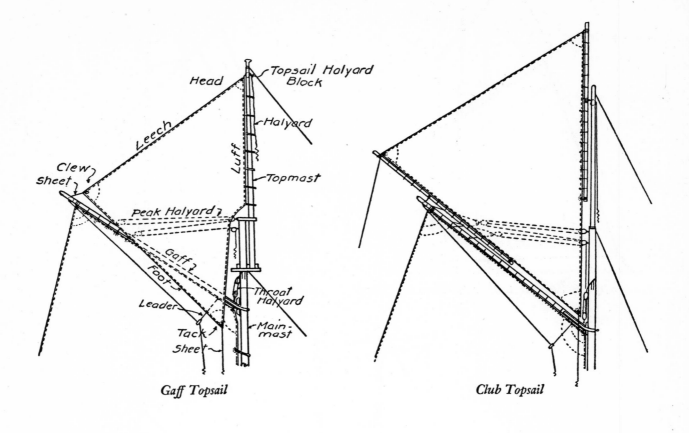

Gaff Topsail

Club Topsail

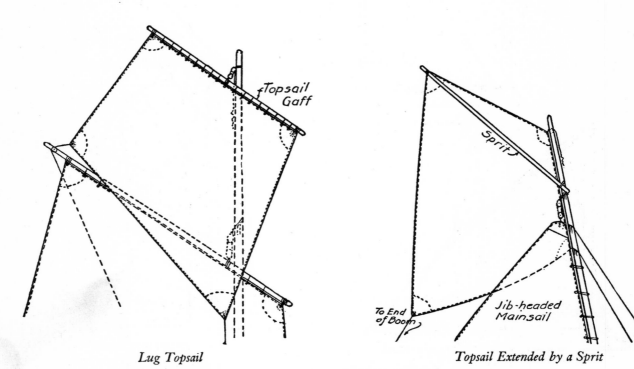

Lug Topsail

Topsail Extended by a Sprit

Fore-and-Aft Topsails

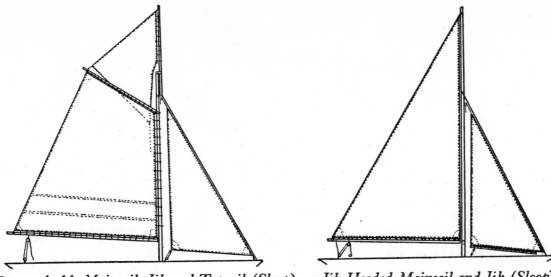

Fore-and-Aft Mainsail, Jib and Topsail (Sloop)   *Jib-Headed Mainsail and Jib (Sloop)*

Spritsail   *Leg-of-Mutton*

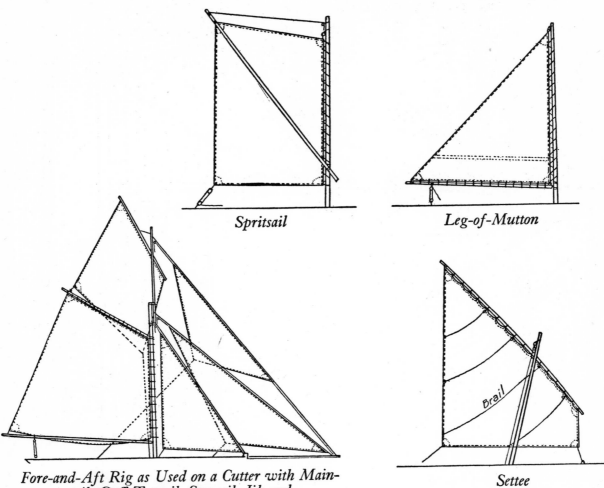

Fore-and-Aft Rig as Used on a Cutter with Main-sail, Gaff-Topsail, Staysail, Jib and Jib Topsail

Brail

Settee

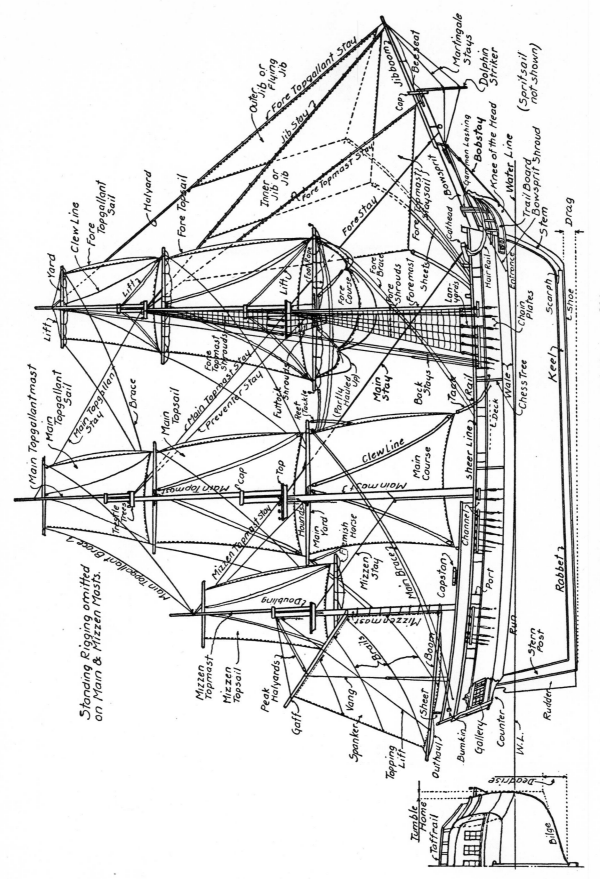

Profile and Sail Plan of a Late 18th Century Ship

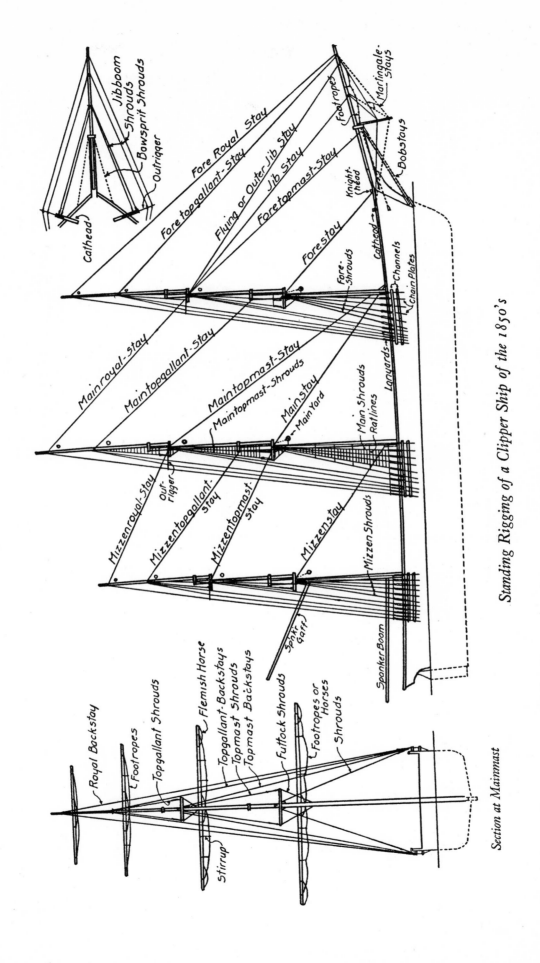

Standing Rigging of a Clipper Ship of the 1850's

Section at Mainmast

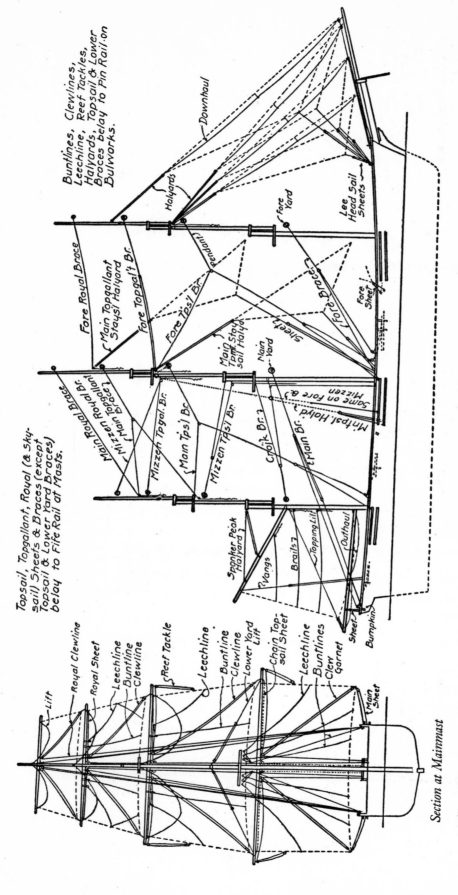

Running Rigging of a Clipper Ship of the 1850's

Buntlines, Clewlines, Leechline, Reef Tackles, Halyards, Topsail & Lower Braces belay to Pin Rail on Bulwarks.

Topsail, Topgallant, Royal (& Sky-sail) Sheets & Braces (except Topsail & Lower Yard Braces) belay to Fife Rail at Masts.

Downhaul

Halyards

Fore Yard

Lee Head Sail Sheets

Fore Royal Brace

Main Topgallant Stays'l Halyard

Fore Topgal't Br.

Fore Tops'l Br.

Pendant

Fore Brace

Fore Sheet

Fore Royal Brace

Main Royal Brace

Main Royal Br. { Main Brace }

Mizzen Topgallant

Mizzen Tpgal. Br.

Main Tps'l Br.

Main Stay Tpt'l sail Halyd

Main Stay sail Halyd

Main Yard

Sheet

Mizzen Tps'l Br.

Mnt'pst Halyd Same on Fore & Mizzen

Crojik Br.?

{ Main Br.

Spanker-Peak Halyard

Vangs

Brails

Topping Lift

Outhaul

Sheet

Bumpkin

Section at Mainmast

Lift

Royal Clewline

Royal Sheet

Leechline

Buntline

Clewline

Reef Tackle

Leechline

Buntline

Clewline

Lower Yard Lift

Chain Top-sail Sheet

Leechline

Buntlines

Clew Garnet

Main Sheet

A Glossary of Sails

ARTEMON   A sail used on Roman ships. It was rectangular in shape, similar to a spritsail, and set from a mast that was raked to a sharp angle over the bow.

BALANCE LUG   See "lugsail."

BALLOON JIB   A large triangular headsail of light material, with a wide foot, used on yachts and "fishermen" in light weather when the wind is abaft the beam.

BENTINCK   A triangular course used on square-rigged ships.

BERMUDA SAIL   A fore-and-aft sail, sometimes so-called because of its great hoist, narrow head, and broad foot. It has much rake aft.

BEZAAN SAIL   A fore-and-aft sail of the 18th century, with a boom and a very short gaff.

BONAVENTURE   The mizzensail carried on the after mast of a four-masted vessel in the Middle Ages.

BONNET   A long, narrow, rectangular piece of sailcloth laced to the bottom of a sail to increase the area and removed to shorten the sail. This method was used before reef points were employed to shorten sail.

BOOM SAIL   When a boom was added to the 18th century "mizzen course" it was known as a "boom sail" or "driver boom sail."

CLUB TOPSAIL   A triangular topsail used above a fore-and-aft mainsail, being bent along its foot and luff to two spars, called clubs, which extend beyond the gaff and topmast.

COURSE   The square sail set from the lower yard of a square-rigged vessel.

CRAB-CLAW   An Oceanic lateen sail, resembling the claw of a crab in shape, made of matting and supported between two curved yards. See illustration of "orou" on page 85.

CROSSJACK   The square sail sometimes hung from the lowest yard on the mizzen-mast of a full-rigged ship.

DADDLER   Another name for "mizzen."

DIPPING LUG   See "lugsail."

DRABBLER	An additional strip of sail cloth laced to the bottom of the "bonnet" to increase the area. Common in the Middle Ages.
DRIVER	Similar to a "ringtail." Sometimes the term "driver" was used to mean a "spanker." Also the after mast on a six-masted schooner.
FISHERMAN STAYSAIL	A quadrilateral sail set between the mainmast and foremast of a schooner.
FLYING JIB	The outer headsail whose tack is set to the jib boom or flying jib boom.
FORE-AND-AFT SAIL	A sail set from a vertical mast or stay, the normal position being fore-and-aft or parallel to the keel.
FORESAIL	On a schooner, the fore-and-aft sail set from the foremast. On a square-rigger, the square sail hung from the lowest yard on the foremast.
FORETOPMAST STAYSAIL	The jib-shaped sail that sets from the foretopmast stay, the first headsail forward of the foremast.
GAFF TOPSAIL	A triangular sail set from a topmast, the clew sheeted to the outer end of the gaff of a fore-and-aft mainsail or lower sail, the sheet from the tack leading to the deck.
GENOA JIB	A reaching jib used on racing yachts.
GRETA GARBO	A nickname given to a quadrilateral jib with two clews and two sheets. A present-day sail used on racing yachts.
HOY SAIL	A tall high-peaked spritsail used on English barges of the 17th century. Vangs were often used.
INNER JIB	The headsail first forward from the foretopmast staysail.
JAMIE GREEN	A sail used on the clipper ships, set beneath the bowsprit and jib boom. It was used mainly when sailing to windward. The halyard hauled the sail to the end of the jib boom and the tack led to the lower end of the martingale boom or dolphin striker. It was sheeted by means of a pendant to the fore-rigging and a whip to the forecastle head. It was cut the same as a topgallant-studding sail, but was longer on the hoist.
JIB	A triangular sail set forward of the foremast, usually from a stay, the tack or lower corner leading to the bowsprit or jib boom. Jibs came into use in the middle of the 18th century and gradually displaced the spritsail.
JIB-HEADED RIG	A rig in which all the sails are triangular.

JIB-O-JIB	A jib set on the fore-topgallant or fore-royal stay. Sometimes set as a jib topsail.
JIB TOPSAIL	A jib set on the outer head stay, the tack being well above the bowsprit or jib boom; usually smaller than other headsails.
LATEEN SAIL	A triangular sail extended by a long yard hung from a mast used chiefly on Mediterranean craft and also on early ships, such as caravels, etc. The yard is in two or more parts, according to length, and is spliced together. It is hoisted by a halyard, usually on the port side, which passes in two parts through a double block at the masthead. A fourfold block is secured to, and some distance above, the deck, and just abaft the mast. A peak halyard takes some of the weight off the yard and peaks it to the required angle. The set of the sail is actually controlled by a heavy tack purchase at the lower end of the yard and by the main sheet. When running free, the tack purchase is let out and the sheet eased way forward, the yard laying athwartships.
LEG-OF-MUTTON	A triangular mainsail used usually on small boats, the upper corner hoisting.
LUGSAIL	A form of fore-and-aft sail bent to a yard or gaff which is slung from one-quarter to one-third of its length forward of the mast. The end of the halyard is usually fastened to an iron hoop, or traveler, which keeps the yard to the mast. The sail is set taut upon its luff rope, which is swayed up so as to stand rigid. It is much used by European fishermen, being simple, and requiring little rigging. *Balance Lug*—A lugsail which is laced to a boom at the foot and has its tack at the mast. This type of lug requires no dipping. *Dipping Lug*—When the tack of a lugsail is made fast at some distance forward of the mast, the sail always has to be hoisted on the lee side of the mast to get best results from it, and, therefore, it must be "dipped" on each new tack and hoisted on the new lee side. *Standing Lug*—When the tack is fastened at the mast it is not necessary to "dip" on each new tack, but the sail is left standing as the mast does not interfere with its set. *Chinese Lug*—Balance lugsails which are extended by battens between the upper and lower yards. The sail is controlled by sheets extending from the outer ends of these battens.
LUG TOPSAIL	A quadrilateral sail set above the mainsail of a lug-rigged vessel, with a gaff along the head, hoisted to a topmast. The gaff extends a short distance forward of the topmast, as in the case of the lug mainsail.

[263]

The clew is sheeted to the outer or after end of the main gaff and the tack sheet leads to the deck. The topsail gaff sets obliquely. While employed most frequently with the lug rig, the lug topsail was also used on 18th century fore-and-afters.

MARCONI RIG	A modern rig with a lofty triangular mainsail and a short boom, with one or two headsails. It is descended from the leg-of-mutton Bermuda rig.
MIZZEN	The sail carried on the after mast of a yawl or ketch or the third mast of a "ship."
MIZZEN COURSE	In the 18th century the fore-and-aft sail suspended either from a lateen yard or gaff on the mizzenmast of a ship. It had no boom.
MOONRAKER	A triangular sail set from the truck and to the yardarms of the highest yard. A "raffee."
MOONSAIL	A sail sometimes carried above the skysail on a square-rigged ship.
OCEANIC LATEEN	A lateen sail made of matting or other material laced between two yards. It is used in certain of the Pacific Islands. See illustration of "thamakau" on page 77.
OCEANIC SPRITSAIL	A sail of various shapes made of matting, etc., supported between sprits, used on canoes of a number of Pacific Islands.
PARACHUTE SPINNAKER	A large spinnaker with a short boom which inflates like a balloon.
RAFFEE	A triangular sail hung from the truck and bent to the yardarms of the highest yard.
REACHING JIB	A large triangular head sail of light material used on yachts and "fishermen" in light weather, when the wind is just forward of abeam.
RINGTAIL	An addition to the after side of a "spanker." Used extensively on clipper ships. If the "spanker" was a trysail the ringtail, or driver, was a triangular sail placed above the former.
ROYAL	The square sail just above the topgallant sail on a square-rigged ship. The roach on the foot is generally 2 feet deep for main and fore royals and 2 feet 6 inches on the mizzen royal.
SAVE-ALL	A "water sail."
SETTEE SAIL	A quadrilateral sail, the head of which was bent to a lateen yard, which hung obliquely to the mast at about one-third the length of the yard, the greater length being the upper portion. The leech is

generally five-sixths the length of the head, and the luff one-fifth of the depth of the leech. Oriental settee sails have a very short luff.

SKYSAIL A square sail set above the royal on a square-rigged ship.

SKYSCRAPER The same as a "moonraker."

SLIDING GUNTER A triangular sail, the upper part of the luff of which is laced to a topmast, which slides up and down the lower mast by means of iron rings fastened to the heel of the topmast. The lower part of the luff of the sail is bent to hoops which encircle the lower, or standing, mast. A sheet is fastened to the clew and leads aft. The sail is hoisted by a halyard, one end being fastened to the heel of the topmast, and the other end reeved through a sheave hole in the lower masthead and then leads down the mast where it is belayed. The sail is furled to the lower mast by lowering the topmast and confining the sail in folds with a furling line.

SPANKER The fore-and-aft sail set from the after mast of a square-rigged ship. It was developed from the lateen-mizzen, first by cutting the sail vertically at the mast and later cutting off the lateen yard at the mast.

SPENCER A fore-and-aft sail carried on the fore- or mainmast of a square-rigged ship, usually set to a standing gaff.

SPINNAKER A large triangular sail made of light material having a wide spread to its foot. It is set from the masthead and the tack is secured to the outer end of a boom, called the "spinnaker boom," set horizontally from the mast to take it. The clew is controlled by a sheet belayed to a cleat on the deck. The boom is guyed by lines leading to the fore and after parts of the boat. The "spinnaker" is used when going before the wind and is set on the weather side (the side opposite the mainsail), in other words, "wing and wing."
The term is also applied by Thames bargemen to the flying jib set from the topmast stay.

SPITFIRE A small storm jib.

SPRITSAIL A small square sail set on a yard, hung below and at right angles to the bowsprit. "Spritsails" were used before the introduction of the fore-and-aft jib, but by the latter part of the 18th century they had been discarded.

SPRITSAIL A quadrilateral sail, the head of which is extended and supported by a small pole, or "sprit," that extends upward diagonally from the mast to the peak. The fore-leech is attached to the mast by a lacing. The

[265]

lower end of the sprit rests in a collar of rope, called a "snotter," which encircles the mast near the foot of the sail. See "hoy sail."

SPRIT TOPSAIL   A small square sail set on a short vertical mast erected at the outer end of the bowsprit on large ships of the 16th and 17th centuries.

SQUARE SAIL   A four-cornered, rectangular sail hung from a horizontal yard at the head.

STAYSAIL   A triangular fore-and-aft sail set from various stays and named for the mast from which the stay leads. On early "frigates" and "men-of-war" quadrilateral staysails were often used.

STAYSAIL RIG   A modern rig used on schooner yachts, in which the mainsail is jib-headed and a main staysail and an upper staysail are set between the fore- and mainmasts. The usual headsails are carried.

STEERING SAILS   An old term for "studding sails."

STUDSAIL   An extension on the leech of a fore-and-aft sail.

STUDDING SAIL   Commonly called "stun's'ls." Light sails, usually quadrilateral in shape, which were set from booms extended outwardly from the yards of a square-rigged ship. These sails were controlled by halyards, outhauls, and sheets, and were named for the square sails adjacent to them.

All studding sails have a horizontal yard at the head. The head of the lower studding sails is two-thirds the length of the head of the fore-course. On large ships the head is generally two strips of canvas, or "cloths," wider (about 44 inches). The depth of the leech is the same as the forecourse. The heads of the main topmast and main topgallant studding sails are one-half the length of the heads of the fore topsail and topgallant sail, respectively. The heads of the fore topmast and fore topgallant studding sails are one cloth (about 22 inches) less in width than those on the main. The inner leeches are 9 inches shorter than those of the respective topsails and topgallant sails.

TOPGALLANT   The square sail next above the topsail or upper topsail on a square-rigged ship. The roach on the foot was 4 feet on large ships and 3 feet on smaller ones.

TOPSAIL   The sail next above the "course" on a square-rigged ship. About 1850 the topsail was divided into an upper and lower topsail for ease in handling. On a fore-and-aft rigged vessel the topsail is triangular and sets above the mainsail gaff.

[266]

TRYSAIL   Generally a triangular sail used in bad weather when the regular working sails cannot be carried. Also used as a "spanker" in connection with a triangular ringtail.

WATERSAIL   A small sail, rectangular in shape, set under the lower studding sail boom on a square-rigged ship.

WINGSAIL   A boomless fore-and-aft sail with a gaff along the head set from the mainmast of the square-rigged ketches of the 18th century. The "wingsail" came into use after about 1725.

WISHBONE RIG   A recently invented rig used on various types of sailing yachts, in which a triangular sail is used as a mainsail, the long side, or luff, being laced to the mast and the clew extended by a double curved gaff, which allows the sail to take its natural curve. A triangular staysail fills in the space underneath, if used on a two-masted vessel. The mainsail, or upper sail, is placed in between the two parts of the gaff.

APPENDICES

APPENDIX A

Nautical Terms

ABAFT	Towards the stern; aft.
AFT	Towards the stern.
BACKSTAY	A stay leading from a mast to the sides of a vessel, some distance aft of the mast.
BALLAST	Weight in the bottom of a vessel to counterbalance the effect of wind on the sails. When a ship is "in ballast" she carries no cargo.
BEAM	The breadth of a vessel at its widest point.
BEND	To secure a sail to a spar.
BILLET HEAD	A wooden scroll used in place of a figurehead.
BLOCK	A grooved sheave or pulley in a case or shell over which a rope is passed. There are many varieties and are made single, double, etc., for any size of rope.
BOBSTAY	A chain, wire rope, or rope guy running diagonally from the end of the bowsprit to the stem.
BOW	The forward part of a vessel.
BOWSPRIT	A spar projecting forward from the bow of a vessel from which one or more head-sails are set.
BOOMKIN	A short spar extending horizontally beyond the stern to take the sheet block of an overhanging sail.
BRACE	A line at the end of a yard by which it is controlled.
BRAIL	A rope leading in from the leech of a fore-and-aft sail to the mast, used to gather in the sail.
BULWARK	The topsides of a vessel's hull above the deck.
BUMPKIN or BUMKIN	A short horizontal spar projecting on either side of the stern, to which leads the main brace, and at the bow to take the fore tack.
BUTTOCK	The rounding part of a vessel's stern.
CARVEL-BUILT	Built with the external planks edge to edge, meeting flush at the seams, flush sided.
CATHEAD	A short timber or beam projecting beyond and on either side of the bow from which the anchor is hoisted.
CEILING	Inside planking of the hull of a vessel.
CHAIN PLATES	Strips of metal bolted to the side of a vessel to take the shrouds and backstays. On large, old-time sailing ships the chain plates were projected outwards from the sides of the vessel in order that the shrouds would clear the rail.

CHANNEL	A ledge or narrow platform bolted to and projecting from the outside of a vessel's hull to spread the rigging.
CHEEK KNEE	Strips along the top and bottom of the trail boards.
CHESS TREE	A timber in which a sheave is set, bolted to the topsides of an old-time square-rigged vessel at a point convenient for hauling down the main tack, the tack leading to the inside of the bulwark.
CLEW	In a square sail, the two lower corners; in a fore-and-aft sail, the lower corner aft.
CLINKER-BUILT	Having the external planks overlapping, the lower edge of a plank overlapping the upper edge of the one below it. This is also called "lapstrake."
COUNTER	The under part of the overhang of the stern.
CROSSTREES	Light timbers resting on the trestle trees at the topmast head for spreading the rigging.
CUDDY	A cabin in a small boat. Also, a cook house on deck.
DEADEYE	A round block of lignum-vitæ in which there are three holes, through which is rove the lanyard.
DEAD RISE	The amount of rise of a vessel's bottom above horizontal at the intersection of the moulded breadth line.
DEPTH OF HOLD	The vertical distance from the top of the keel to the top of the main deck beams.
DOLPHIN STRIKER	A short spar projecting downward beneath the bowsprit, forming a member of the truss supporting the jib boom.
DRAFT	The depth a vessel sinks in the water when afloat, or the vertical distance from the surface of the water to the lowest point of the keel.
DRAG	The vertical distance that the after end of the keel is below the forward end when the vessel is afloat.
ENTRANCE	The forward part of a vessel at the water line.
FIFE RAIL	A rail for pins around a mast, to which halyards and other lines are belayed.
FLEMISH HORSE	A short footrope at the end of a yard.
FOOTROPE	A rope slung underneath the yard, bowsprit, or jib boom on which the crew stands when furling a sail.
FOREFOOT	The point at which the stem joins the keel.
FREEBOARD	The distance from the top of the upper deck down to the water.
GAFF	A spar bent along the head of a fore-and-aft sail, extending aft from the mast. It is hoisted by "throat" halyards at the mast and by "peak" halyards at the outer end.
GARBOARD STRAKE	The plank adjacent the keel.
GUNWALE	The top of any rail of a boat or vessel.
HAIR RAIL	The top member of two or three curved timbers, extending from either side of the figurehead to the bow or cathead, to brace the head or projecting stem, used on old-time ships.

HALYARD or **HALLIARD**	A rope or tackle for hoisting a sail or a yard.
HORSES	Footropes. Also an iron rod secured to the deck, on which a sheet block travels.
JACKSTAY	A rod along the top of a yard to which the sails are bent.
JIB BOOM	A spar extending beyond the bowsprit to take the outer headsails. Also a spar or boom bent to the foot of a jib.
KEEL	A longitudinal timber or built-up timbers, extending along the center line of the bottom, which forms the backbone of the hull of a vessel and from which rise the frames, or ribs, stem and sternpost.
KEELSON	A timber stringer bolted on the keel to reenforce it.
KNIGHTHEADS	Upright timbers inside of and on either side of the stem; the bowsprit sets between them.
KNOT	The speed of a vessel or current in nautical miles (6,080.27 feet) per hour. A measurement of speed, not of distance. To say "knots per hour" is unnecessary. A rope or ropes tied into combinations of turns.
LANYARDS	Ropes that lead through the deadeyes and used to "set up" (tighten) the shrouds and stays.
LARBOARD	The old term for the port, or left, side of a vessel, facing forward.
LAZY JACKS	Ropes leading down vertically from the topping lift to the boom to hold the sail when taking it in.
LEE	The side of a ship opposite that from which the wind blows.
LEECH	The outer edges of a square sail and the after edge of a fore-and-aft sail.
LENGTH OVER-ALL	The distance from the foremost part of the stem to the aftermost part of the stern. "Length between perpendiculars": The distance from the fore part of the stem to the after part of the sternpost where they intersect the top of the upper deck beams.
LIFT	A line running diagonally from the masthead to the end of a yard. It takes the weight of the yard.
LUFF	The forward edge of a fore-and-aft sail. To luff a vessel is to bring her up toward the direction of the wind.
MARTINGALE BOOM	A dolphin striker.
MOULDED BREADTH	The measurement over the frames at the greatest breadth (not to the outside of the planking or plates).
MOULDED DEPTH	The vertical distance from the top of the keel to the top of the upper deck beams at the side of a vessel (taken at the middle of the length). This applies to ships with one, two, or three decks. In the case of a spar-decked ship, the distance is to the top of the main deck beam.
PARREL	A ring around the mast secured to the middle of a yard by which the latter is held to the mast.
PEAK	The upper and after corner of a fore-and-aft sail.

POOP	The raised deck abaft the mizzenmast, generally over a cabin.
QUARTER	The portion of a vessel abaft the after rigging.
RABBET	A longitudinal recess cut in the face of a timber to receive the planking, as along the top of the keel, and the inside of the stem and sternpost.
RAIL	The top of the bulwarks. See also "hair rail."
RAKE	The angle that the stem, sternpost, or mast makes with the perpendicular.
ROACH	A curve in the side of a sail.
RUN	The after part of a vessel at the water line where her lines converge toward the sternpost.
RUNNING RIGGING	Lines which are used to control the sails, such as halyards, buntlines, clew lines, etc.
SHEER	The amount of upward sweep or curve of the deck or rail.
SHEET	A rope used to control a sail.
SHROUDS	Rope or wire-rope stays which brace a mast laterally, extending from the masthead to the chain plates on the sides of a vessel. The lower ends are made fast to turnbuckles or deadeyes and lanyards, which in turn are secured to the chain plates.
SPAR DECK	The upper deck of a flush-decked naval vessel.
STANDING RIGGING	Ropes or wire ropes which permanently support the spars, such as shrouds and other stays, and are not moved when working the sails.
STEEVE	The angle the bowsprit makes with the horizontal.
STEM	The foremost upright timber in the hull of a vessel, all the planks or plates being rabbeted or riveted to it.
STERN	The after part of a vessel.
STERNPOST	An upright timber joined to and erected above the after end of the keel, to which the rudder is hung.
STRAKE	A plank or planks running the length of a vessel.
THROAT	The upper corner of a fore-and-aft sail adjacent the mast.
TIE or TYE	The single part of a halyard which hoists a yard.
TILLER	A bar of wood or iron connected with the head of the rudder post, leading forward, by which the rudder is moved to steer the vessel.
TOPPING LIFT	A line with a tackle by which the outer end of a boom is supported or hoisted.
TRAIL BOARD	A curved board extending from the figurehead to the bow, often carved or embellished.
TRANSOM	Transverse timbers secured to the sternpost.
TRANSOM STERN	A flat type of stern.
TRAWL	A long fishing line, anchored and buoyed at the ends, having many small lines bearing hooks. Also, a large bag-shaped net dragged along the bottom in sea fishing.

TUMBLE HOME	The amount the topsides of the hull of a vessel go in toward the center from the perpendicular above the water line.
TRESTLE TREES	Short timbers running fore and aft on either side of a mast that rest on the "hounds." They support the "top platform" and "crosstrees."
VANGS	Lines leading from the outer end of a gaff to the rails to steady it.
WALE	A strake of planking running fore and aft on the outside of the hull, heavier than the regular planking.
WEATHER	Toward the direction of the wind; the weather side of a ship is toward the wind.

APPENDIX B

Notes

Note 1, page 122. A relief on the wall of Queen Hatshepsut's temple in Thebes shows a barge about 300 feet long transporting two obelisks and towed by thirty rowing tug boats in three rows of ten each. As the shafts weighed approximately 350 tons apiece and were 97 feet in length, it was quite an engineering feat for these early people to cut, load, unload and set such weights, as well as to build a vessel of this size from their comparatively slender resources. The barge was strengthened by heavy longitudinal trusses in the Egyptian manner.

In the tombs of the kings of the 12th dynasty (circa 2000 B.C.) numerous models of boats were found. Some of them are canoe-shaped craft made of papyrus reeds, with upturned tapering ends. Similar reed canoes are still in use on Lake Tana at the head of the Blue Nile.

Note 2, page 130. A quaint touch on the gaiassas is the earthen pot hanging from the mast some feet above the deck. The crew's food is kept in these pots out of the reach of the rats which infest the vessel. This is also the custom in parts of the Orient.

Note 3, page 131. Before the 15th century labor was hired, but subsequently slaves, war and political prisoners, and other unfortunates did the rowing on the galleys. The rowers were chained to their seats and forced to remain aboard for long periods.

Note 4, page 133. For an informative treatise on the history of the Gloucester schooners see the articles by H. I. Chapelle in *Yachting*, November and December, 1933, and April, 1934.

Note 5, page 157. The Portuguese muletta uses a sort of a trawl net when employed in fishing. The boat is laid broadside to the wind when trawling, drifting to leeward. The purpose of the numerous sails is to balance the craft in its sidewise drift and leeboards are employed to regulate the speed. Ordinarily, when sailing, only the working canvas is used.

Note 6, page 193. A treaty port is one wherein foreigners can do business under their own laws. After the Sino-British "Opium War," 1839–42, five treaty ports were opened in which foreigners were given special concessions, including very low tariffs on imports. Through these ports China was opened to western commerce.

Note 7, page 205. Taku is the name of the main island of the group, which is usually known as the Mortlock Is. It is interesting to note that the government of the Territory of New Guinea has purchased Taku Is. from the Europeans who had dispossessed and even indentured the natives. Haddon states that the land is now held in trust for the natives and they are back on their own land. Some of the older generation who are still alive are teaching the younger folks their old crafts and rituals, in order to revive the old customs, as a governmental experiment.

Note 8, page 208. The *Charles W. Morgan* was built at New Bedford in 1841. She now sets in a sand-filled cofferdam on the shore of Buzzard's Bay at South Dartmouth, Mass.

Note 9, page 208. The first iron commercial sailing ship was the *Ironsides*, launched in 1838 in Liverpool by Jackson, Gordon and Company. For histories of the British clippers see *The China Clippers* and *The Colonial Clippers*, by Basil Lubbock.

APPENDIX C

Craft of Oceania

The islands of Oceania are divided into groups, as follows:

POLYNESIA consists of the islands in the territory extending from Easter Island on the east westward to New Zealand, including the Hawaiians, Marquesas Islands, Tuamotu Archipelago, Cook Islands, Austral Islands, Tongan Archipelago, Samoa, Niue, Ellice Islands, and Manihiki.

MELANESIA—New Caledonia, Loyalty Islands, New Hebrides, Santa Cruz Islands, Fiji, New Britain, the Louisiades, Solomon Islands, Bismarck Archipelago, New Guinea, marginal islands such as Tikopia, Rennel, Ontong Java, etc.

MICRONESIA—Caroline Islands, Marianas Islands (Ladrones), Gilbert Islands, Marshall Islands, and Palau Islands.

AUSTRALIA, MALAY ARCHIPELAGO, including Borneo, Netherlands Indies, etc.

Since the influx of the white man into the Pacific islands during the past century and a half, there has been a general retrogression in the construction of the native canoe. This has been due to the gradual adoption of the European types of vessel and also to the great diminishing of the population, especially in the eastern isles. The highest level of culture and boat craft was reached over two hundred years ago.

It is conceded that the Micronesians were superior to the peoples of the other groups in navigation and boat designing. They were sea rovers and raiders and their fast "flying proas" were admirably suited to their needs. The natives of Micronesia invented the flattened lee side of the hull, which reduced the drift to leeward; the lee platform; and the pivoting mast placed amidships, which enabled the canoe to sail either end forward, thereby always keeping the outrigger to weather. The fastest canoes were built in the Marianas and Palau Islands. The double-ended, built-up dugout or dugout canoe with single outrigger was (and is) used exclusively, except in the Truk Islands of the central Carolines, where a double canoe was also in use. The rig of the sailing canoes of Micronesia was the Oceanic lateen.

The Polynesians were great voyagers and explorers. Their cruises were lengthy and extended. The Society Islanders traveled as far north as the Hawaiians, southward to the ice region and to far-off New Zealand. Because of the space required for passengers, supplies and water on their exploratory voyages, the large seagoing double canoe was developed. For local use the natives employed a small dugout paddling canoe with a single outrigger.

While the double canoe existed in practically all of Polynesia, it was not known to have been used to any great extent in the islands of Melanesia and Micronesia, with the exception of Fiji, New Caledonia, New Guinea, and the Truk Islands. The large, platformed, sailing double and multiple canoes of New Guinea, such as the "orou" and "lakatoi," were needed to accommodate the huge cargoes of pottery used for bartering with the neighboring villages.

Summarizing further, dugout or built-up dugout sailing and paddling canoes, with an outrigger on one side only, are distributed throughout Oceania and Indonesia. Double outrigger canoes (outrigger on both sides of the hull) are used in the Nissan Islands of the Solomon group, Cape York Peninsula in Queensland, Mawata district of Papua, the eastern islands of the Torres Straits, Netherlands New Guinea, the Moluccas, the Celebes, and the Philippines; also in Madagascar, Zanzibar, etc.

Single outrigger canoes with two booms are usual throughout Polynesia and Micronesia, with the exception of Fiji, Ellice Islands, and Tokelau Islands. Multiple booms are employed on the outrigger canoes of Fiji, Tokelau, and Ellice Islands, and nearly all the Melanesian Islands. Both two-boomed and multiple-boomed outriggers are in use in Tonga, Samoa, and New Guinea. Plank-built canoes without outrigger of the "mon" type are found only in the Solomon Islands. The Oceanic spritsail rig was used in Hawaii, Marquesas Islands, Society Islands, and New Zealand. The Oceanic lateen sail, in various forms, was, and is to a limited extent, employed in the remainder of Oceania.

As one works eastward from Indonesia, the picturesque native canoes become scarcer. In most of the Polynesian Islands only the small outrigger canoes remain, the double canoes and seagoing vessels having long since disappeared.

(Note: In the illustrations of craft with outriggers, it will be noted that in the elevations the float is shown below the water line of the hull. While incorrect, this was done in order that the outrigger could be shown and also to give an idea of the connectives.

In such cases where models of extinct craft in museums differ from the description given by Messrs. Haddon and Hornell in their *Canoes of Oceania*, the writer has followed the data given in the latter.)

APPENDIX D
Bibliography

AFLALO, F. G., "The Sea-fishing Industry of England and Wales."

ALBION, R. G., "Square Riggers on Schedule."

ALLEN GARDNER, "Our Naval War with France."

ANDERSON, JOHN, "Ships."

ANDERSON, R. and R. C., "The Sailing Ship."

ANSON, PETER F., "Mariners of Brittany," "Fishing Boats and Fisher Folk."

BLAKE, WM. MAXWELL, Articles in "Yachting."

BRADY, WILLIAM, "Kedge Anchor."

CARR, F. G. G., "Sailing Barges."

CARTWRIGHT, CHAS., "Tale of Our Merchant Ships."

CHAPELLE, H. I., "History of American Sailing Ships," "American Sailing Craft," Articles in "Yachting."

CHATTERTON, E. K., "Sailing Ships and Their Story."

CLARK, A. H., "Clipper Ship Era."

CONNOLLY, JAMES B., "Book of Gloucester Fishermen."

CULVER, HENRY, and GORDON GRANT, "Book of Old Ships."

CUTLER, C. C., "Greyhounds of the Sea."

DAVIS, CHAS. G., "Ships of the Past."

DOW, G. F., "Slave Ships and Slaving."

FOLIN, MARQUIS DE, "Bateaux et Navires."

HADDON, A. C., "Canoes of Melanesia."

HALL, HENRY, "Shipbuilding Industry of the United States."

HENDERSON, W. J., "Elements of Navigation."

HERUBEL, MARCEL A., "Sea Fisheries."

HOBBS, E. W., "Sailing Ships at a Glance."

HOLLIS, IRA N., "The Frigate *Constitution*."

HOLMES, G. C. V., "Ancient and Modern Ships."

HOPKINS, R. T., "Small Sailing Ships."

HORNELL, JAMES, "Canoes of Polynesia, Fiji, and Micronesia."

JENKINS, J. T., "Sea Fisheries."

KIPPING, ROBERT, "Sails and Sailmaking."

KNOX, DUDLEY, "A History of the U. S. Navy."

KRÄMER, AUGUSTIN, "Hawaii, Ostmikronesien, und Samoa."

LEVER, DARCY, "Young Officers' Sheet Anchor."

LOVETTE, L. P., "Naval Customs, Tradition, and Usage."

LUBBOCK, BASIL, "China Clippers," "Sail," and "The Blackwall Frigates."

MAGOUN, F. A., "The Frigate *Constitution*."

MALINOWSKI, B., "Argonauts of the Western Pacific."

MASON, F. A., "North Sea Fishers."

McKAY, R. C., "Some Sailing Ships."

MITMAN, CARL, U. S. National Museum.

MOORE, SIR ALAN, "Last Days of Mast and Sail."

MORISON, SAM'L E., "Maritime History of Massachusetts."

MORRIS, E. P., "The Fore-and-Aft Rig in America."

NORDHOFF, C. B., and HALL, J. N., "Faery Lands of the South Seas."

PARIS, Admiral F. E., "Essai sur la Construction Navale des Peuples Extra-Européens" and "Souvenir de Marine."

PAULLIN, C. O., "Early Voyages of American Naval Ships to the Orient."

PRATT, FLETCHER, "The Navy."

PRITCHETT, R. T., "Sketches of Shipping and Craft Round the World."

ROGERS, STANLEY, "Sea Lore."

ROOSEVELT, THEODORE, "Naval War of 1812."

SMYTH, H. WARRINGTON, "Mast and Sail in Europe and Asia."

SPEARS, JOHN R., "Story of the New England Whalers," "Story of the American Merchant Marine."

STEEL, DAVID, "Elements and Practice of Seamanship."

STONE, HERBERT L., "History of the *America's* Cup."

SWAN, WILLIAM U., "Fate of the Cup Defenders" in "Yachting."

TORR, CECIL T., "Ancient Ships."

VILLIERS, ALAN J., "Cape Horn Grain Race," "Rounding the Horn in a Windjammer."

WRIGHT, SIDNEY, "Romance of the World's Fisheries."

Periodicals

"Yachting"

"U. S. Naval Institute PROCEEDINGS"

"National Geographic Magazine"

"Yachting Monthly"

"Oceania"

"Mariner's Mirror"

Annual Reports of Smithsonian Institution

Museums

National Museum, Washington, D.C.

British Museum

Science Museum, South Kensington, London, England

Berlin Museum, Berlin, Germany

Deutsches Museum, Munich, Germany

Museum für Völkerkunde, Hamburg, Germany

Köln Museum, Cologne, Germany

Peabody Museum, Salem, Massachusetts

Musée de Marine, Louvre, Paris, France

Philadelphia Comm. Museum, Philadelphia, Pennsylvania

Bernice P. Bishop Museum, Honolulu, Hawaii

Colombo Museum, Colombo, Ceylon